This guide to the coast path from Minehead to Bude (124½ miles) covers the first part, the Somerset and North Devon section, of the 630-mile South West Coast Path and is the first book in this three-part series. It was originally walked, researched and written by **HENRY STEDMAN** and **JOEL NEWTON** (photo below, with **DAISY**).

This third edition was rewalked and updated by Daniel McCrohan, accompanied every step of the way by his two young research assistants, Simon and Yoyo McCrohan.

DANIEL MCCROHAN (photo top, with **Simon** and **Yoyo**) has been writing guidebooks for both Lonely Planet and Trailblazer for almost 15 years. He specialises in far-flung parts of East and South Asia, but relishes any opportunity to explore his British homeland, especially if it means another chance to go camping! Daniel has updated Trailblazer guides to *Hadrian's Wall Path*, the *South Downs Way*, *Pembrokeshire Coast Path*, *Coast to Coast Path*, and the other two books in this South West Coast Path trilogy. He also updated the most recent edition of Trailblazer's *Trans-Siberian Handbook* as part of an epic three-month journey through China, Mongolia and Russia.

For this trip, Daniel and his two adventure-loving children Simon and Yoyo hiked and camped their way along the Somerset, Devon and Cornish coastline testing the best pasties and ice creams on offer, and ensuring no café or tearoom was left unvisited. Along the way they saw five snakes, twelve dolphins, a herd of feral goats and the mother of all thunderstorms, but were all in agreement that the highlight of the trip was the celebratory final-day swim in Bude's magnificent sea pool.

You can follow Daniel's global travels through his website (💻 danielmccrohan.com) or on Twitter (@danielmccrohan).

Exmoor & North Devon Coast Path (SWCP Part 1)

First edition: 2012; this third edition 2022

Publisher Trailblazer Publications
The Old Manse, Tower Rd, Hindhead, Surrey, GU26 6SU, UK, ✉ trailblazer-guides.com

British Library Cataloguing in Publication Data
A catalogue record for this book is available from the British Library

ISBN 978-1-912716-24-1

© **Trailblazer** 2012, 2017 & 2022: Text and maps

Series Editor: Anna Jacomb-Hood
Editor & layout: Nicky Slade **Proofreading**: Henry Stedman
Cartography: Nick Hill **Index**: Jane Thomas **Photographs (flora)**: © Bryn Thomas
All other photographs: © Daniel McCrohan (unless otherwise indicated)

The maps in this guide were prepared from out-of-Crown-copyright Ordnance Survey maps amended and updated by Trailblazer.

Acknowledgements

My biggest thanks this time goes to my two incredible children, Simon and Yoyo, for being brave enough to take up the challenge of hiking up and down a 200km-long coast path whilst carrying everything needed for a two-week camping trip. More than that, though, you were both wonderful company, making this trip more fun than almost any other. Thank you for your songs, your games, your enthusiasm and your kindness. I love you both. Also thank you (and sorry) to my darling wife Taotao for holding the fort while we were gone. Next time you're coming with us!

On the coast path, thank you to all the campsite managers who continue to make hikers feel so welcome. It's your help and generosity that makes hiking the path so rewarding. Well, that and the cream teas. Particular thanks goes to Sparkhayes Farm Campsite (Porlock), Newberry Valley Campsite (Coombe Martin), Westacott Farm Campsite (Westward Ho!) and Stoke Barton Farm Campsite (Hartland Quay). Also thanks to Base Lodge Hostel in Minehead for opening up during renovations so that we weren't left homeless on the night before our walk began.

Back at Trailblazer HQ, thanks to Henry and Joel for their stellar work on the previous editions, to Nick Hill (mapping), Nicky Slade (editing), Henry Stedman (proofreading) and Jane Thomas (index). And of course a huge thank you to Bryn Thomas, not only for commissioning me to update another Trailblazer guidebook, but for doing so at a time of unprecedented uncertainty.

Last but not least, thank you to all our readers who contacted us with tips and recommendations for this latest edition, including: Gabi Blauer, Chris Ellingham, Bryan Gray, Jeff Handley, Nicola Haynes, Isabel Heycock, Elissa Klapper, Chris Layton, Tony Maynard-Smith, Helen Older, Keri and Pauline, Morten Planer, and Andy Riddle.

A request

The author and publisher have tried to ensure that this guide is as accurate and up to date as possible. Nevertheless, things change. If you notice any changes or omissions that should be included in the next edition of this book, please write to Trailblazer (address above) or email us at ✉ info@trailblazer-guides.com. A free copy of the next edition will be sent to persons making a significant contribution.

Warning: coastal walking and long-distance walking can be dangerous

Updated information will be available on: ✉ trailblazer-guides.com

Photos – Front cover & this page: Sandy Mouth (© Simon McCrohan). **Overleaf**: Croyde Beach.

Printed in China; print production by D'Print (☎ +65-6581 3832), Singapore

EXMOOR &
North Devon
COAST PATH

SW COAST PATH PART 1 – MINEHEAD TO BUDE
68 large-scale maps & guides to 30 towns and villages
PLANNING – PLACES TO STAY – PLACES TO EAT

HENRY STEDMAN, JOEL NEWTON &
DANIEL McCROHAN

TRAILBLAZER PUBLICATIONS

INTRODUCTION

Exmoor and North Devon Coast Path

PART 1: PLANNING YOUR WALK

Practical information for the walker

Budgeting 29

Itineraries

What to take

Getting to and from the Coast Path

PART 2: MINIMUM IMPACT WALKING & OUTDOOR SAFETY

Minimum impact walking

Outdoor safety

PART 3: THE ENVIRONMENT & NATURE

Conservation

Flora and fauna

ABOUT THIS BOOK

This guidebook contains all the information you need. The hard work has been done for you so you can plan your trip without having to consult numerous websites and other books and maps. When you're packed and ready to go, there's comprehensive public transport information to get you to and from the trail and detailed maps (1:20,000) to help you find your way along it. It includes:

● All standards of accommodation with reviews of campsites, camping barns, hostels, B&Bs, pubs/inns, guesthouses and hotels
● Walking companies if you want an organised tour, and baggage-transfer services if you just want your luggage carried
● Suggested itineraries for all types of walkers
● Answers to all your questions: when to go, degree of difficulty, what to pack, and how much the whole walking holiday will cost
● Walking times in both directions and GPS waypoints
● Cafés, pubs, tearooms, takeaways, restaurants and food shops
● Rail, bus & taxi information for all villages and towns on the path
● Street plans of the main towns and villages both on and off the path
● Historical, cultural and geographical background information

---

❏ THIS EDITION AND THE COVID-19 PANDEMIC

This particular edition of the guide was researched at a time when the entire country was just emerging from some pretty tight restrictions. Most of the hotels, cafés, pubs, restaurants, and tourist attractions have now reopened, but some are still offering a more limited service than they were pre-pandemic.

Most **accommodation** is back open, albeit with some changes such as later check-ins and earlier check-outs to allow for extra cleaning.

The majority of **pubs, restaurants and cafés** are open – though some are still operating reduced opening hours or have a limited menu. You may need to book a table in advance.

Most **train** and **bus services** were operating to reduced timetables but should now be back to normal. However, it is likely face coverings will still be required on (or in) all forms of public transport.

Museums and galleries may require booking (especially for tours) and may also restrict the number of people inside at any one time.

In this book all we can do is record the opening times as they currently stand, or as the owners of the various establishments are predicting they will be by the time this is published. Do forgive us where your experience on the ground contradicts what is written in the book; please email us – **info@trailblazer-guides.com** – so we can add your information to our updates page on the website.

Hopefully, by the time you read this, Coronavirus, lockdowns and other ubiquitous words from the last two years will be nothing but a bad memory of a surreal time. And if that's the case, the operating hours of the establishments en route will be back to 'normal'.

For the latest information visit ▢ gov.uk/coronavirus.

INTRODUCTION

This book covers the first 124½ miles (200.3km) of the South West
Coast Path (hereafter known as SWCP), Britain's longest national
trail. The trail in this book
starts at Minehead in **This book covers the first 124½**
Somerset and, after navi- **miles of the 630-mile**
gating the whole of North **South West Coast Path**
Devon's coastline, ends just across the border at Bude in Cornwall.
Together with the two other books in this 'mini-series', the entire
length of this 630-mile-long coast path is covered.

This first section of the path is also by some distance the short-
est of the three. But size isn't everything, as they say, and there's
plenty here to tempt the discerning walker. Look at a map of the
British Isles and this part of the coastal path – meandering as it does
along some of Britain's most exquisite shoreline, backed by a vast
swathe of green, a verdant outlook unbroken save for tiny villages
and hamlets scattered here and there – is a logical place to go for an
amble. That vast swathe of green is Exmoor National Park, the most
delightful of wildernesses, through which the route saunters along
the coastal cliffs for 34 miles and takes in Great Hangman, at 318m
(1043ft) the highest point on the entire trail. Nor does the fun stop
there for no sooner does the path leave the park than it immediately

Above: The final clifftop stretch from Hartland Quay to Bude includes a
series of tortuous ups and downs but you'll soon be soaking those over-
worked feet in the cool waters at Summerleaze Beach.

The walk around Hartland Peninsula is the toughest, most isolated and the most spectacular walking – in most experts' opinions – on the entire SWCP

joins the North Devon coast, luxuriating in its designation as an Area of Outstanding Natural Beauty (AONB). It is here you'll find enormous beaches stretching for miles; Braunton Burrows, part of a UNESCO Biosphere Reserve and the largest sand dune system in the country; plenty of pretty little historical towns and gorgeous villages where one can rest and recuperate, including the breathtaking harbour of Clovelly; and we haven't even mentioned the walk around Hartland Peninsula, the toughest, most isolated and the most spectacular walking – in most experts' opinions – on the entire SWCP. Clearly, God was in a rumbustious mood when He designed this gorgeous little corner of England.

The North Devon AONB continues all the way to the border with Cornwall, though this book actually finishes just across the border at Bude – a more logical end to a walk, with fine accommodation, good restaurants in which to celebrate and half-decent (by the standards of the South-West at least!) transport links back to the everyday world.

Below: A typically quaint thatched cottage in the village of Bossington. The trail takes you through numerous picturesque villages.

Sounds perfect doesn't it? A dozen days or so of walking along romantic, windswept cliffs, through Elysian fields and sylvan valleys, a small yet vital part of a mammoth odyssey around England's most idiosyncratic corner. But such rewards are not gained easily; for one thing, the weather in this blessed corner of England takes a perverse pleasure in its unpredictability – though it does have more than its fair share of good weather too, especially compared to the rest of the UK. But there's also some hard walking to be done; by many people's estimates, this is actually the toughest leg of the entire SWCP, with plenty of fiercely undulating sections guaranteed to torment calf muscles and sap morale. Indeed, it can't be denied that there are a couple of days that will truly test your mettle.

Above: The start of the trail in Minehead is marked with a sculpture of a giant hand holding a South-West Coast Path map.
(© Simon McCrohan).

But then again, few if any will disagree that the obstacles and difficulties this path presents to those who dare to pit themselves against it, are far outweighed by its compensations.

History

The Somerset and North Devon section of the South West Coast Path is the youngest part, having only been created and added to the rest of the path in 1978 – five years after the Cornish section was declared open. The entire path, however, including this section, existed way before its designation as a national trail, having been used by the coastguard for centuries to protect against smugglers and aid maritime safety. The nature of the coastguard's job meant that the path had to follow the cliff-tops closely to provide their officers with far-reaching views over land and sea – and to allow them to visit every beach and cove along the way. By chance, these are the exact same qualities that discerning walkers look for in a coastal path!

How long do you need?

Most people take about 10-11 days to complete the walk; count on a fortnight away in total to give you time to travel there and back. Of course, if you're fit there's no reason why you can't go a little faster, if that's what you want to do,

❏ THE SOUTH-WEST COAST PATH

Typing 'Minehead to Poole Harbour, Dorset' into Google Maps reveals that travelling between the two can be completed in a matter of 2½ hours by car, along a distance of 98.1 miles. Even walking, along the most direct route, takes only around 28 hours, so Google Maps says, with the path an even shorter one at just 88.2 miles.

It is these two points that are connected by the South-West Coast Path (SWCP). This most famous – and infamous – of national trails is, however, a good deal longer than 89.3 miles. Though estimates as to its exact length vary – and to a large part are determined by which of the alternative paths one takes at various stages along the trail – the most widely accepted estimate of the path is that it is about 630 miles long (1014km). That figure, however, often changes due to necessary alterations of the path caused by erosion and other factors.

So why, when you could walk from Minehead to South Haven Point in just 29 hours, do most people choose to take 6-8 weeks? The answer is simple: the SWCP is one of the most beautiful trails in the UK. Around 70% of those 630 miles are spent either in national parks, or regions that have been designated as Areas of Outstanding Natural Beauty. The variety of places crossed by the SWCP is extraordinary too: from sunkissed beaches to sandy burrows, holiday parks to fishing harbours, esplanade to estuary, on top of windswept cliffs and under woodland canopy, the scenery that one travels through along the length of SWCP has to be the most diverse of any of the national trails. Of course, maintaining such a monumental route is no easy task. A survey in 2000 stated that the trail boasted 2473 signposts and waymarks, 302 bridges, 921 stiles, and 26,719 steps. These figures are, of course, out of date now, though they do still give an idea of both how long the trail is, and how much is involved in building and maintaining it to such a high standard. The task of looking after the trail falls to a dedicated team from the official body, Natural England. Another important organisation, and one that looks after the rights of walkers is the South West Coast Path Association (see box p42), a charity that fights for improvements to the path and offers advice, information and support to walkers. Their campaigns help to ensure that England's right-of-way laws – which keep the footpath open to the public even though it does, on occasion, pass through private property – are fully observed.

History of the path

In 1948 a government report recommended the creation of a footpath around the entire South-West peninsula to improve public access to the coast which, at that time, was pretty dire. It took until 1973 for the Cornwall Coast Path to be declared officially open and another five years for the rest of the South-West Coast Path to be completed. The section covered in this book, North Devon and Exmoor, is the first part that most coastal walkers complete, though it was actually the last section to be opened to the public, in 1978.

The origins of the path, however, are much older than its official designation. Originally, the paths were established – or at least adopted, there presumably being coastal paths from time immemorial that connected the coastal villages – by the local coastguard in the 19th century, who needed a path that hugged the shoreline closely to aid them in their attempts to spot and prevent smugglers from bringing contraband into the country. The coastguards were unpopular in the area as they prevented the locals from exploiting a lucrative if illegal activity, to the extent that it was considered too dangerous for them to stay in the villages; as a result, the authorities were

and finish the walk in eight days or even less, though you will end up having a different sort of walk to most of the other people on the trail. For, whilst theirs is a fairly relaxing holiday, yours will be more of a sport. What's more, you won't have much time to laze in the sun on the beaches, scoff scones in tearooms, visit an attraction or two, or sup local beers under the shade of a pub parasol – which does rather beg the question as to why you've come here in the first place! There's nothing wrong with this approach, of course, but **don't try to push yourself too fast, or too far**. That road leads only to exhaustion, injury or, at the absolute least, an unpleasant time.

Most people take about 10-11 days to complete the walk; count on a fortnight away in total

When deciding how long to allow for the walk, those intending to camp and carry their own luggage shouldn't underestimate just how much a heavy pack can slow them down. On pp30-1 there are some suggested itineraries covering different walking speeds.

If you have only a few days, don't try to walk it all; concentrate instead on one area such as the coast path through Exmoor, the beaches around

obliged to build special cottages for the coastguards that stood (and, often, still stand) in splendid isolation near the path – but well away from the villages.

The lifeboat patrols also used the path to look out for craft in distress (and on one famous occasion used the path to drag their boat to a safe launch to rescue a ship in distress – see p100). When the coastguards' work ended in 1856, the Admiralty took over the task of protecting England's shoreline and thus the paths continued to be used.

The route – Minehead (Somerset) to Poole Harbour (Dorset)
The SWCP officially begins at Minehead in Somerset (its exact starting point marked by a sculpture of a giant hand holding a map, see p9), heads west right round the bottom south-west corner of Britain then shuffles back along the south coast to South Haven Point, overlooking Poole Harbour in Dorset.

On its lengthy journey around Britain's south-western corner the SWCP crosses national parks such as Exmoor as well as regions that have been designated as Areas of Outstanding Natural Beauty (including North, South and East Devon as well as Cornwall and Dorset) or Sites of Special Scientific Interest (Braunton Burrows being just one example – an area that also enjoys a privileged status as a UNESCO Biosphere Reserve), and even a couple of UNESCO World Heritage sites, too, including the Jurassic Coast of East Devon and Dorset and the old mining landscape of Cornwall and West Devon.

Other features passed on the way include: the highest cliffs on mainland Britain (at Great Hangman – also the highest point on the coast path at 318m/1043ft, with a cliff-face of 244m); the largest sand-dune system in England (at Braunton Burrows); England's most westerly point (at Land's End) and Britain's most southerly (at the Lizard); the 18-mile barrier beach of Chesil Bank; one of the world's largest natural harbours at Poole; and even the National Trust's only official nudist beach at Studland!

The path then ends at South Haven Point, its exact finish marked by a second SWCP sculpture. The path also takes in four counties – Somerset, Devon, Cornwall and Dorset, and connects with over 15 other long-distance trails; the southern section from Plymouth to Poole also forms part of the 3125-mile long European E9 Coastal Path that runs on a convoluted route from Portugal to Estonia. *(cont'd overleaf)*

❏ **THE SOUTH-WEST COAST PATH** *(cont'd from p11)*

Walking the South-West Coast Path

In terms of difficulty, there are those people who, having never undertaken such a trail before, are under the illusion that coastal walking is a cinch; that all it involves is a simple stroll along mile after mile of golden, level beach, the walker needing to pause only to kick the sand out from his or her flip-flop or buy another ice-cream.

The truth, of course, is somewhat different, for coastal paths tend to stick to the cliffs above the beaches rather than the beaches themselves (which is actually something of a relief, given how hard it is to walk across sand or shingle). These cliffs make for some spectacular walking but – given the undulating nature of Britain's coastline, and the fact the course of the SWCP inevitably crosses innumerable river valleys, each of which forces the walker to descend rapidly before climbing back up again almost immediately afterwards – some exhausting walking too. Indeed, it has been estimated that anybody who completes the entire SWCP will have climbed more than four times the height of Everest (35,031m to be precise, or 114,931ft) by the time they finish!

Given these figures, it is perhaps hardly surprising that most people take around eight weeks to complete the whole route, and few do so in one go; indeed, it is not unusual for people to take years or even decades to complete the whole path, taking a week or two here and there to tackle various sections until the whole trail is complete.

Woolacombe and Croyde, or the more low-key estuary path along a disused railway from Braunton to Westward Ho!. Or you can really challenge yourself by taking on the trail between lovely Clovelly and Bude.

How difficult is the path?

The South West Coast Path (SWCP) is just a walk (albeit a very, very long one!), so there's no need for crampons, ropes, ice axes, oxygen bottles or any other climbing paraphernalia. All you need to complete the walk is some suitable clothing, a bit of money, a rucksack full of determination and a half-decent pair of calf muscles.

That said, the part of the SWCP that is covered by this book is reputed to be the most challenging section, with plenty of steep ups-and-downs. It is also a fairly wild walk in places – to cross Exmoor National Park is to traverse one of the remotest corners of the country. There are also plenty of places on the regular trail where it would be possible to fall from a great height, even if you

When the going gets tough there's always ice cream!

strayed from the path by only a few metres. Still, with the path well signposted all the way along and the sea keeping you company for the entire stretch, it's difficult to get lost.

See pp30-31 for some suggested itineraries covering different walking speeds

As with any walk, you can minimise the risks by preparing properly. Your greatest danger on the walk is likely to be from the weather, which can be so unpredictable in this corner of the world, so it is vital that you dress for inclement conditions and always carry a set of dry clothes with you.

When to go

SEASONS

'My shoes are clean from walking in the rain.' **Jack Kerouac**

Britain is a notoriously wet country and South-West England does nothing to crush that reputation. Few walkers manage to complete the walk without suffering at least one downpour; two or three per walk are more likely, even in summer. That said, it's equally unlikely that you'll spend a week in the area and not see any sun at all, and even the most cynical of walkers will have to admit that, during the **walking season** at least, there are more sunny days than showery ones. The season, by the way, starts at Easter and builds to a

Above: The smaller beaches, such as this one at Bude, can get busy in summer. Others such as Woolacombe stretch for several miles and never seem crowded even in summer.

crescendo in August, before steadily tailing off in October. Few people attempt the entire path after the end of October though there are still plenty of people on day walks. Many places close in November for the winter.

There is one further point to consider when planning your trip. Firstly, remember that most people set off on the trail at a weekend. This means that you'll find the trail quieter **during the week** and as a consequence you may find it easier to book accommodation.

Spring

Find a dry fortnight in springtime (around the end of March to mid June) and you're in for a treat. The wild flowers are coming into bloom, lambs are skipping in the meadows and the grass is green and lush. Of course, finding a dry week in spring is not easy but occasionally there's a mini-heatwave at this time.

INTRODUCTION

Above: Under the trees on The Hobby Drive, approaching Clovelly; even in summer you should be prepared for some wet days.

Another advantage with walking at this time is that there will be fewer walkers and finding accommodation is relatively easy, though do check that where you want to stay is open. Easter is the exception; it's the first major holiday in the year when people flock to the coast.

Summer

Summer, on the other hand, can be a bit too busy, at least in the towns and tourist centres, and weekends in August can be both suffocating and insufferable. Still, the chances of a prolonged period of sunshine are of course higher at this time of year than any other, the days are much longer, and all the facilities and public transport are operating. Our advice is this: if you're flexible and want to avoid seeing too many people on the trail, avoid the school holidays, which basically means ruling out the tail end of July, all of August and the first few days of September. Alternatively, if you crave the company of other walkers summer will provide you with the opportunity of meeting plenty, though do remember that you **must book your accommodation in advance**, especially if staying in B&B-type accommodation. However, you'll need to factor in that most such places only accept advance bookings for a minimum of two nights in the summer. Despite the higher than average chance of sunshine, take clothes for any eventuality – it will probably still rain at some point.

Autumn

September is a wonderful time to walk; many tourists have returned home and the path is clear. The weather is usually reliably sunny too, at least at the beginning of September. The first signs of winter will be felt in October but there's nothing really to deter the walker. In fact there's still much to entice you, such as the colours of the heathland, which come into their own in autumn; a magnificent blaze of brilliant purples and pinks, splashed with the occasional yellow flowers of gorse (it is more usual in spring but can thrive in autumn).

By the end of October, however, the weather will begin to get a little wilder and the nights will start to draw in. The walking season is almost at an end and most campsites and some B&Bs and hostels may close.

Winter

November can bring crisp clear days which are ideal for walking, although you'll definitely feel the chill when you stop on the cliff tops for a break. Winter temperatures rarely fall below freezing but the incidence of gales and storms definitely increases. You need to be fairly hardy to walk in December and January and you may have to alter your plans because of the weather. By

February the daffodils and primroses are already appearing but even into March it can still be decidedly chilly if the sun is not out.

While winter is definitely the low season with many places closed, this can be more of an advantage than a disadvantage. Very few people walk at this time of year, giving you long stretches of the trail to yourself. When you do stumble across other walkers they are as happy as you to stop and chat. Finding B&B accommodation is easier as you rarely have to book more than a night ahead (though it is still worth checking in advance as some B&Bs close out of season), but if you are planning to camp, or are on a small budget, you will find places to stay much more limited.

WEATHER

Before departing on your walk, tell yourself this: at some point on my walk it is going to **rain**. That's not to say it will, but at least if it does you won't be too disappointed and will hopefully have come prepared for this, clothes-wise. Besides, walking in the rain can be fun, at least for a while: the gentle drumming of rain on hood can be quite relaxing, the path is usually quiet, and if it really does chuck it down at least it provides an excuse to linger in tearooms and have that extra scone. And as long as you dress accordingly and take note of the safety advice given on pp56-9, walking in moderate rain is no more dangerous than walking at any other time – though do be careful, particularly on exposed sections, if the path becomes slippy or the wind picks up.

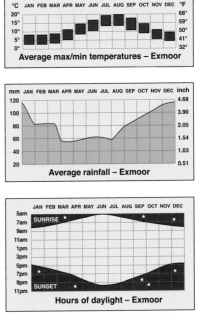

Average max/min temperatures – Exmoor

Average rainfall – Exmoor

DAYLIGHT HOURS

If walking in winter, autumn or even early spring, you must take account of how far you can walk in the available light. It won't be possible to cover as many miles as you would in summer. Conversely, in the summer months there is enough available light until at least 9pm – so don't use that as an

Hours of daylight – Exmoor

excuse for finishing your day's walk early! Remember, too, that you will get a further 30-45 minutes of usable light before sunrise and after sunset depending on the weather.

❏ FESTIVALS AND ANNUAL EVENTS

Before leaving home it may be wise to be aware of any cultural events that could turn your peaceful seaside stroll into something resembling the Rio Carnival! You may wish to consider either avoiding or participating in the following events whilst planning your walk.

June

● **Ilfracombe Victorian and Steampunk Celebration** (🖳 visitilfracombe.co.uk) sees locals and visitors dress up in Victorian costumes for a week-long celebration of Ilfracombe's past.

● **GoldCoast Oceanfest** (🖳 goldcoastoceanfest.co.uk) Ostensibly a weekend music festival in Croyde Bay though with as much emphasis on sport, especially surfing.

● **Barnstaple Fringe Theatre Festival** (🖳 theatrefest.co.uk) Over 100 performances from numerous theatre companies taking place over four days in late June.

July

● **Minehead & Exmoor Music Festival** (🖳 mineheadmusicfestival.org) Four concerts featuring the Festival Orchestra spread out over a week in late July; held at Minehead's Regal Theatre.

August

● **Combe Martin Carnival** (🖳 visitcombemartin.com) Annual week-long event held in mid August with raft and wheelbarrow races as well as fireworks and a much-anticipated parade.

● **Bude Jazz Festival** (🖳 jazzfestivalbude.co.uk) A four-day festival, usually at the end of August/beginning of September, featuring top UK and international musicians.

● **Ilfracombe Carnival** (🖳 visitilfracombe.co.uk) A procession of floats parades though the town on the August bank holiday weekend.

September

● **Appledore Book Festival** (🖳 appledorebookfestival.co.uk) Held over a week in late September, this festival attracts many highly regarded authors to the stage.

● **Barnstaple Fair Carnival** (🖳 barnstaplecarnival.org.uk) Held for four days beginning on the Wednesday before 20th September with carnivals and processions culminating in a firework 'extravaganza'.

● **Clovelly Lobster and Crab Feast** (🖳 clovelly.co.uk/events) Family day out with lobster and crab dishes cooked on the quay.

This list is by no means comprehensive. For further information on other festivals in the area visit: 🖳 visitdevon.co.uk, or 🖳 exmoor.com.

If you're carrying on along the SWCP you'll find the fun continues over the border in Cornwall too, including Boscastle Walking Week in late March. Further details on festivals around the Cornish coast can be found at 🖳 cornwall.gov.uk and in Trailblazer's guide to *Cornwall Coast Path*, part of this series of books for the SWCP.

Opposite: Looking out through the trees towards Foreland Point (Map 10).
Overleaf: The sweeping descent to Bossington Beach (Map 5).(Photo © Simon McCrohan).

Practical information for the walker

ROUTE FINDING

© HENRY STEDMAN

For most of its length the coast path is well signposted. At confusing junctions the route is usually indicated by a finger-post sign with 'coast path' written on it. At other points, where there could be some confu-
sion, there are wooden waymark posts with an acorn symbol and a yellow arrow to indicate in which direction you should head. The waymarking is the responsibility of the local authorities along the trail who have a duty to maintain the path. Although they generally do a good job, occasionally you will come across sections of the trail where waymarking is ambiguous, or even non-existent, but with the detailed trail maps and directions in this book and the fact that you always have the sea to one side it would be hard to get really lost.

Using GPS with this book

Given the above, modern Wainwrights may scoff at the idea of using GPS technology on a walk like this. More open-minded walkers, though, will accept that GPS technology can be an inexpensive, well-established if non-essential navigational aid. In no time at all a GPS receiver with a clear view of the sky will establish your position and altitude in a variety of formats, including the British OS grid system, to within a few metres. These days most **smartphones** have a GPS receiver built in and mapping software available to run on it.

The maps in this book's route guide section include numbered waypoints; these correlate to the list on pp207-8, which gives the latitude/longitude position in a decimal minute format as well as a description. Where the path is vague, or there are several options, you will find more waypoints. You can download the complete list of these waypoints for free as a GPS-readable file (that doesn't include the text descriptions) from the Trailblazer website: ⬜ trailblazer-guides.com (click on GPS waypoints).

Bear in mind that the vast majority of people who tackle this path do so perfectly well without GPS technology.

(Opposite) Taking a well-earned rest on the cliffs of Duckpool (Map 52), with views south down the Cornish coast to Bude and beyond.

ACCOMMODATION

The route guide (Part 4) lists a fairly comprehensive selection of places to stay along the length of the trail. You have two main options: camping or using B&Bs and hotels. While there ought to be a third option too, that of staying in hostels, there aren't enough on this stretch of the coast path to make this a realistic alternative. Few people stick to just one of these options the whole way, preferring, for example, to camp most of the time but spend every third night in a guesthouse, or perhaps use hostels where possible but splash out on a B&B every once in a while.

When booking accommodation that is far from the path, remember to ask if a pick-up and drop-off service is available (usually only B&Bs provide this service); at the end of a tiring day it's nice to know a lift is available to take you to your accommodation rather than having to traipse another two or three miles off the path to get to your bed for the night. (This is particularly true at the end of this section of the SWCP, around Hartland Point, where there are only a few B&Bs and they are usually a fair walk from the path – and the walking is arduous enough as it is around this peninsula.)

The facilities' table on pp32-3 provides a quick snapshot of what type of accommodation is available in each of the towns and villages along the way, while the tables on p30 and p31 provide some suggested itineraries.

Camping

There are campsites most of the way along the South West Coast Path. That said, few people choose to camp every night. You're almost bound to get at least one night where the rain falls relentlessly, soaking equipment and sapping morale, and it is then that many campers opt to spend the next night drying out in a hostel or B&B. There are, however, many advantages with camping; it's more economical, for a start (see p29).

If you do decide to camp the whole way along the stretch of the SWCP described in this book, you will find some days where you either have to walk a very, very long way, or where you'll be forced to either wild camp (though remember it is illegal to do so without the permission of the landowner) or stay in a bothy (of which there three along the trail). The stretch around the Taw-Torridge Estuary, leading past Barnstaple, is particularly devoid of campsites (there's only one between Croyde and Appledore, and no suitable spots for wild camping), as is the stretch between Westward Ho! and Hartland Quay, which has no campsites at all, but does have some bothy and wild-camping potential.

Campsites vary; some are just a quiet corner of a farmer's field, while others are full-blown holiday parks with a few spaces put aside for tents; since their main customers are families on their annual holidays, backpackers are often low on their list of priorities. Nearly all the campsites in this book have showers (the exception being Tarka Trail Camping, p158, near Fremington), although, as with the quality of the site, the standard of their facilities can also vary.

Camping is an option at YHA Elmscott (see p193) but there is space for only three tents. As mentioned above, **wild camping** (ie not in a regular campsite) **is not allowed**. If you are forced to wild camp, try to pitch late, and leave early, never light camp fires (use a camping stove if you need to cook), and be sure to take absolutely everything with you when you leave.

Camping is not an easy option; the route is wearying enough without carrying your accommodation around with you. However, you could also look into employing a baggage-transfer company (see p26). Of course this does mean it will cost more and that you will lose a certain amount of freedom as you have to decide on your destination at least a day before – and stick to it – so that you and your bag can be reunited every evening.

Rates vary from site to site. Most of the sites in this book have a special rate for coastal-path hikers (usually around £10pp – be sure to tell them you're walking the coast path!). However, at some campsites you may end up paying for a full pitch, which can be as much as £20 or £30 in peak summer season.

Note that although every effort has been made to ensure that this book is up-to-date, things can change quickly. While planning your itinerary, it's a good idea to contact the campsites that you are planning to stay at, just to ensure that they are still operational.

Bothies

There are three National Trust-run 'bothies' along this stretch of the SWCP. Unlike genuine bothies found in, say, the Scottish Highlands, these are not free (though they are cheap), and they must be booked in advance. A booking, though, does get you the whole place to yourself. These bothies offer very basic lodgings – you will need to have your own bedding, for example – so they are really only an option for campers who are carrying all their gear.

The three official bothies on this trail are renovated stone huts with one or two sleeping platforms onto which you place your roll mat and sleeping bag. They have a cold-water sink, but no showers, and only an outdoor compost toilet. They also have electricity and some basic lighting. Two are very close to each other, just before you reach Lynmouth (see Maps 10 & 11), while a third is between Westward Ho! and Clovelly (see Map 41). There are one or two ramshackle huts along the path that could, at a push, also be used as emergency bothies, but the shelter in these is minimal.

To book any of the National Trust-run bothies, see 🖳 nationaltrust.org.uk. They tend to cost around £20-30 for the whole bothy, which will sleep two to four people.

Hostels

The Exmoor and North Devon Coast Path is not well served by hostels – there are large swathes where hostels don't exist – so it isn't possible to stay one every night. Only two YHA hostels remain open: Minehead, and Elmscott, near Hartland Quay, and the Minehead one is too far from the path to be convenient. There are also two independent hostels at Minehead and Ilfracombe (or three if you count the more expensive boutique-like hostel at Woolacombe).

Most hostels have dorm rooms (sleeping up to seven people) and private rooms, some of which are en suite but mostly facilities are shared. They also have a whole range of facilities from drying rooms to internet access and/or wifi as well as fully equipped kitchens for guests to use. Some have a shop selling

PLANNING YOUR WALK

emergency groceries, snacks and souvenirs. Hostels are good places to meet fellow walkers, swap stories and compare blisters.

If you are travelling in April/May or September you may find some hostels entirely taken over by school groups, leaving walkers shut out. Contact the YHA or the relevant hostel to find out the exact opening dates. It's worth noting that if you are walking with a partner and therefore would otherwise be sharing the cost of a room in a B&B, the cost of staying in a hostel (around £16-30pp for a dorm bed), once breakfast has been added on, is not that much cheaper than staying in a B&B.

Contact the **Youth Hostels Association of England and Wales** (YHA; ☎ 0800 019 1700 or ☎ 01629-592700, 🖳 yha.org.uk) for details of membership and also to book either of their two hostels.

Bed and breakfast accommodation
Bed and Breakfasts (**B&Bs**) are a great British institution and many of those along the South-West Coast Path are absolutely charming.

❏ **SHOULD YOU BOOK YOUR ACCOMMODATION IN ADVANCE?**
When walking any section of the South-West Coast Path it's essential that you have your night's accommodation booked by the time you set off in the morning, whether you're planning to stay in a hostel or a B&B. Nothing is more deflating than to arrive at your destination at the day's end only to find that you've then got to walk a further five miles or so, or even take a detour, because everywhere in town is booked.

That said, there's a certain amount of hysteria regarding the booking of accommodation, with many websites, B&Bs and other organisations suggesting you book at least six months in advance. Whilst it's true that the earlier you book the more chance you have of getting precisely the accommodation you require, booking so far in advance does leave you vulnerable to changing circumstances and may mean you lose all your deposits if you are forced to change your plans. By not booking so far in advance, you give yourself the chance to shift your holiday plans to a later date should the unforeseen arise.

It's worth noting that the lack of **B&B-style accommodation** is not as bad as some suggest, at least not outside the high season (ie the summer period coinciding with the long school holidays in the UK). Outside this period, and particularly in April/May or September, as long as you're flexible and willing to take what's offered, with maybe even a night or two in a hostel if that's all there is, you should get away with booking just a few nights in advance, or indeed just the night before. The exceptions to this rule are at weekends and in the high season, when everywhere is busy. It is essential to be aware that **most places require a minimum booking of two nights in high season** unless the booking is near the actual date required.

Campers, however, have more flexibility and can almost always just turn up and find a space there and then, though ringing in advance would give you more certainty. The exception is at large holiday parks, such as Upper Lynstone Caravan Park in Bude, where you should phone well in advance especially at weekends and in summer.

If staying in **hostels**, the same applies though do be careful when travelling out of high season as sometimes hostels are fully booked by school groups and shut altogether from around November to Easter. Once again, it's well worth phoning at least one night before and well before that if it's a weekend.

Nearly all the B&Bs on this route have either en suite rooms or rooms with private facilities; only a few have rooms with shared facilities. The rooms usually contain either a double bed (known as a double room), or two single beds (known as a twin room). Some rooms sleep three (Tr) or four people (Qd); these are often called family rooms. Generally this means there is a double bed (which two people may need to share) with one or two single beds, or bunk beds.

Note that in winter some B&Bs close; for those that stay open, make sure that beforehand they will have their heating in your room turned on!

An evening meal (usually £15-20) is often provided at the more remote or bigger places, but almost always needs to be booked at least 24 hours in advance. (Note that if you have any dietary requirements – eg if you're vegetarian, or need a gluten-free meal – you should mention this when requesting the meal.) Alternatively, if you want to eat out, there's nearly always a pub or restaurant nearby or, if it's far, the B&B owner may give you a lift to and from the nearest place with food.

The difference between a B&B and a **guesthouse** is minimal, though some of the better guesthouses are more like hotels, offering evening meals and a lounge for guests. **Pubs** and **inns** also offer bed and breakfast accommodation and prices are generally no more than in a regular B&B. **Hotels** usually *do* cost more than B&Bs, and some might be a little incensed by a bunch of smelly walkers turning up and treading mud into their carpet. Most on the South-West Coast Path, however, are used to seeing walkers and welcome them warmly.

Rates Proprietors quote their **tariffs** either on a **per person** (pp) basis, or **per room**. Room rates are the same whether one or two people share. Accommodation in this guide starts at around £25pp (assuming two people are sharing) for the most basic B&Bs rising to around £50pp for more luxurious places. Most charge around £30-40pp. Prices in hotels start at around £35pp; however, sometimes rates are for the room only and breakfast is additional. Solo walkers should take note: single rooms are not easy to find so you will often end up occupying a double/twin room and may have to pay a single occupancy supplement (from £10), or even the full room rate.

Most places now have their own website and offer online/email **booking** but for some you will need to phone. Note that it can be worth contacting the proprietors direct as this may lead to better rates than via an online booking agent. Most places ask for a deposit (about 50%) which is generally non-refundable if you cancel at short notice. Some places may charge 100% if the booking is for one night only, or they may require a stay of at least two nights (see box opposite). Always let the owner know as soon as possible if you have to cancel your booking so they can offer the bed to someone else.

Airbnb

The rise of Airbnb (⌨ airbnb.co.uk) has seen private homes and apartments opened up to overnight travellers on an informal basis. While accommodation is primarily based in cities, the concept is spreading to tourist hotspots in more rural areas, but do check thoroughly what you are getting and the precise location. While the first couple of options listed may be in the area you're after, others may be too far afield for walkers. At its best, this is a great way to meet local people in a relatively unstructured environment, but do be aware that these places are not registered B&Bs, so standards may vary, and prices may not necessarily be any lower.

FOOD AND DRINK

Breakfast and lunch

Stay in a B&B and you'll be filled to the gills with a cooked **English breakfast**. This usually consists of a bowl of cereal followed by a plateful of eggs, bacon, sausages, mushrooms, tomatoes and possibly baked beans or black pudding, with toast and butter, and all washed down with coffee, tea and/or juice. Enormously satisfying the first time you try it, by the fourth or fifth morning you may start to prefer a lighter continental breakfast. If you have had enough of these cooked breakfasts and/or plan an early start, ask if you can have a packed lunch instead of breakfast. Your host or hostel can usually provide a **packed lunch** at an additional cost (unless it's in lieu of breakfast), though of course there's nothing to stop you preparing your own lunch (but do bring a penknife if you plan to do this), or going to a pub or café.

Plan ahead: certain stretches of the walk are virtually devoid of eating places (the stretch from Porlock Weir to Lynmouth/Lynton, and from Combe Martin to Ilfracombe, or the final stretch from Hartland Quay to Bude) so read ahead about the next day's walk in Part 4 to make sure you never go hungry.

Cream teas

Whatever you do for lunch, don't forget to leave some room for a cream tea, a morale, energy and cholesterol booster all rolled into one delicious package: a pot of tea accompanied by scones served with cream and jam, and sometimes a cake or two. The jury is out on whether you should put the jam on first (as is preferred in Cornwall) or the cream (as preferred in Devon). Either way, do not miss the chance of at least one cream tea.

Evening meals

Pubs are as much a feature of the walk as seagulls and sheep, and in some cases the pub is as much a tourist attraction as any Roman fort or ruined priory. The Ship Inn at Porlock, The Rising Sun at Lynmouth, The Hunters Inn, nestled in the Heddon Valley, The Pack o' Cards at Combe Martin, harbour-side Red Lion Hotel at Clovelly, 13th-century Bush Inn at Morwenstow... the list goes on.

Most pubs have become highly attuned to the desires of walkers and offer lunch and evening meals (often with a couple of local dishes and almost always a few vegetarian, vegan and gluten-free options), some locally-brewed beers, a garden to relax in on hot days and a roaring fire to huddle around on cold ones. The standard of the food varies widely, though is usually served in big portions, which is often just about all that matters to walkers at the end of a long day. In many of the villages the pub is the only place to eat out. Note that pubs may close in the afternoon, especially in the winter months, so check in advance if you are hoping to visit a particular one, and also if you are planning lunch there as food serving hours can change.

That other great British culinary institution, the **fish & chip shop**, can be found in virtually every town on the trail. As well as the chippies, there are other **takeaways** (such as Chinese and Indian) in the larger towns en route.

Buying camping supplies
There is a grocery shop of some description in most of the places along the route, though most are small (and often combined with the post office) and finding precisely what you went in for is unlikely. If self-catering, therefore, your menu for the evening will depend upon what you found in the store that day. Part 4 details what shops are on the path.

Drinking water
On a hot day in some of the remoter parts after a steep climb or two you'll quickly dehydrate, which is at best highly unpleasant and at worst mightily dangerous. Always carry water with you and in hot weather drink three to four litres a day. Don't be tempted by the water in the streams; if the cow or sheep faeces in the water don't make you ill, the chemicals from the pesticides and fertilisers used on the farms almost certainly will. Using iodine or another purifying treatment will help to combat the former, though there's little you can do about the

---

❑ TRADITIONAL FOOD IN SOMERSET AND DEVON

● **Somerset** As a major centre of farming and fishing, it's not surprising that the South West is a key supplier of food to the rest of Britain and can boast some pretty fine local specialities. In Somerset – literally, 'Land of the Summer People' – fruit is unsurprisingly bountiful with **apples**, the main ingredient for their legendary cider (see box on p24), particularly renowned. However, the **cheeses** of Somerset are perhaps its most famous export, with the name Cheddar used throughout the world, though only The Cheddar Gorge Cheese Company actually produces the cheese within the parish of Cheddar.

● **Devon** Say 'Devon' to most Brits and in addition to images of sparkling coastlines and rolling hills, the county's name will also conjure up the delights of **clotted cream** (a thick cream with a high fat content, made by gently heating and cooling full-cream cow's milk) which is best enjoyed as part of a traditional **cream tea** with a scone or two and some whortleberry jam. This is an Exmoor speciality, **whortleberry** being the local name for wild bilberry (though they go by several other names including blueberry, heidelberry, huckleberry, hurtleberry and wimberry) and locally they're called 'worts' or 'urts'. **Dairy products** in general are plentiful in this corner of the country, including delicious yoghurts and ice-cream.

In the sea, South Devon **crab** is reputed to be the tastiest in the world and smoked eels are a speciality in these parts too. Other **fish** caught in the Bristol Channel include thornback ray, bass, conger, dogfish, flounder, whiting, dab pout, cod and codling. There's also shellfish: lobsters, crabs, scallops, langoustines, clams and mussels, which are often caught by boats from the smaller coastal villages.

Even if you're on a tight budget the ubiquitous **fish & chips** can be satisfying if cooked with fresh fish. At the other end of the scale there are plenty of restaurants around the coast offering mouth-watering dishes concocted from locally caught fish.

latter. It's a lot safer to fill up from taps instead. Most places will be more than
happy to fill up a thirsty hiker's water bottle – and don't forget that water from
taps in public toilets is perfectly safe to drink.

❏ BEERS AND CIDERS

Beers The process of brewing beer is believed to have been in Britain since the
Neolithic period and is an art local brewers have been perfecting ever since. Real ale
is beer that has been brewed using traditional methods. Real ales are not filtered or
pasteurised, a process which removes and kills all the yeast cells, but instead undergo
a secondary fermentation at the pub which enhances the natural flavours and brings
out the individual characteristics of the beer. It's served at cellar temperature with no
artificial fizz added, unlike keg beer which is pasteurised and has the fizz added by
injecting nitrogen dioxide.

Based in the Somerset town of Wiveliscombe on the border of the national park,
Exmoor Ales (🖳 exmoorales.co.uk) produces six permanent ales, including Exmoor
Ram (a 3.5% Golden Ale) and Exmoor Beast (a 6.6% dark Porter), named after
Exmoor's most famous modern mystery (see box p62), and six seasonal ales. Nearby,
Cotleigh Brewery (🖳 cotleighbrewery.com) was originally based in Devon but
moved to Wiveliscombe after just one year of trading. They brew three permanent
cask ales and around a dozen seasonal ales, each named after a member of the local
avifauna such as Barn Owl or Buzzard. Devon is also well served, with numerous
micro-breweries operating within its borders, including **Barum Brewery** (🖳
reforminn.co.uk/barum-brewery), a tiny brewery based at the Reform Inn in Pilton
near Barnstaple. They are responsible for the dangerously strong 6.6% ABV
Barnstablasta, one of 14 different ales brewed on the premises.

Country Life Brewery (🖳 countrylifebrewery.co.uk) is located in a quirky family theme park called The Big Sheep (🖳 thebigsheep.co.uk), in the village of
Abbotsham, near Bideford; you can watch the brewing process and pick up a couple
of bottles of tipples such as Black Boar (4.5%) or Old Appledore Ale (3.7%). Further
west along the trail, **Forge Brewery** (🖳 forge-brewery.co.uk) is located in the tiny
village of Woolley, between Hartland and Bude, and is continuing a proud tradition
of brewing that was started by the Augustinian monks at the abbey. They have ten real
ales to choose from.

Ciders A pint of cider on this section of the walk is pretty much as obligatory as blisters. Somerset in particular is known for its cider farms with: **Sheppy's** (🖳 sheppys
cider.com) at Bradford-on-Tone, which has been made by the Sheppy family for six
generations; **Torre Cider** (🖳 torrecider.farm) at Washford, Watchet; **Parson's Choice
Cider** (🖳 parsonschoicecider.co.uk) at West Lyng; **Perry's Cider** (🖳 perryscider
.co.uk) of Ilminster; and **Hecks** (🖳 heckscider.com) at Street, with the Heck family
also on their sixth generation of cider makers. The **Somerset Cider Brandy Co** (🖳
somersetciderbrandy.com), at Martock, was granted the UK's first ever cider-distilling
licence in 1989 to make their award-winning Somerset Cider Brandy, with each bottle
traceable back to its source orchard. Though none is particularly near the path, all have
online shops if you'd like a taste of Somerset sent to your home after your walk.

Scrumpy, or rough cider, is a particular form of cider, easy to differentiate from
the weaker, more mass-market keg ciders, being cloudy, fizz-free and with bits floating in it too! The only thing to remember before drinking scrumpy is that it should be
done in moderation – it's powerful stuff. After you've drunk it, you'll be lucky to
remember anything at all.

PLANNING YOUR WALK

The smartphone app Refill (🖥 refill.org.uk) might also be handy. It shows on a digital map any premises happy to fill up people's water bottles for free.

MONEY

There are several banks on the trail, most equipped with an **ATM** (cash machine/cashpoint). You'll also find ATMs in some shops and stores though these may charge around £1.75 to withdraw money. The only place where you need to be careful is from Westward Ho! to Bude where there are no ATMs on the path (the nearest place to get money being Hartland, 2½ miles inland). Make sure you take enough cash out at Westward Ho!. Another way of getting money in your hand is to use the **cashback system**: find a store or a pub that will accept a debit card and when you are paying for whatever you are buying (usually a minimum of £5) ask them to advance cash against the card you are using.

Although many local stores, pubs and B&Bs accept credit or debit cards, some don't and others have a minimum spend on a card so it is essential to carry cash with you.

Using the Post Office for banking

Several banks have agreements with the Post Office (PO) allowing customers to make cash withdrawals free of charge using a debit card at branches throughout the country. Given that many towns and villages have post offices this is a very useful facility. However, check with the Post Office Helpline (☎ 0345 722 3344, 🖥 postoffice.co.uk/branch-finder) that your bank has an agreement with the post office and that the post offices en route are still open and offer a cash withdrawal service. If using the website put in the place name and you will be told if there is a PO there or nearby as well as the opening days/hours and services.

OTHER SERVICES

There is **internet access** in the libraries along the trail, and in some tourist information centres, which also usually have free **wi-fi**. Most pubs, restaurants, cafés and B&Bs also have free wi-fi, and even some campsites.

In addition to a grocery store most small towns have a **launderette**, **chemist/pharmacy**, **public toilets** and a **phone box**. Smaller villages may have a grocery store and public toilets, but are unlikely to have much else.

For hiking and camping gear, there are **outdoor equipment shops** in Minehead, Porlock, Combe Martin, Barnstaple and Bude.

WALKING COMPANIES

It is, of course, possible to turn up with your boots and backpack at Minehead and just start walking, with little planned save for your accommodation (see box on p20). The following companies, however, are in the business of making your holiday as stress-free and enjoyable as possible.

Baggage transfer

For those who don't fancy being burdened while on the path, it is possible to arrange to have your luggage transferred to your destination at the end of each day. The main baggage company on the SWCP is the aptly named **Luggage Transfers** (☎ 01326-567247, ☎ 0800-043 7927, 💻 www.luggagetransfers.co .uk), who cover the whole of the path, charging from £15 for two bags (max weight 23kg per piece of luggage); any journey can be quoted for. They deliver

---

❑ INFORMATION FOR FOREIGN VISITORS

● **Currency** The British pound (£) comes in notes of £50, £20, £10 and £5, and coins of £2 and £1. The pound is divided into 100 pence (usually referred to as 'p', pronounced 'pee') which come in silver coins of 50p, 20p, 10p and 5p, and copper coins of 2p and 1p.

● **Money** Up-to-date **rates of exchange** can be found on 💻 xe.com/currencyconvert er, at some post offices, or at any bank or travel agent. These days rarely used, **travellers' cheques** can be cashed only at banks, foreign exchanges and some of the large hotels; it makes much more sense to use a combination of **debit card and cash**.

● **Business hours** Most **grocery shops** are open Monday to Saturday 9am-5pm though some open as early as 7.30/8am; many also open on Sundays but not usually for the whole day. **Supermarkets** are open daily 8am-8pm (often longer) and on Sunday from about 9am to 5 or 6pm, though main branches of supermarkets generally open 10am-4pm or 11am-5pm.

Main **post offices** generally open Monday to Friday 9am-5pm and Saturday 9am-12.30pm; **banks** typically open at 9.30/10am Monday to Friday and close at 3.30/4pm, though in some places both post offices and banks may open only two or three days a week and/or in the morning, or limited hours, only.

ATMs (**cash machines**) located outside a bank, shop, post office or petrol station are open all the time, but any that are inside will be accessible only when that place is open. Most are free to use, but note that those with a charge, such as Link machines (💻 link.co.uk/consumers/locator) may not accept foreign-issued cards.

Pub hours are less predictable as each pub may have different opening hours. However, most pubs on the Path open daily 11am-11pm (some close at 10.30pm on Sunday) but **some close in the afternoon**.

The last entry time to most **museums and galleries** is usually half an hour, or an hour, before the official closing time.

● **Public holidays** Most businesses in the South-West are shut on 1 January, Good Friday (March/April), Easter Monday (March/April), the first and last Monday in May, the last Monday in August, 25 December and 26 December.

● **School holidays** State-school holidays in England are generally as follows: a one-week break late October, two weeks over Christmas and the New Year, a week mid February, two weeks around Easter, one week at the end of May/early June (to coincide with the bank holiday at the end of May) and six weeks from late July to early September. Private-school holidays fall at the same time, but tend to be slightly longer.

● **Documents** If you are a member of a National Trust organisation in your country bring your membership card as you should be entitled to free entry to National Trust properties and sites in the UK.

● **Travel/medical insurance** All visitors to Britain should be properly insured, including comprehensive health coverage. Before Brexit on 1st January 2021, the

anywhere including campsites (as long as you have rung the campsite by the night before to give your name).

Alternatively, some of the **taxi** firms listed in this guide can provide a similar service within a local area if you want a break from carrying your bags for a day or so. Also, don't rule out the possibility of your B&B/guesthouse owner taking your bags ahead for you; plenty of them are glad to do so. Depending on the distance they may make no charge at all, or charge £10-15; this may be less than a taxi so is worth enquiring about.

European Health Insurance Card (EHIC) entitled EU nationals (on production of the card) to necessary medical treatment under the National Health Service (NHS) while on a temporary visit here. Since Brexit this system is still valid for the time being but check the current situation (🖳 nhs.uk/nhs-services, then click on Visiting or moving to England) before travelling. In any case, not all treatment will be covered and it is not a substitute for proper medical cover on your travel insurance for unforeseen bills and for getting you home should that be necessary. Also consider getting cover for loss and theft of personal belongings, especially if you are camping or staying in hostels, as there will be times when you'll have to leave your luggage unattended.

● **Weights and measures** Milk in Britain is still sometimes sold in pints (1 pint = 568ml), as is beer in pubs, though most other **liquids** including petrol (gasoline) and diesel are sold in litres.

Distances on road and path signs are given in miles (1 mile = 1.6km) rather than kilometres, and yards (1yd = 0.9m) rather than metres. The population remains divided between those who still use inches (1 inch = 2.5cm), feet (1ft = 0.3m) and yards and those who are happy with metric measurements; you'll often be told that 'it's only a hundred yards or so' to somewhere, rather than a hundred metres or so.

Most **food** is sold in metric weights (g and kg) but the imperial weights of pounds (lb: 1lb = 453g) and ounces (oz: 1oz = 28g) are frequently displayed too.

The **weather** – a frequent topic of conversation – is also an issue: while most forecasts predict temperatures in Celsius (C), some people continue to think in terms of Fahrenheit (F; see the temperature chart on p15 for conversions).

● **Smoking** Smoking in enclosed public spaces is banned. The ban relates not only to pubs and restaurants, but also to B&Bs, hostels and hotels. These latter have the right to designate one or more bedrooms where the occupants can smoke, but the ban is in force in all enclosed areas open to the public – even if they are in a private home such as a B&B. If you light up in a no-smoking area, which includes almost any indoor public place, you could be fined £50, but it will be the owners of the premises who suffer most if they fail to stop you, with a potential fine of £2500.

● **Time** During the winter, the whole of Britain is on Greenwich Meantime (GMT). The clocks move one hour forward on the last Sunday in March, remaining on British Summer Time (BST) until the last Sunday in October.

● **Telephone** From outside Britain the international country access code for Britain is ☎ 44 followed by the area code minus the first 0, and then the number you require. Within Britain, to call a landline number with the same code as the landline phone you are calling from, the code can be omitted. If your mobile phone is registered overseas, consider buying a local SIM card to keep costs down. See also box p39.

● **Emergency services** For police, ambulance, fire or coastguard dial ☎ 999, or the EU standard number ☎ 112.

Self-guided holidays

Useful for those who simply don't have the time to organise their trip, several companies now offer what are known as self-guided holidays, where your accommodation, transport at the start/end of the walk and baggage transportation along the trail are arranged for you.

Unless specified, all the companies below offer walks on the whole South-West Coast Path (SWCP) and they can tailor-make holidays if required. Detailed information and maps are also provided as a matter of course, thereby allowing you to just turn up and start marching!

● **Absolute Escapes** (☎ 0131-610 1210, 🖥 www.absoluteescapes.com; Edinburgh) Only offer walks on the other parts of the SWCP but can tailor make a holiday for this section of the SWCP.

● **Contours** (☎ 01629-821900, 🖥 www.contours.co.uk; Derbyshire) They divide the SWCP into ten sections and their itineraries from Minehead to Westward Ho! last six, seven and eleven days. They offer dog-friendly hikes.

● **Encounter Walking Holidays** (☎ 01208-871066, 🖥 encounterwalkinghol idays.com; Cornwall) Specialise in assisting overseas walkers along the route.

● **Explore Britain** (☎ 01740-650900, 🖥 www.explorebritain.com; Co Durham) Walks include Minehead to Barnstaple (6 days) and Minehead to Woolacombe (5 days).

● **Footpath Holidays** (☎ 01985-840049, 🖥 www.footpath-holidays.com; Wilts) Arrange a 6-day Exmoor Coast walk from Minehead to Instow, and a 5-day section along the North Devon Coast from Instow to Bude.

● **Great British Walks** (☎ 01600-713008, 🖥 www.great-british-walks.com; Monmouth) SWCP north section from Minehead to St Ives (Cornwall) in a variety of itineraries of 6-8 walking days.

● **Let's Go Walking!** (☎ 01837-880075, 🖥 www.letsgowalking.co.uk; Devon) Offers 8-day walks (Minehead to Barnstaple & Barnstaple to Crackington Haven (Cornwall), with an optional trip to Lundy Island.

● **Macs Adventure** (☎ 0141-530 8886, 🖥 www.macsadventure.com; Glasgow) Have walks covering the whole SWCP including Minehead to Westward Ho! (7 days) and Westward Ho! to Padstow (6-8 days).

● **Mickledore** (☎ 017687-72335, 🖥 www.mickledore.co.uk; Keswick) Offers itineraries along the whole SWCP.

● **Nearwater Walking Holidays** (☎ 01326-279278, 🖥 www.nearwaterwalk ingholidays.co.uk; Truro) Walks covering the whole path as well as sections.

● **Walk the Trail** (☎ 01326-567252, 🖥 www.walkthetrail.co.uk; Cornwall) Cover the whole of the SWCP, with itineraries for all levels of walking ability.

Group/guided walking tour

This is ideal for those who want the extra safety, security and companionship that comes with walking in a group. Accommodation, meals, transport to and from the trail, baggage transfer – all of these are usually included in the price.

● **HF Holidays** (☎ 0345-470 7558, 🖥 www.hfholidays.co.uk; Herts) Offers guided walks to various parts of the SWCP including the 7-night Somerset & North Devon Coast Path (Minehead to Croyde).

Budgeting

England is not a cheap place to go travelling. The accommodation providers on the South-West Coast Path are well-accustomed to seeing tourists and charge accordingly. You may think before you set out that you are going to try to keep your budget to a minimum by camping every night and cooking your own food but it's a rare walker who sticks to this rule. Besides, the B&Bs and pubs on the route are amongst the path's major attractions and it would be a pity not to sample the hospitality in at least some of them.

If the only expenses of this walk were accommodation and food, budgeting for the trip would be a piece of cake. Unfortunately, in addition there are all the little **extras** that push up the cost of your trip. Getting to and from the path can be very expensive. Then there's beer, cream teas, ice creams, laundry, souvenirs, entrance fees, buses here and there, baggage carriers... it's surprising how much all of these things add up.

CAMPING

Coastal-path hikers with small 'one-man' tents tend to be charged around £10 per night (though it can be much more in a large holiday park). You could therefore survive on less than £20 per person (pp) per day if you use the cheapest campsites, don't visit a pub, avoid all the museums and tourist attractions in the towns, and cook all your own food. But even then, unforeseen expenses will probably nudge your daily budget above this figure. Include the occasional pint, and perhaps a pub meal every now and then, and the figure will be nearer £30pp a day.

HOSTELS

Rates at hostels tend to be around £15-20pp, although YHA rates are cheaper if you are a member. These rates don't usually include breakfast but you may be able to order one for around £5-10, and you can often cook your own meals in the communal kitchens. Overall, expect to spend £30-40pp per day if staying in hostels.

B&Bs, PUBS, GUESTHOUSES AND HOTELS

[See also pp18-21] Assuming two people are sharing a double room, B&B rates start at £25pp per night but are usually £30-40pp, and can be more than £50pp. If you are walking alone, you'll sometimes have to pay the full room rate and so may need to fork out as much as £70-80 per night. Add the cost of lunch and dinner and you should reckon on about £45-50pp minimum with two people sharing; much more if you're on your own. Staying in a guesthouse or hotel will push the minimum up to £55-60pp.

Itineraries

To help plan your walk the **colour maps** at the end of the book have **gradient profiles** and there is also a **planning map** (see opposite inside back cover). The **table of town and village facilities** (pp32-3) gives a rundown on the essential information you will need regarding accommodation possibilities and services. Alternatively, you could follow one of the **suggested itineraries** below.

SUGGESTED ITINERARIES

The itineraries in the boxes below are based on different accommodation types (camping or B&B-style accommodation), each divided into three options depending on your walking speed. They are only suggestions so feel free to adapt them. Don't forget to **add on your travelling time** before and after the walk. If using public transport to get to the start and end of the walk see the **public transport map and service details and map** on pp48-50. Once you have an idea of your approach turn to Part 4 for detailed information on accommodation, places to eat and other services in each village and town on the route. Also in Part 4 you'll find summaries of the route to accompany the detailed trail maps.

PLANNING YOUR WALK

			CAMPING			
Relaxed		**Medium**		**Fast**		
Place	**Approx Distance**	**Place**	**Approx Distance**	**Place**	**Approx Distance**	
Night	miles km		miles km		miles km	
0 Minehead*	0	Minehead*	0	Minehead*	0	
1 Porlock*	7¼ 11.7	Porlock*	7¼ 11.7	Lynton*	22 35.4	
2 Lynton*	15¼ 24.6	Lynton*	15¼ 24.6	Watermouth	16 25.8	
3 Combe Martin	14 22.5	Combe Martin	14 22.5	Croyde	20½ 33	
4 Woolacombe	14¼ 22.9	Woolacombe	14¼ 22.9	Fremington	16¾ 27	
5 Croyde	6¼ 10.1	Croyde	6¼ 10.1	Abbotsham*	16¾ 27	
6 Fremington	16¾ 27	Fremington	16¾ 27	Stoke*	16 25.8	
7 Northam	7½ 12.1	Abbotsham*	16¾ 27	Bude	16 25.8	
8 Abbotsham*	9¼ 14.9	Stoke*	16 25.8			
9 Stoke*	16 25.8	Bude	16 25.8			
10 Elmscott	3½ 5.6					
11 Bude	13½ 21.7	* campsite is at least 1 mile from the path				

NOTES
● Approx distances are to campsites rather than to the towns/villages.
● To break the long walk between Porlock and Lynton, you could stay at Foreland Point Bothy (p98).
● To reduce the long walk to Stoke by around 3 miles, you could stay at Peppercombe Bothy (p178) rather than at Abbotsham.

STAYING IN B&B-STYLE ACCOMMODATION

Relaxed		Medium		Fast	
Place	**Approx Distance**	**Place**	**Approx Distance**	**Place**	**Approx Distance**
Night	miles km		miles km		miles/km
0 Minehead	0	Minehead	0	Minehead	0
1 Porlock Weir	9 14.5	Porlock Weir	9 14.5	Lynmouth	21¼ 34.2
2 Lynmouth	12¼ 19.7	Lynmouth	12¼ 19.7	Ilfracombe	19½ 31.4
3 Combe Martin	13¾ 22.1	Combe Martin	13¾ 22.1	Croyde	14¾ 23.7
4 Ilfracombe	5¾ 9.3	Woolacombe	14¼ 22.9	Barnstaple	13½ 21.7
5 Woolacombe	8½ 13.7	Braunton	14¾ 23.7	W'ward Ho!	18½ 29.8
6 Croyde	6¼ 10.1	Instow	12½ 20.1	Clovelly	11 17.7
7 Barnstaple	13½ 21.7	Westward Ho!	11 17.7	H'land Quay	10½ 16.9
8 Instow	7½ 12.1	Clovelly	11 17.7	Bude	15½ 25
9 Appledore	6¼ 10.1	Hartland Quay	10½ 16.9		
10 Westward Ho!	4¾ 7.6	Morwenstow	8 12.9		
11 Clovelly	11 17.7	Bude	7½ 12.1		
12 Hartland Quay	10½ 16.9				
13 Morwenstow	8 12.9				
14 Bude	7½ 12.1				

WHICH DIRECTION?

It's more common for walkers attempting the entire trail to start from Minehead and head west. This is also the logical way to walk, and thus the way we have chosen to describe the route in Part 4. If this is your first taste of the South-West Coast Path – but you think you may like to do it all one day – obviously this is the way to head, with the Cornwall section next up. Furthermore, Bude is a more picturesque place to celebrate the end of your walk than Minehead.

That said, this may of course be the final leg of your walk on the South-West Coast Path and thus Bude to Minehead would probably be the way to go. What's more, the prevailing wind usually comes from the west, so by walking to Minehead you'll find you have the weather behind you, pushing you on rather than driving in your face. If you prefer to swim against the tide of popular opinion and walk west to east you should find it easy to use this book, too.

❏ **WOOLACOMBE TO WESTWARD HO! – TWO OR THREE STAGES?**
Between Woolacombe and Westward Ho! there are nearly 40 miles of mostly flat and easy walking. For this reason, some choose to cover the miles in just two stages. Whilst doing so means you will get back to the more spectacular parts of the SWCP faster, you also risk exhausting yourself before the final three days to Bude, which are very strenuous indeed. Completing these 40 miles over a longer period of time will allow you to thoroughly explore the towns and villages on the way. There is plenty of accommodation en route so a plethora of itineraries is possible.

This book covers this section in three stages, but it could easily be divided into just two, or four or more.

W ←

VILLAGE AND TOWN FACILITIES

← BUDE Walking West – Minehead to Bude

Place* & Distance* approx miles / *km*	Bank (ATM)	Post Office	Info	Eating Place	Food Shop	Camp-site	Hostel Barn	B&B Hotel
Minehead 0	✓	✓	TIC	✓✓	✓	✓(+1¼)	YHA/H	✓✓
Bossington 6/*9.7*				✓				✓
(Porlock) **t/o 1¼/*2*** (+½)	✓	✓	TIC	✓✓	✓	✓		✓✓
Porlock Weir 1¾/*2.8*				✓✓	✓			✓✓
Countisbury 10¾/*17.3*				✓		B		✓
Lynmouth 1½/*2.4*			NPC	✓✓		B		✓✓
Lynton ¼/*0.4*	✓	✓	TIP	✓✓	✓			✓✓
Combe Martin 13½/*21.7*	✓	✓	TIP	✓✓	✓	✓		✓✓
Watermouth 2/*3.2*				✓✓		✓		✓
Hele 2¾/*4.4*				✓✓	✓			
Ilfracombe 1/*1.6*	✓	✓	TIC	✓✓	✓		H	✓✓
Lee Bay 3/*4.8* (& Lee +¼)				✓				
Woolacombe 5½/*8.8*	✓	✓	TIC	✓✓	✓	✓	H	✓✓
Croyde 6¼/*10*	✓§	✓		✓✓	✓	✓		✓✓
Saunton 2¼/*3.6*				✓		✓(+1¼)		✓
Braunton 6¼/*10*	✓	✓	TIC	✓✓	✓			✓✓
Chivenor 1¼/*2*				✓✓				
Barnstaple 3¾/*6*	✓	✓	TIC	✓✓	✓			✓✓
Fremington Quay 2½/*4*				✓		✓		
Instow 5/*8*		✓		✓✓	✓			✓✓
Bideford & E-Wtr 2¾/*4.4*	✓	✓	TIC	✓✓	✓			✓✓
(Northam) **t/o 1¼/*2*** (+½)						✓		✓✓
Appledore 2¼/*3.6*	✓	✓	TIP	✓✓	✓			✓✓
Westward Ho! 4¾/*7.6*	✓	✓		✓✓	✓			✓✓
(Abbotsham) **t/o 1¾/*2.8*** (+¾)				✓		✓(+¾)		
Peppercombe 3¼/*5.2*				✓(+¾)		B		✓
Clovelly 6/*9.7*			VC	✓✓				✓✓
Hartland Quay 10½/*16.9*				✓				✓
(Stoke ½/*0.8* from Hartland Quay)						✓		✓
(Hartland 2½/*4* from HQ)	✓§	✓		✓✓	✓			✓✓
(Elmscott) **t/o 2/*3.2*** (+¾)						✓	YHA	✓
(Morwenstow) **t/o 5½/*8.8*** (+½)				✓✓				✓
Bude 8/*12.9*	✓	✓	TIC	✓✓	✓	✓		✓✓

NOTES *PLACE & DISTANCE Places in **bold** are on the path; places in brackets and not in bold – eg (Porlock) – are a short walk off the path. DISTANCE is given from the place above. Distances are between **places on the route** or to the **main turnoff (t/o)** to places in brackets. For example the distance from Bossington to the turnoff for Porlock is 1¼ miles. Bracketed distances eg (+1) show the additional distance in miles off the route – eg Porlock village is ½ mile from the Coast Path.

PLANNING YOUR WALK

VILLAGE AND TOWN FACILITIES
Walking East – Bude to Minehead ▷MINEHEAD▷   E →

PLACE* & DISTANCE* APPROX MILES / KM	BANK (ATM)	POST OFFICE	INFO	EATING PLACE	FOOD SHOP	CAMP-SITE	HOSTEL BARN	B&B HOTEL
Bude 0	✓	✓	TIC	〰〰	✓	✓		〰〰
(Morwenstow) t/o 8 / *12.9* (+½)				〰				✓
(Elmscott) t/o 5½ / *8.8* (+¾)						✓	YHA	✓
Hartland Quay 2 / *3.2*				✓				✓
(Stoke ½ / *0.8* from Hartland Quay)						✓		✓
(Hartland 2½ / *4* from HQ) ✓§ ✓	✓§	✓		〰〰	✓			〰〰
Clovelly 10½ / *16.9*			VC	〰〰				〰〰
Peppercombe 6 / *9.7*				✓(+¾)		B		✓
(Abbotsham) t/o 3¼ / *5.2* (+¾)				✓		✓(+¾)		
Westward Ho! 1¾ / *2.8*	✓	✓		〰〰	✓			〰〰
Appledore 4¾ / *7.6*	✓	✓	TIP	〰〰	✓			〰〰
(Northam) t/o 2¼ / *3.6* (+½)						✓		〰
Bideford & E-Wtr 1¼ / *2* ✓	✓	✓	TIC	〰〰	✓			〰〰
Instow 2¾ / *4.4*		✓		〰〰	✓			〰〰
Fremington Quay 5 / *8*				✓		✓		
Barnstaple 2½ / *4*	✓	✓	TIC	〰〰	✓			〰〰
Chivenor 3¾ / *6*				〰				
Braunton 1¼ / *2*	✓	✓	TIC	〰〰	✓			〰〰
Saunton 6¼ / *10*				✓		✓(+1¼)		✓
Croyde 2¼ / *3.6*	✓§	✓		〰〰	✓	✓		〰〰
Woolacombe 6¼ / *10*	✓	✓	TIC	〰〰	✓	✓	H	〰〰
Lee Bay 5½ / *8.8* (& Lee +¼)				✓				
Ilfracombe 3 / *4.8*	✓	✓	TIC	〰〰	✓		H	〰〰
Hele 1 / *1.6*				〰	✓			
Watermouth 2¾ / *4.4*				〰		✓		✓
Combe Martin 2 / *3.2*	✓	✓	TIP	〰〰	✓	✓		〰〰
Lynton 13½ / *21.7*	✓	✓	TIP	〰〰	✓			〰〰
Lynmouth ¼ / *0.4*			NPC	〰〰		B		〰〰
Countisbury 1½ / *2.4*				✓		B		✓
Porlock Weir 10¾ / *17.3*				〰	✓			〰〰
(Porlock) t/o 1¾ / *2.8* (+½) ✓	✓	✓	TIC	〰〰	✓	✓		〰〰
Bossington 1¼ / *2*				✓				✓
Minehead 6 / *9.7*	✓	✓	TIC	〰〰	✓	✓(+1¼)	YHA/H	〰〰

B&B/HOTEL ✓ = one place 〰 = two 〰〰 = three or more
HOSTEL/BARN YHA = YHA hostel H = independent hostel
CAMPSITE Bracketed distance eg (½) shows mileage from Coast Path B = bothy
EATING PLACE ✓ = one place 〰 = two 〰〰 = three or more
INFO TIC/P = Tourist Info Centre/Point NPC = National Park Centre VC = Visitor Centre
BANK/ATM ✓ = no charge for ATM use ✓§ = ATM with charges for withdrawal

PLANNING YOUR WALK

THE BEST DAY AND WEEKEND WALKS

Trying to pick one particular section that is representative of the entire trail is impossible because each is very different. The wilds of Exmoor, the beaches of Woolacombe and Croyde, the estuaries of Bideford and Barnstaple, and the windswept cliff-top beauty of Hartland – each region enjoys its own character. It would be erroneous to think that visiting one section could give you a flavour of the entire region. That said, if you don't have the time to walk the entire route

❏ **OTHER TRAILS**
Whilst the South-West Coast Path follows the coastline of Exmoor, other walking trails meander through its interior and some, at points, cross over or join the coastal path, offering plenty of opportunities for short (or long) diversions off the trail. Such trips are beyond the scope of this book but the following selection, plus a glance at an Ordnance Survey map, will give you some idea of the other walks available.

● **The Coleridge Way** (🖥 visit-exmoor.co.uk/coleridge-way) Starting in Nether Stowey, where Coleridge lived from 1797, The Coleridge Way crosses 36 miles of the Quantock Hills, Brendon Hills and Exmoor, ending in Porlock (where the Man who notoriously interrupted the writing of the poet's *Kubla Khan* originated).

In 1956 the Quantock Hills was the first area of England to be designated an Area of Outstanding Natural Beauty (AONB). The trail is well-serviced by pubs and tea-rooms.

● **The Tarka Trail** (🖥 tarkatrail.org.uk) Following in the paw-steps of Henry Williamson's famous *Tarka the Otter*, this 180-mile path runs in a figure-of-eight shape and centres on Barnstaple. It joins the SWCP at Lynton and colludes with it as far south as Bideford.

The stretch between Braunton and Meeth is part of Sustrans' National Cycle Network, and there's a section where you even take a train! Whilst the chances of seeing an otter are slim there is an abundance of other wildlife to be seen.

● **Devon's Coast to Coast (Two Moors Way & Erme-Plym Trail)** (🖥 explore devon.info – select Walking tab, then Long walks) The 15-mile/24km Erme-Plym Trail begins in Wembury on the South Devon coast and travels as far north as Ivybridge where The Two Moors Way (100 miles/160km) begins. Climbing onto Dartmoor can be strenuous but the effort is worth it.

The trail then heads north, traversing the length of Dartmoor to Drewsteignton before passing through Morchard Bishop and Witheridge, eventually entering Exmoor from the south before culminating in Lynmouth. Splendid scenery and real solitude are just two of the joys of this trip.

● **The Samaritans Way** (🖥 bristolramblers.org.uk – select Other Walking Opportunities tab) Beginning at Clifton Suspension Bridge in Bristol, this 100-mile jaunt heads south through the Mendip Hills to Glastonbury before turning west and passing through the Quantock Hills and Exmoor to end in Lynton.

For those after a really long walk, The Samaritans Way can be joined to The Cotswold Way via The River Avon trail which runs from Bath to Bristol.

● **West Somerset Coast Path** (WSCP; 🖥 ldwa.org.uk) Significantly shorter than the SWCP, the WSCP travels approximately 25 miles from the tiny settlement of Steart, via the Quantock Hills AONB, passing both Watchet harbour and Dunster beach en route to Minehead. This means that if you wish to, you could make the SWCP even more of a challenge!

the following will allow you to savour at least some of the joys of the Exmoor and North Devon Coast Path. The main obstacle to preparing a short itinerary of a few days or less along the coast path is the lack of regular transport connections to towns and villages on the way. For example, on possibly the most spectacular part of the entire SWCP, Clovelly to Bude, public transport is scarce and it is thus very difficult to divide this section into day walks. However, if you have three days spare this section is both achievable and most definitely worth it!

All these routes link up with public transport (see pp48-50).

Day walks

Minehead to Porlock   **(7½ miles/12.1km; see pp79-89)**
A splendid introduction to Exmoor with varied terrain, tremendous views out to sea as well as the option of an alternative rugged route. Parts of this walk are quite tough – although the hardest part may well be ending it and going home after just one day.

Lynton to Combe Martin   **(13½ miles/21.7km; see pp105-17)**
Get up early for this one: a long and strenuous day's walk that will truly whet your appetite for both Exmoor and the coastal path. Highlights include the extraordinary Valley of Rocks and the SWCP's highest point – Great Hangman.

Woolacombe to Croyde   **(6¼ miles/10.1km; see pp133-9)**
An easy to moderate day's walk that could be completed in one morning. There is the option of either walking through Woolacombe Warren or making your way along the beach before both paths unite for a stroll around Baggy Point: the views from here over Croyde Bay and Saunton Sands are terrific.

Croyde to Braunton   **(8¾ miles/14.1km; see pp139-48)**
Ambling hand-in-hand with the Tarka Trail around Saunton Down and through the Braunton Burrows, this is an easy to moderate day's walk.

Bideford to Westward Ho!   **(8¼ miles/13.3km; see pp164-75)**
An easy day's walk that includes both the lovely village of Appledore – an ideal location for lunch – and Northam Burrows Country Park.

Weekend walks – 2-3 days

Exmoor: Porlock Weir to Combe Martin (26 miles/41.9km; see pp92-117)
A strenuous couple of days with an overnight stop in Lynmouth/Lynton; this section offers some of the best walking in England.

Beaches and Burrows: Ilfracombe to Braunton (23½ miles/37.8km; see pp120-48) This is a relatively easy couple of days; highlights include the beaches of Woolacombe and Saunton as well as Braunton Burrows.

The best of the best: Westward Ho! to Bude (37 miles/59.6km; see pp172-205) A long, strenuous and truly spectacular three-day walk; the scenery is some of the best on the entire SWCP. Highlights include the village of Clovelly and the remarkably dramatic views of the sunset over the Atlantic at Hartland Quay.

PLANNING YOUR WALK

What to take

KEEP YOUR LUGGAGE LIGHT

Experienced backpackers know that there is some sort of complicated formula governing the success of a walk, in which the enjoyment of the walk is inversely proportional to the amount carried.

Carrying a heavy rucksack slows you down, tires you out and gives you aches and pains in parts of the body that you never knew existed. It is imperative, therefore, that you take a good deal to consider what to pack and that you are ruthless when you do; if it's not essential, don't take it.

HOW TO CARRY IT

If you are using the baggage-transfer service (see p26), you must comply with their regulations regarding the weight and size of the luggage.

Even if you are using this service, you will still need to carry a small **day-pack**, filled with those items that you will need during the day: water bottle or pouch, this book, map, sun-screen, sun hat, wet-weather gear, some food, camera, money and so on.

If you have decided to forego the services of the baggage carrier you will have to consider your **rucksack** even more carefully. Ultimately its size will depend on your plans for sleeping and eating. If you are camping and cooking for yourself you will probably need a 65- to 75-litre rucksack, which should be large enough to carry a small tent, sleeping bag, cooking equipment, eating utensils and food. Those not carrying their home with them should find a 40- to 60-litre rucksack sufficient.

When choosing a rucksack, make sure it has a stiffened back and can be adjusted to fit your own back comfortably. Don't just try the rucksack out in the shop: take it home, fill it with things and then try it out around the house and take it out for a short walk. Only then can you be certain that it fits. Make sure the hip belt and chest strap (if there is one) are fastened tightly as this helps distribute the weight more comfortably with most of it being carried on your hips. Carry a small daypack inside the rucksack, as this will be useful to carry things in when leaving the main pack at the hostel or B&B.

One reader wrote in with the eminently sensible advice of taking a **waterproof rucksack cover**. Most rucksacks these days have them 'built in' to the sack, but you can also buy them separately for less than a tenner. Lining your bag with a **bin liner** is another sensible, cut-price idea. It's also a good idea to keep everything wrapped in **smaller plastic bags** inside the rucksack. That way, even if it does pour with rain, everything should remain dry. It also makes things easier to find, provided you can remember which plastic bags contain which items!

PLANNING YOUR WALK

FOOTWEAR

Boots

For many people, only a decent pair of strong, durable walking boots is good enough to survive the rigours of the South West Coast Path. Others, however, make do with more lightweight running shoes or trail shoes, particularly if walking in summer. Hiking boots have the advantage of providing good ankle support (the ground can occasionally be rough and stony and twisted ankles are not uncommon), and are usually waterproof: these days most people opt for a synthetic waterproof lining (Gore-Tex or similar), though a good-quality leather boot with dubbin should prove just as reliable in keeping your feet dry. Running shoes or trail shoes have the advantage of being much lighter and more comfortable, and though they aren't waterproof, they're often quick-drying meaning you should always be able to at least begin your walk each morning with dry feet.

In addition, many people bring some extra footwear (trainers, sandals, Crocs, flip-flops etc) to wear off the trail. This is not essential but it's nice to get out of your hot and smelly walking shoes during the evening.

Socks

If you haven't got a pair of the modern hi-tech walking socks the old system of wearing a thin liner sock under a thicker wool sock is just as good. Bring a few pairs of each.

CLOTHES

In a country notorious for its unpredictable climate it is imperative that you pack enough clothes to cover every extreme of weather, from burning hot to bloomin' freezing at any time of the year.

Modern hi-tech outdoor clothes come with a range of fancy names and brands but they all still follow the basic two- or three-layer principle, with an inner base layer to transport sweat away from your skin, a mid-layer for warmth and an outer layer to protect you from the wind and rain.

A thin lightweight **thermal top** of a synthetic material is ideal as the base layer as it draws moisture (ie sweat) away from your body. Cool in hot weather and warm when worn under other clothes in the cold, pack at least one thermal top. Over the top in cold weather a mid-weight **polyester fleece** should suffice. Fleeces are light, more water-resistant than the alternatives (such as a woolly jumper), remain warm even when wet and pack down small in rucksacks; they are thus ideal walking gear. Over the top of all this a **waterproof jacket** is essential. 'Breathable' jackets cost a small fortune (though prices are falling all the time) but they do prevent the build-up of condensation.

Leg wear

Many walkers find walking trousers an unnecessary investment. Any light, quick-drying trouser should suffice. Jeans are heavy and dry slowly and are thus not recommended. A pair of waterproof trousers *is* more than useful, however, while on really hot sunny days you'll be glad you brought your shorts. Thermal **long johns** take up little room in a rucksack and could be vital if the weather

PLANNING YOUR WALK

starts to close in. **Gaiters** are not essential but, again, those who bring them are always glad they did, for they provide extra protection when walking through muddy ground and when the vegetation around the trail is dripping wet after bad weather or morning dew.

Underwear
Three or four changes of underwear is fine. Any more is excessive, any less unhygienic. Because backpacks can cause bra straps to dig painfully into the skin, women may find a **sports bra** more comfortable.

Other clothes
You may like to consider a woolly **hat** and **gloves** – you'd be surprised how cold it can get up on the cliffs even in summer. A **sun hat** is vital given the strength of the sun sometimes (see p59).

TOILETRIES

Once again, take the minimum. **Soap**, **towel**, a **toothbrush** and **toothpaste** are pretty much essential (although those staying in B&Bs will find that most provide soap and towels anyway). Some **toilet paper** could also prove vital on the trail, particularly if using public toilets (which occasionally run out).

Other items: **razor**; **deodorant**; **tampons/sanitary towels** and a high factor **sun-screen** should cover just about everything.

FIRST-AID KIT

A small first-aid kit could prove useful for those emergencies that occur along the trail. This kit should include **aspirin** or **paracetamol**; **plasters** for minor cuts; **Compeed**, **Second Skin** or some other treatment for blisters; a **bandage** or elasticated joint support for supporting a sprained ankle or a weak knee; **antiseptic wipes**; **antiseptic cream**; **safety pins**; **tweezers** and **scissors**.

GENERAL ITEMS

Essential
Everybody should have a **map**, **torch**, **water bottle or pouch**, **spare batteries**, **penknife**, **whistle** (see p57 for details of the international distress signal), some **emergency food** and a **watch** (preferably with an alarm to help you make an early start each day). Those with weak knees will find a **walking pole** or **sticks**

❏ CANINE COMPANIONS
The South-West Coast Path is a dog-friendly path and many are the rewards that await those prepared to make the extra effort required to bring their best friend along the trail. However, you shouldn't underestimate the amount of work involved in bringing your pooch to the path. Indeed, just about every decision you make will be influenced by the fact that you've got a dog. The best starting point is to study the advice on pp209-10, and the village & town facilities table (pp32-3) so you can plan where to stay and eat, and where to buy food for your mutt.   **Henry Stedman**

❑ MOBILE PHONE RECEPTION AND INTERNET CONNECTIONS
While many people view their walk in this remote corner of England as an escape from the modern world, for some people a decent connection with the outside world is vital. In our research we found EE (🖥 ee.co.uk) provided the best coverage for mobile and (up to) 4G internet connections (with Vodaphone pretty good too).

Those who need to stay in touch online, and who are taking a laptop, may like to consider investing in a dongle (a small device that plugs into a USB port and connects your computer to the internet) – though pretty much all accommodation options, cafés and pubs offer free wi-fi, so it's only really necessary if you need to get online on the trail and aren't carrying a smartphone.

essential. Those who've also walked in Scotland will recognise the importance of taking **insect repellent** to ward off midges, though they're not so bad here. **Sun screen**, however, is vital; see p59.

A **mobile phone** is invaluable too – and reception is usually pretty good on this stretch of the SWCP – not only for emergencies, but also for arranging a lift from the path to your B&B, for booking a table at a restaurant, or for calling campsites; just don't forget the **charger**! If you know how to use it properly you'll also find a **compass** handy.

Useful items and luxuries
Suggestions here include a **book** for days off or on train and bus journeys, a **camera** (if you don't have a smartphone with a reasonable camera), a pair of **sunglasses**, **binoculars**, a **vacuum flask** for hot drinks and an **iPad/iPod** or **MP3 player**.

National Trust and English Heritage **membership cards**, as well as student (ISIC) and YHA hostel cards could save you money on the trail. Some sort of ID, such as a driving licence, might also prove useful. Note that you need to show photo ID or your passport (or a copy of it) to stay in YHA hostels.

CAMPING GEAR

Campers will find a sleeping bag essential. A two- to three-season bag should suffice for summer. In addition, you will also need a decent bivvy bag or tent, a sleeping mat, fuel and stove, cutlery and pans, a cup and a scrubber for washing up.

MONEY

ATMs (cash machines) are fairly common along the Exmoor and North Devon Coast Path as are banks and post offices (see p25). However, not everybody accepts **debit** or **credit cards** as payment – though many B&Bs, most restaurants and even some campsites now do. You should still carry a fair amount of **cash** with you, just to be on the safe side. Crime on the trail is thankfully rare but it's always a good idea to carry your money safely in a **moneybelt**.

MAPS

It would be perfectly possible to walk long stretches of the coastal path unaided by map or compass. Just keep the sea to your right (or left, depending on which way you're heading) and you can't go too far off track. The **hand-drawn maps in this book**, which cover the trail at a scale of 1:20,000, should provide sufficient aid in areas where navigation is slightly more problematic.

Nevertheless, having other maps will paint a more fulfilling picture of your surroundings and will allow you to plan much more effectively for any accommodation or other facilities that lie off the trail. **Ordnance Survey** (OS; 🖥 ordnancesurvey.co.uk) produce their maps to two scales: the 1:25,000 Explorer series in orange and the 1:50,000 Landranger in pink (which is less useful for walking purposes). Alongside the paper versions OS also produce an 'Active' edition of both which is 'weatherproof' (covered in a lightweight protective plastic coating).

Those needed for the stretch of the SWCP covered by this book are as follows: Explorer: Outdoor Leisure (OL) 9 Exmoor; 139 Bideford, Ilfracombe and Barnstaple; 126 Clovelly and Hartland, and 111 Bude, Boscastle and Tintagel. The fourth map is really essential only if you plan to continue past Bude, as the section of path missing between OL126 and Bude is only about a mile or two of fairly uneventful walking. If you don't feel that such precise cartography is needed the Landranger may be sufficient; of the 14 to cover the SWCP you will need the following three to cover the initial 115 miles: 181 Minehead and Brendon Hills; 180 Barnstaple and Ilfracombe; and 190 Bude and Clovelly.

While it may be extravagant to buy all these maps, Ramblers (see box on p42) allows members to borrow them for a small charge. Alternatively, members of Backpackers are entitled to discounts. Some public libraries in the UK also have OS maps that can be borrowed by library members.

❏ DIGITAL MAPPING

Most smartphones have a GPS chip so you can see your position overlaid onto a digital map on your phone. There are numerous software packages that provide Ordnance Survey (OS) maps for a smartphone, tablet, PC or GPS unit. Maps are downloaded over the internet, then loaded into an app, also available by download, from where you can view them, print them and create routes on them.

It is important to ensure any digital mapping software on your smartphone uses pre-downloaded maps stored on your device, and doesn't need to download them on-the-fly, as this may be expensive and will be impossible without a signal. Note that battery life will be significantly reduced, compared to normal usage, when you are using the built-in GPS and running the screen for long periods.

Many websites have **free routes** you can download for the more popular digital mapping products; anything from day walks to complete Long Distance Paths. **Memory Map** (🖥 memory-map.co.uk) currently sell OS 1:25,000 mapping covering the whole of the UK for £166. They also have annual subscriptions from £25.

For a subscription of £2.99 for one month, or £23.99 for a year (on their current offer) **Ordnance Survey** (see above) will let you download and then use their UK maps (1:25,000 scale) on a mobile or tablet without a data connection for a specific period.

Harvey Maps (🖳 harveymaps.co.uk) produce a series of maps that cover all the designated National Trails to a scale of 1:40,000. For full coverage of the SWCP you will need three, but if you are intending to walk the section covered by this book just Map One (Minehead to St Ives) will suffice. This of course will save on weight and cost compared to buying the four OS maps, though the OS has more detail and will show you what is further inland.

For those who like the comfort of having an OS map with them, but are not overly concerned by what is too far away from the trail, a great companion to this guidebook, is AZ's (🖳 collins.co.uk/collections/a-z-adventure-maps) adventure booklet: *South West Coast Path 1: North Devon & Somerset*, which includes Ordnance Survey mapping (scale 1:25,000) of the trail described in this book. There are a further four in AZ's SWCP series.

RECOMMENDED READING

Guidebooks
If you're willing to also carry separate maps, undoubtedly the most detailed guide to the accommodation, tide tables and other useful information on the entire SWCP is the South West Coast Path Association's companion to the path, called simply **The South West Coast Path** and currently priced at £16. Alongside this annual guide they also produce and sell pamphlets for each section which can be found in tourist information centres en route or ordered via post or online for £2; see 🖳 southwestcoastpath.org.uk for details.

Flora and fauna
For identifying obscure plants and peculiar-looking beasties as you walk, Collins and New Holland publish a pocket-sized range to Britain's natural riches. The Collins Gem series are tough little books; current titles include guides to *Trees*, *Birds*, *Mushrooms*, *Wild Flowers*, *Wild Animals*, *Insects* and *Butterflies*.

In addition, for any budding crustacean connoisseur there is a *Seashore* book; there is also a handbook to the *Stars*, which could be of particular interest for those who are considering sleeping under them.

Also in the Collins series, there's an adapted version of Richard Mabey's classic bestseller *Food for Free* – great for anyone intent on getting back to nature, saving the pennies, or just with an interest in what's edible outside of a supermarket. You could also consult *Wild Food: Foraging for Food in the Wild*, written by Jane Eastoe and published by the National Trust.

Covering much the same topics as the Gem series, New Holland's Concise range comes in a waterproof plastic jacket and includes useful quick reference foldout charts. Both series contain a wealth of information.

It's also worth investigating the rapidly increasing range of flora and fauna identification apps that are becoming available for your phone.

Autobiography
Raynor Winn's rightly lauded memoir, *The Salt Path* (2018), is an incredible account of one couple's journey walking the entire South West Coast Path after becoming homeless, and is highly recommended.

☐ **SOURCES OF FURTHER INFORMATION**

Online information

● 🖥 **nationaltrail.co.uk/south-west-coast-path**, **fb** The official and most useful website to Britain's longest national trail. Good for background information on the trail and has the latest news on the path, details about river crossings and army ranges, as well as information on accommodation, itineraries and distance/timing calculators.

● 🖥 **southwestcoastpath.org.uk**, **fb** The site for the **South West Coast Path Association (SWCPA)**, a charity that exists to support users of the path. Many of the features on the official site are replicated here – distance calculators, river-crossing details etc – though there is much more detail here too. The Association is also very active politically, pressurising government bodies to ensure that the path is highly maintained along its length. Membership is available at £26.50/34.50 for single/joint memberships for UK residents (£34.50 for both single and joint membership for non-UK residents) and includes a copy of their guidebook and a twice-yearly magazine.

● 🖥 **southwestcoastalpath.co.uk** Unusual website concentrating on day walks on short stretches of the Path, with information on accommodation, pubs and restaurants.

● 🖥 **exmoor-nationalpark.gov.uk**, **fb** The official site of the Exmoor National Park – home to both the country's longest wooded coastline and, so they claim, England's tallest tree, a 61.3m-tall Douglas Fir.

● 🖥 **northdevon-aonb.org.uk**, **fb** Official website for North Devon Areas of Outstanding Natural Beauty. Good for background information on geology, flora & fauna.

Tourist information centres (TICs)

As one of the busiest tourist areas of the country, the South-West is reasonably well served by tourist information centres, and there are quite a few on this stretch of the coast path. They provide all manner of local information and advice as well as selling things like maps, guidebooks and souvenirs. Some also provide an accommodation-booking service (in many cases a 10% deposit is payable which is deducted from the final bill and sometimes there's a booking charge as well). You'll find TICs at: **Minehead** (see p75); **Porlock** (see p86); **Ilfracombe** (p123); **Woolacombe** (p130); **Braunton** (p146); **Barnstaple** (p152); **Bideford** (p164) and **Bude** (p202). There's also the excellent Exmoor National Park Centre in **Lynmouth** (p100).

In addition, there are less-useful Tourist Information Points (TIPs – often little more than a desk with leaflets) in the post office in **Lynton**, the museum in **Coombe Martin** and the library in **Appledore**. The Visitor Centre in **Clovelly** (see p182) does have some general tourist information but tends to focus mainly on Clovelly itself.

Organisations for walkers

● **The Backpackers' Club** (🖥 backpackersclub.co.uk) A club aimed at people who are involved or interested in lightweight camping through walking, cycling, skiing and canoeing. They produce a quarterly magazine, provide members with a comprehensive advisory and information service on all aspects of backpacking, organise weekend trips, offer discounts for maps and at outdoor stores, and also publish a farm-pitch directory. Membership is £20/30 a year for individuals/families.

● **The Long Distance Walkers' Association** (🖥 ldwa.org.uk) Membership (from £15/22.50 a year for individuals/families) includes a copy of their journal *Strider* three times per year giving details of challenge events and local group walks as well as articles on the subject. Members also receive a discount on maps.

● **Ramblers** (🖥 ramblers.org.uk) Looks after the interests of walkers throughout Britain. They publish a large amount of useful information including their quarterly *Walk* magazine. The website also has a discussion forum. Members can borrow OS maps for a small charge. Annual membership costs £36.60/49 individual/joint.

The beautifully illustrated *A Brush with the Coast* (2015) is a watercolour-filled delight of a book by artist Sasha Harding, and documents her hike along the SWCP with her dog as she searches for inspiration for her next art exhibition.

Dog-owning hikers will also warm to Mark Wallington's *Travels with Boogie: 500 Mile Walkies* (1996), a humorous account of his time spent on the trail. Accompanied by the more-loathed-than-loved Boogie the dog, man and beast survive all that the path can throw at them on a diet of tinned soup and Kennomeat. If you have ever walked a long distance with a dog many of the author's anecdotes will ring true. Another dog-goes-walking book, *Two Feet, Four Paws* (2009) is Spud Talbot-Ponsonby's tale of her time circumnavigating Britain (Chapter 15: Bristol to Boscastle is the relevant chapter).

For something more poetic, *Walking Away: Further Travels with a Troubadour on the South West Coast Path* (2015) is an often-hilarious travelogue by Poet Laureate Simon Armitage. An account of his time walking and reciting odes along the SWCP between Minehead and Land's End, it is a follow-up to *Walking Home: Travels with a Troubadour on the Pennine Way* (2012).

For fans of English rock band Mott the Hoople there is former member Overend Watts' account of his time on the trail: *The Man Who Hated Walking: The South West Coast Path* (2013).

Fiction

The Tarka Trail is a local path named after Henry Williamson's much-loved *Tarka the Otter* (1927), just one of many books in which Williamson's extraordinary ability to evoke the Devonshire countryside gilds every page.

Perhaps the most famous book, however, is the most dense 19th-century classic, *Lorna Doone: A Romance of Exmoor* (1869), by Richard Doddridge Blackmore. Margaret Drabble's witty 1998 novel *The Witch of Exmoor* is also set near the Lyn Valley. Possibly the only piece of fiction to inspire the naming of an English village, *Westward Ho!* (1855) is a Spanish Armada adventure-romp written by Charles Kingsley (see p167).

History

Hope Bourne had four books published during her 91-year lifetime that vividly describe life in the wilds of Devon, beginning with 1963's *Living on Exmoor* and ending with 1993's *My Moorland Life*. One thousand years of farming, quarrying and the Home Guard are crammed into Felicity Goodall's *Lost Devon* (2007), which is good for those with an interest in the lost heritage of the county; while for those interested in the development of the moor's landscape and archaeology, *The Field Archaeology of Exmoor* (2001) by Hazel Riley and Robert Wilson-North is published by English Heritage.

A broader, more conventional historical summary can be found in Mary Siraut's *Exmoor: The Making of an English Upland* (2009). Local historian Dennis Corner has written several books on the local area including *Porlock in those Days* (1992). Derrick Warren's *Curious Devon* (2008) examines the quirkier side of the county, while for something a little darker there's John Van Der Kiste's *Grim Almanac of Devon* (2008) that recounts 366 of the county's more macabre episodes.

Getting to and from the Coast Path

Given that it is one of the most popular holiday destinations in the UK, the South-West is surprisingly poorly served by public transport connections. Indeed, getting to the start of your walk can be quite laborious – and returning home at the end can be equally painful.

Those who wish to take a train will soon discover that neither Minehead nor Bude has a mainline rail connection. The best way to get to Minehead by train is to go to Taunton, Barnstaple, or Tiverton Parkway. Barnstaple, Exeter and Okehampton are best for Bude; see opposite for more details.

National Express coach services go to Minehead only in the summer months, serving the Butlins there rather than the centre of town and the fare is

PLANNING YOUR WALK

❏ GETTING TO BRITAIN

● **By air** Exeter (🖳 exeter-airport.co.uk); Bristol (🖳 bristolairport.co.uk), Southampton (🖳 southamptonairport.com) and Bournemouth (🖳 bournemouthairport.com) have international flights though mostly from Europe only; for details on Newquay Airport see p47. However, none of these airports is well connected to Minehead (or Bude), so for this reason London's Heathrow (🖳 heathrow.com) may be the most convenient.

See box on p47 for details of National Express coach services from Heathrow, Exeter and Bristol. There are also rail services between Bristol Temple Meads (take a bus from the airport) and Taunton. From Heathrow you can take the Heathrow Express (🖳 heathrowexpress.com) to Paddington and from there take a train to Taunton (see box opposite). From Taunton you can catch Buses of Somerset No 28 service (see box on p48) to Minehead at the start of the trail.

● **Eurostar** (🖳 eurostar.com) operates a high-speed passenger service via the Channel Tunnel between Paris, Brussels and Lille and London. The Eurostar terminal in London is at St Pancras International station with connections to the London Underground and to all other main railway stations in London. Trains to Somerset and Devon leave from Paddington station.

For more information on rail services to Britain see **Railteam** (🖳 railteam.eu).

● **From Europe by coach** Eurolines (🖳 eurolines.com) have a wide network of long-distance bus services connecting over 500 destinations in 25 European countries to London (Victoria Coach Station). Visit the Eurolines website for details of services from your country. Check carefully: often, once expenses such as food for the journey are taken into consideration, it doesn't work out much cheaper than flying, particularly when compared to the prices of some of the budget airlines, although it is a more environmentally friendly option.

● **From Europe by car** Ferries operate on several routes between mainland Europe and Britain. Look at 🖳 ferrysavers.com or 🖳 directferries.co.uk for a full list of companies and services.

Eurotunnel (🖳 eurotunnel.com) operates 'le shuttle' train service for vehicles via the Channel Tunnel between Calais and Folkestone.

quite expensive. A weekly service to Bude operates only on a Saturday mid-June to early September. See pp46-7 for options for coach travel.

Given the above, the temptation to drive (see p46) to the start of your walk is understandable. This may be the most convenient way to get here but it will also probably be the most expensive and you may not feel comfortable abandoning your car in a car park (see also p47 for details of long-stay parking) for a couple of weeks. Then, of course, there are the ecological downsides of driving to consider.

NATIONAL TRANSPORT

By train

Neither Minehead nor Bude is served by a regular rail service (though see box below). **Taunton**, however, *is* well connected by rail (Bristol is less than an hour away, Exeter half an hour and even London Paddington is within a 2-hour journey) and there are regular bus services (Buses of Somerset No 28) from there on to Minehead (1½hrs). This journey is, whilst slow, enjoyable: if you have already travelled by train from London, or indeed any other metropolis, you will feel life pleasantly decelerating around you as you approach the northern end of Exmoor.

❑ RAIL SERVICES
Note: not all stops are listed.
● London Paddington to Penzance via Reading, Taunton, Exeter, Plymouth & Bodmin Parkway, Mon-Sat approx 12/day, Sun approx 8/day, some services go via Bristol, some call at Tiverton Parkway.
● Cardiff to Taunton via Bristol (some services continue to Tiverton Parkway, Exeter & Plymouth), Mon-Fri 1/hr, Sat & Sun no direct services.
● Edinburgh to Plymouth via Newcastle, York, Leeds, Birmingham, Bristol, Taunton, Tiverton Parkway & Exeter, Mon-Sat 6-day, Sun 4/day for the full route.
● Exeter to Barnstaple (The Tarka Line), Mon-Sun 1/hr.

The West Somerset Railway Arriving in Minehead by rail is undoubtedly the most attractive way of arriving (apart from walking from Porlock, of course!), the steam train chuffing its way through the rolling Somerset countryside before terminating its journey right in the centre of town, just a few steps from the seafront and only a couple of hundred metres from the start of the SWCP itself.

Unfortunately, the only train service that operates a service to/from Minehead is the West Somerset Railway (☎ 01643-704996, 💻 west-somerset-railway.co.uk, **fb**), and whilst it may be one of the most picturesque services imaginable, it is also one of the most pointless, in that it doesn't go anywhere particularly useful. Running between Minehead and Bishops Lydeard, on the way to Taunton, the railway offers a choice of transportation by either steam or diesel, the entire journey taking around 1¼ hours to cover the 20 miles.

If you're determined that this is how you want to arrive, Bishops Lydeard is a half-hour bus ride from Taunton on Buses of Somerset's 28 service (see box p48). The timetable differs daily so it would be wise to check the website (or phone ahead) for up-to-date timetabling information.

As for the other end of the walk, the nearest railway stations to Bude are at Exeter, Okehampton and Barnstaple, and each boasts some sort of bus service to Bude (see pp48-50).

Barnstaple is actually the only location on the path that *is* served by a regular rail service, though it's a 3½-hour journey from London, 2 hours from Taunton and a good 80 minutes from Exeter. The quickest way from Barnstaple to Minehead (2hrs) is to take a bus to Lynmouth (Filers Travel's No 309/310) and then the Exmoor Coaster to Minehead; although the latter only operates between mid July and early September meaning that during the rest of the year you'll need to pay for a taxi from Lynton to Minehead (approximately £40).

From Barnstaple there is a limited service (Stagecoach No 85) to Bude. Alternatively Stagecoach's No 319 to Hartland connects with their 218/219 service to Bude but none of these operates on a Sunday; see pp48-50 for details.

National Rail (☎ 0345-7484950, 🖥 nationalrail.co.uk) is the best source of rail information. The lines throughout the South-West are run by **Great Western Railway** (☎ 0345-7000125, 🖥 gwr.com). **Arriva Cross Country Trains** (🖥 crosscountrytrains.co.uk) also run services linking the Midlands, North and Scotland with the South-West.

Finally, one tip when buying **tickets**: it's always worth checking the fares on the relevant train company's website or on 🖥 thetrainline.com. You'll normally find significant reductions, especially if booking 8-12 weeks in advance and also if you are able to travel on a particular service. However, be aware of additional charges such as a booking fee, or fees for using a debit/credit card.

If you plan to take a bus when you arrive consider getting a **plusbus** (🖥 plusbus.info) ticket and if you want to book a taxi **Traintaxi**'s website (🖥 traintaxi.co.uk) gives details of the companies operating at railway stations.

By coach

Although coach travel can take significantly longer than getting a train and is susceptible to traffic jams – especially in the summer months when the South-West is choked with tourists – it is generally cheaper than train travel and, on some of today's newer coaches, it can also be far more salubrious than coach travel of old.

National Express (see box opposite; 🖥 nationalexpress.com) runs several services to Taunton (from here take Buses of Somerset No 28 to Minehead); one service also goes to Barnstaple, Braunton and Ilfracombe.

Megabus (🖥 uk.megabus.com), part of Stagecoach, is a cheap and expanding bus company with a limited service between London Victoria and Bude or Birmingham and Bude, both stopping en route at Barnstaple & Bideford.

By car

Driving to the start of the path raises as many questions as it does answers: Where do you leave your car while you're walking? Will it be safe? And how are you going to get back to it at the end of your trip? Furthermore, given the ever-rising price of fuel and the fact that you'll probably have to pay to leave your car somewhere, taking your car will almost certainly be the least financially viable option. Then, of course, there are environmental concerns to consider

❏ **NATIONAL EXPRESS COACH SERVICES**
Note: not all stops are listed. National Express was running a reduced timetable at the time of research but more services were due to resume; see 🖥 nationalexpress.com for the latest information.
100 Birmingham to Bristol (3/day)
101 Birmingham to Plymouth via Bristol, Taunton & Exeter (2/day)
102 Birmingham to Plymouth via Exeter, Torquay & Paignton (2/day)
103 Birmingham to Poole via Bristol (1/day)
105 Birmingham to **Minehead** via Bristol (1/day)
401 London Victoria to Bristol (1/day)
404 London Victoria to Penzance via Heathrow Airport, Bath, Taunton & Exeter (1/day)
406 London Victoria to Penzance via Heathrow Airport, Weston-super-Mare, Taunton & Exeter (1/day)
501 London Victoria to Exeter via Heathrow Airport & Taunton 3/day
502 London Victoria to **Ilfracombe** via Bristol, Taunton, **Barnstaple** & **Braunton** (1-2/day)

– some people will simply feel uncomfortable driving their own private car a considerable distance to get to and from the Path when the journey bookends what would otherwise be a largely environmentally-friendly holiday.

For those who do decide to drive, a great way to look at the varying options with regards to **route planning** is to use the AA's website and route planner (🖥 theaa.com/route-planner/route).

Both Minehead and Bude have **long stay parking**. This involves paying cash into a machine (usually) for your first seven days and then paying for longer online or via your phone, or completing the whole arrangement online. For up-to-date information on prices and processes for organising this and for which car parks you can use in Minehead, consult 🖥 www.somersetwestand taunton.gov.uk; for Bude see 🖥 www.cornwall.gov.uk.

One idea that is popular with drivers is to park in Barnstaple – the railway station has long-term parking where you can pay (from £3.90 per day) for seven days and update it by phone if necessary. The advantage with parking in Barnstaple is that your vehicle is left at a point approximately half-way along the trail – allowing you to leave items in the car and pick them up when you walk past – or jump in and drive home if you've found the walking too taxing! It also means you won't have quite such an arduous journey to get back to the car from Bude at the end of the trip.

By air

In addition to the airports mentioned in the box on p44, there is the option of flying (mostly domestic flights) into Newquay (🖥 cornwallairportnewquay .com). However, Newquay lies 70 miles along the coast from Bude. What's more, it isn't particularly well placed even for Bude (and not really a realistic option for Minehead) – a bus between Newquay and Bude takes at least three hours.

PLANNING YOUR WALK

☐ BUS SERVICES

No	Route	Operator (see p50)
Exmoor Coaster	Minehead to Lynmouth via Porlock, summer daily 6/day	Buses Somerset
5B	Exeter to Barnstaple via Bideford, Instow & Fremington, Mon-Sat 8-10/day	Stagecoach
6/6A	Bude to Exeter via Okehampton, Mon-Sat 7/day, Sun & public holidays 3/day	Stagecoach
10	Minehead to Porlock & Porlock Weir, Mon-Fri 6-7/day, Sat 4/day	AW/R/BS
12	Bude to Plymouth via Launceston, Mon-Sat 8/day	Plym'th Citybus
15A/15C	Bideford/East-the-Water circular (some services continue to Barnstaple), Mon-Sat 2/hr	Stagecoach
21	Ilfracombe to Westward Ho! via Braunton, Chivenor, Barnstaple, Fremington, Instow & Bideford, Mon-Sat 2/hr, Sun & public holidays 1/hr	Stagecoach
21A	Barnstaple to Appledore via Fremington, Instow, Bideford & Northam, Mon-Sat 2/hr, Sun 1/hr between Ilfracombe & Appledore	Stagecoach
21C	Croyde to Barnstaple via Saunton Sands, Braunton & Chivenor, Mon-Sat 2/hr, summer Sun 1/hr	Stagecoach
28	Taunton to Minehead via Bishops Lydeard, Mon-Sat 7/day, Sun 7/day	Buses Somerset
31	Ilfracombe to Mortehoe via Woolacombe, Mon-Sat 1/hr, Sun 5/day	Taw & Torridge
35	Ilfracombe to Lee, Tue & Fri 2/day	Ilf Comm Trspt
85	Barnstaple to Holsworthy via Bideford, Mon-Sat 4-5/day, including 1-2/day to/from Bude	Stagecoach
95	Bude to Truro via Wadebridge, Mon-Sat 6/day, Sun 6/day between Bude & St Columb Major	Go Cornwall Bus
155	Exeter to Barnstaple via Tiverton, Mon-Sat 5-6/day	Stagecoach
217	Morwenstow to Bude, Mon-Sat 3/day inc 1/day which continues to/from Holsworthy	Go Cornwall Bus
218/219	Hartland to Bude, Mon-Sat 6/day	Go Cornwall Bus
300	Lynmouth to Ilfracombe via Lynton, Combe Martin, Watermouth & Hele, mid July to early Sep Mon-Fri 2/day, June-Oct Sun 4/day	Taw & Torridge
301	Combe Martin to Barnstaple via Ilfracombe, Mon-Sat approx 1/hr	Filers Travel
302	Combe Martin to Woolacombe via Ilfracombe, mid July to early Sep Mon-Fri 3/day plus 3/day Ilfracombe to Woolacombe	Filers Travel
303	Barnstaple to Woolacombe via Heanton, Velator, Braunton & Mortehoe, Mon-Sat 4-5/day	Filers Travel
309/310	Lynton to Barnstaple, Mon-Sat 1/hr (of which 3/day start/end in Lynmouth)	Filers Travel
319	Barnstaple to Hartland via Bideford, Abbotsham & Clovelly, Mon-Sat 4/day, of which 1/day continues to Bude	Stagecoach

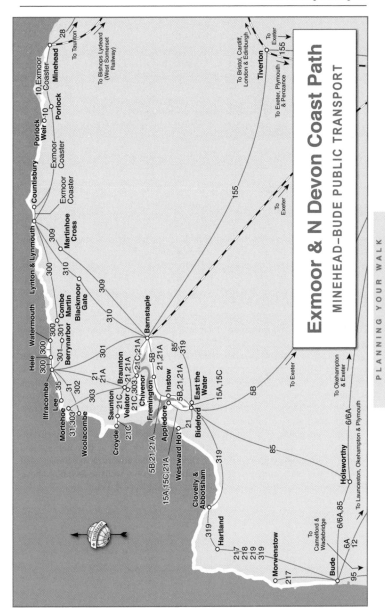

Exmoor & N Devon Coast Path
MINEHEAD–BUDE PUBLIC TRANSPORT

PLANNING YOUR WALK

❏ **BUS OPERATOR CONTACT DETAILS**

- **AW/R/BS** = minibus service operated jointly by **AtWest** (🖳 atwest.org.uk),
  Ridlers (🖳 ridlers.co.uk) and Buses of Somerset (see below).
- **Buses of Somerset** (☎ 0345-646 0707, 🖳 firstbus.co.uk/somerset)
- **Filers Travel** (☎ 01271-863819, 🖳 filers.co.uk)
- **Go Cornwall Bus** (☎ 0808-196 2632, 🖳 gocornwallbus.co.uk)
- **Ilf Comm Trspt = Ilfracombe Community Transport** (🖳 ilfcomminibuses)
- **Plymouth Citybus Service** (☎ 01752-662271, 🖳 plymouthbus.co.uk)
- **Stagecoach** (🖳 stagecoachbus.com)
- **Taw & Torridge Coaches Ltd** (☎ 01805-603400, 🖳 tawandtorridge.co.uk)

LOCAL TRANSPORT

Bus services

All places along the trail (or at least those with inhabitants) boast at least some sort of bus service except for Hartland Quay, the penultimate stop on the path. (From here you'll need to walk 2½ miles inland to Hartland to catch a bus.)

Most buses servicing points on the trail run at least once a day (usually more) but often only from Monday to Saturday (although note that the 300 service runs Mon-Fri & Sun but not Sat). Services are reduced out of season, and are sometimes non-existent (or at least reduced) on Sundays even in peak season. Most services run to a Sunday timetable on public holidays. Do be sure to check timetables, and ask around locally, if you think you might need to rely on a particular service.

Another problem with public transport in the area is the time it takes to get anywhere. Things are further complicated by the fact that local buses have been organised by county, so while Minehead and Bude may have good connections within their respective counties (Somerset and Cornwall), they have pretty lousy connections with their neighbour Devon, which means that if you want to cross a county border you'll often have to change buses somewhere along the way.

Planning ahead is a must as services change and may have been cut. Timetables for the services should be available for free at bus stations and tourist information centres (the North Devon booklet covers most services) and can also be found online on either the operator's own website (see box above for contact details) or 🖳 travelinesw.com (also an app: traveline sw).

Minimum impact walking

By visiting this rural corner of England you are having a positive impact, not just on your own wellbeing but on local communities as well. Your presence brings money and jobs into the local economy and also encourages pride in, and awareness of, the region's environment and culture.

However, the environment should not just be considered in terms of its value as a tourist asset. Its long-term survival and enjoyment by future generations will only be possible if both visitors and local communities protect it now. The following points are made to help you reduce your impact on the environment, encourage conservation and promote sustainable tourism in the area.

ECONOMIC IMPACT

Support local businesses

Rural businesses and communities in Britain have been hit hard in recent years by a seemingly endless series of crises. Most people are aware of the Countryside Code (see p54) – not dropping litter and closing the gate behind you are still as pertinent as ever – but in light of the economic pressures there is something else you can do: **buy local**.

Look and ask for local produce (see box p23) to buy and eat; not only does this cut down on the amount of pollution and congestion that the transportation of food creates (the so-called 'food miles'), but also ensures that you are supporting local farmers and producers; the very people who have moulded the countryside you have come to see and who are in the best position to protect it. If you can find local food which is also organic so much the better.

It's a fact of life that money spent at local level – perhaps in a market, or at the greengrocer, or in an independent pub – has a far greater impact for good on that community than the equivalent spent in a branch of a national chain store or restaurant. While no-one would advocate that walkers should boycott the larger supermarkets, which do, after all, provide local employment, it's worth remembering that businesses in rural communities rely heavily on visitors for their very existence. If we want to keep these shops and post offices, we need to use them.

ENVIRONMENTAL IMPACT

A walking holiday in itself is an environmentally friendly approach to tourism. The following are some ideas on how you can go a few steps further in helping to minimise your impact on the environment while walking the South West Coast Path.

Use public transport whenever possible
While we recognise that public transport along this section of the South West Coast Path is not ideal, it is preferable to using private cars as it benefits everyone: visitors, locals and the environment.

Never leave litter
Leaving litter shows a total disrespect for the natural world and others coming after you. As well as being unsightly, litter can be harmful to wildlife, pollutes the environment and can be dangerous to farm animals. Please carry a plastic bag so you can dispose of your rubbish in a bin in the next village. It would be very helpful if you could pick up litter left by other people too.
● **Is it OK if it's biodegradable?** Not really. Apple cores, banana skins, orange peel and the like are unsightly, encourage flies, ants and wasps and ruin a picnic spot for others.
● **The lasting impact of litter** A piece of orange peel left on the ground takes six months to decompose; silver foil 18 months; a plastic bag 10 years; clothes 15 years; and an aluminium can 85 years.

Respect all wildlife
Care for all wildlife you come across along the path; it has as much right to be there as you. As tempting as it may be to pick wild flowers, leave them in place so the next person who passes can enjoy them too. Don't break branches off or damage trees in any way.

If you come across wildlife, keep your distance and don't watch for too long. Your presence can cause considerable stress, particularly if the adults are with young, or in winter when the weather is harsh and food is scarce. Young animals are rarely abandoned. If you come across young birds, keep away so that their mother can return.

Outdoor toiletry
As more and more people discover the joys of walking in the natural environment issues such as how to go to the loo outdoors rapidly gain importance. How many of us have shaken our heads at the sight of toilet paper strewn beside the path, or even worse, someone's dump left in full view? Human excrement is not only offensive to our senses but, more importantly, can infect water sources.

Where to go The coast path is a high-use area and many habitats will not benefit from your fertilisation. As far as 'number twos' are concerned try whenever possible to use public toilets. There's no shortage of public toilets along the coast path and they are all marked on the trail maps. However, there are those times when the only time is now. If you have to go outdoors, help the environment to deal with your deposit in the best possible way by following these guidelines:

● **Choose your site carefully** It should be at least 30 metres away from running water and out of reach of the high tide and not on any site of historical or archaeological interest. Carry a small trowel or use a sturdy stick to dig a small hole about 15cm (6") deep to bury your faeces in. Faeces decompose quicker when in contact with the top layer of soil or leaf mould; by using a stick to stir loose soil into your deposit you will speed decomposition up even more. Do not squash it under rocks as this slows down the decomposition process. If you have to use rocks as a cover make sure they are not in contact with your faeces.

● **Pack out toilet paper and tampons** Toilet paper, tampons and sanitary towels take a long time to decompose whether buried or not. They can easily be dug up by animals and may then blow into water sources or onto the trail. The best method for dealing with these is to pack them out. Put the used item in a paper bag placed inside a plastic bag and dispose of it at the next toilet.

ACCESS

Britain is a crowded cluster of islands with few places where you can wander as you please. Most of the land is a patchwork of fields and agricultural land and the environment through which the Exmoor & North Devon Coast Path marches is no different. However, there are countless public rights of way (see below), in addition to the main trail, that criss-cross the land.

This is fine, but what happens if you feel a little more adventurous and want to explore the moorland, woodland and hills that can also be found near the walk? Access to the countryside has always been a hot topic in Britain. In the 1940s soldiers coming back from World War II were horrified and disgruntled to find that landowners were denying them the right to walk across the moors; ironically the very country that they had been fighting to protect. The battle was finally won in 2005 as new legislation (see p56) came into force granting public access to thousands of acres of Britain's wildest land.

All those who enjoy access to the countryside must respect the land, its wildlife, the interests of those who live and work there and other users; we all share a common interest in the countryside. Knowing your rights and responsibilities gives you the information you need to act with minimal impact.

Rights of way
As a designated National Trail (see box on p61) the coast path is a public right of way. A public right of way is either a footpath, a bridleway or a byway. The SWCP is a footpath for almost all its length which means that anyone has the legal right to use it on foot only.

Rights of way are theoretically established because the owner has dedicated them to public use. However, very few paths are formally dedicated in this way. If members of the public have been using a path without interference for 20 years or more the law assumes the owner has intended to dedicate it as a right of way. If a path has been unused for 20 years it does not cease to exist; the guiding principle is 'once a highway, always a highway'.

On a public right of way you have the right to 'pass and repass along the way' which includes stopping to rest or admire the view, or to consume refreshments. You can also take with you a 'natural accompaniment' (!) which includes a dog, but it must be kept under close control.

Farmers and land managers must ensure that paths are not blocked by crops or other vegetation, or otherwise obstructed, that the route is identifiable and the surface is restored soon after cultivation. If crops are growing over the path you have every right to walk through them, following the line of the right of way as closely as possible. If you find a path blocked or impassable you should report it to the appropriate highway authority. Highway authorities are responsible for maintaining footpaths. In Somerset and North Devon the highway authorities are Somerset and North Devon county councils respectively. The council is also the surveying authority with responsibility for maintaining the official definitive map of public rights of way.

❏ THE COUNTRYSIDE CODE

The countryside is a fragile place which every visitor should respect. The Countryside Code, originally described in the 1950s as the Country Code, was revised and relaunched in 2004, in part because of the changes brought about by the CRoW Act (see p56); it was updated again in 2012, 2014 & 2016 and again in 2020 to include considerations regarding COVID-19. The Code seems like common sense but sadly some people still appear to have no understanding of how to treat the countryside they walk in. An adapted version of the 2020 Code, launched under the logo 'Respect. Protect. Enjoy.', is given below:

Respect other people

• **Consider the local community and other people enjoying the outdoors** Be sensitive to the needs and wishes of those who live and work there. If, for example, farm animals are being moved or gathered keep out of the way and follow the farmer's directions. Being courteous and friendly to those you meet will ensure a healthy future for all based on partnership and co-operation.

• **Leave gates and property as you find them and follow paths unless wider access is available** A farmer normally closes gates to keep farm animals in, but may sometimes leave them open so the animals can reach food and water. Leave gates as you find them or follow instructions on signs. When in a group, make sure the last person knows how to leave the gates.

Follow paths unless wider access is available, such as on open country or registered common land (known as 'open access land'). Leave machinery and farm animals alone – if you think an animal is in distress try to alert the farmer instead.

Use gates, stiles or gaps in field boundaries if you can – climbing over walls, hedges and fences can damage them and increase the risk of farm animals escaping. The path is well supplied with stiles where it crosses field boundaries. If you have to climb over a gate because you can't open it always do so at the hinged end. Also be careful not to disturb ruins and historic sites.

Minimise erosion by not cutting corners or widening the path.

Wider access

The access situation to land around the coast path is a little more complicated. Trying to unravel and understand the seemingly thousands of different laws and acts is never easy in any legal system. Parliamentary Acts give a right to walk over certain areas of land such as some (but by no means all) common land and some specific places such as Dartmoor and the New Forest. However, in other places, such as Bodmin Moor and many British beaches, right of access is not written in law. It is merely tolerated by the landowner and could be terminated at any time.

Some landowners, such as the Forestry Commission, water companies and the National Trust, are obliged by law to allow some degree of access to their land. Land covered by schemes such as the Environmental Stewardship Scheme or Countryside Stewardship Scheme gives landowners a financial incentive to manage their land for conservation and to provide limited public access. There are also a few truly altruistic landowners who have allowed access over their land and these include organisations such as the RSPB, the Woodland Trust, and some local authorities. Overall, however, access to most of Britain's country-

● **Follow the path but give way to others when it is narrow** (unless they give way to you).

Protect the natural environment
● **Leave no trace of your visit and take your litter home** Take special care not to damage, destroy or remove features such as rocks, plants and trees. Take your litter with you; litter and leftover food doesn't just spoil the beauty of the countryside, it can be dangerous to wildlife and farm animals.
● **Keep dogs under effective control** This means you should keep your dog on a lead or in sight at all times, be aware of what it's doing and be confident it will return to you promptly on command.

Across farmland dogs should always be kept on a short lead; during lambing time they should not be taken at all.

Always clean up after your dog and get rid of the mess responsibly – 'bag it and bin it'.
● **Don't have BBQs or fires** Fires can be as devastating to wildlife and habitats as they are to people and property – so be careful with naked flames and cigarettes at any time of the year.

Enjoy the outdoors
● **Plan ahead, check what facilities are open and be prepared** You're responsible for your own safety: be prepared for natural hazards, changes in the weather and other events.

Wild animals, farm animals and horses can behave unpredictably if you get too close, especially if they're with their young – so give them plenty of space. Check the weather forecasts and tide times.
● **Follow advice and local signs** In some areas temporary diversions may be in place; take notice of these and other local trail advice.

MINIMUM IMPACT & OUTDOOR SAFETY

side is forbidden to Britain's people, in marked contrast to the general rights of access that prevail in other European countries.

Right to roam

For many years groups such as Ramblers (see box p42) and the British Mountaineering Council (🖥 thebmc.co.uk) campaigned for new and wider access legislation. This finally bore fruit in the form of the Countryside and Rights of Way Act of November 2000, colloquially known as the CRoW Act, which granted access for 'recreation on foot' to mountain, moor, heath, down and registered common land in England and Wales. In essence it allows walkers the freedom to roam responsibly away from footpaths, without being accused of trespass, on about four million acres of open, uncultivated land.

On 28 August 2005 the South-West became the sixth region in England/Wales to be opened up under this act; however, restrictions may still be in place from time to time – check the situation on 🖥 gov.uk/right-of-way-open-access-land/use-your-right-to-roam. Natural England (see p63) has mapped the new agreed areas of open access and they are also clearly marked on all the latest Ordinance Survey Explorer (1:25,000) maps. In the future it is hoped that the legislation can be extended to include other types of land such as cliff, foreshore, woodland, riverside and canal side.

Outdoor safety

AVOIDANCE OF HAZARDS

Swimming

If you are not an experienced swimmer or familiar with the sea, plan ahead and swim only at beaches where there is a lifeguard service, such as Woolacombe, Croyde and Saunton. On such beaches you should swim between the red and yellow flags as this is the patrolled area. Don't swim between black and white chequered flags as these areas are only for surfers. A red flag indicates that it is dangerous to enter the water. If you are not sure about anything ask one of the lifeguards; after all they are there to help you.

If you are going to swim at unsupervised beaches never do so alone and always take care. Some beaches are prone to strong rips. Never swim off headlands or near river mouths as there may be strong currents. Always be aware of changing weather conditions and tidal movement. The South-West has a huge tidal range and it can be very easy to get cut off by the tide.

If you see someone in difficulty do not attempt a rescue until you have contacted the coastguard (see opposite). Once you know help is on the way try to assist the person by throwing something to help them stay afloat. Many beaches have rescue equipment in red boxes should you find yourself needing it.

A safe alternative to swimming in the open sea is to swim in a **sea pool** – public seawater pools usually sited on a rocky surf coast, so that waves can wash into the pool. There are two wonderful examples on this stretch of the SWCP: one in Westward Ho! and one in Bude.

Walking alone

If you are walking alone you must appreciate and be prepared for the increased risk. Take note of the safety guidelines below.

Safety on the Coast Path

Sadly every year people are injured walking along the trail, though usually it's nothing more than a badly twisted ankle. Parts of Exmoor can be pretty remote, however, and it certainly pays to take precautions when walking. Abiding by the following rules should minimise the risks:

● Avoid walking on your own if possible.
● Make sure that somebody knows your plans for every day you are on the trail. This could be the place you plan to stay in at the end of each day's walk or a friend or relative whom you have promised to call every night. That way, if you fail to turn up or call, they can raise the alarm.
● If the weather closes in suddenly and fog or mist descends and you become uncertain of the correct trail, do not be tempted to continue. Just wait where you are and you'll find that mist often clears, at least for long enough to allow you to get your bearings. If you are still uncertain and the weather doesn't look like improving, return the way you came to the nearest point of civilisation and try again another time when conditions have improved.
● Always fill your water bottle or pouch at every available opportunity (but don't empty it until you are certain you can fill it again) and ensure you have some food such as high-energy snacks.
● Always carry a torch, compass, map, whistle and wet-weather gear with you; a mobile phone can be useful though you cannot rely on getting good reception (see p39).
● Wear strong sturdy footwear with good grip, and consider wearing walking boots with ankle support.
● Be extra vigilant with children.

Dealing with an accident

● Use basic first aid to treat the injury to the best of your ability.
● Try to attract the attention of anybody else who may be in the area. The **international distress (emergency) signal** is six blasts on a whistle, or six flashes with a torch.
● If possible leave someone with the casualty while others go to get help. If there are only two people, you have a dilemma. If you decide to get help, leave all spare clothing and food with the casualty.
● In an emergency dial ☎ 999 and ask for the coastguard. They are responsible for dealing with any emergency that occurs on the coast or at sea. Make sure you know exactly where you are before you call.
● Report the exact position of the casualty and their condition.

WEATHER AND WEATHER FORECASTS

The trail suffers from extremes of weather so it's vital that you always try to find out what the weather is going to be like before you set off for the day. It is a good idea to pay attention to **wind and gale warnings**. The wind on any coastline can get very strong and if it is strong it is advisable not to walk, particularly if you are carrying a pack which can act as a sail. If you are on a steep incline or above high cliffs it is also dangerous.

Even if the wind direction is inland it can literally blow you right over (unpleasant if there are gorse bushes around!), or if it suddenly stops or eddies (a common phenomenon when strong winds hit cliffs) it can cause you to lose your balance and stagger in the direction in which you have been leaning, ie towards the cliffs!

Another hazard on the coast is **sea mist or fog** which can dramatically decrease visibility. If a coastal fog blows over take extreme care where the path runs close to cliff edges.

Most hotels, some B&Bs and TICs will have pinned up somewhere a summary of the **weather forecast**. Alternatively, you can get a forecast through ⌨ bbc.co.uk/weather, or ⌨ metoffice.gov.uk/public/weather.

Pay close attention to the weather forecast and alter your plans for the day accordingly. That said, even if the forecast is for a fine sunny day, always assume the worst and pack some wet-weather gear.

BLISTERS

If you decide to wear hiking boots, it is important to break them in before embarking on a long walk. Make sure the boots are comfortable and try to avoid getting them wet on the inside. If wearing trainers, be sure to wear ones you have worn before – even lightweight trainers can rub your skin if they are brand new. Whatever your choice of footwear, it's advisable to air your feet at every opportunity, keep them clean and change your socks regularly; using talcum powder can help to keep them dry. If you feel any hot spots, stop immediately and apply a few strips of zinc oxide tape – or a blister plaster – and leave it on until it is pain free or the tape starts to come off. If you don't have zinc oxide tape, ordinary plasters are better than nothing.

If you have left it too late and a blister has developed you should surround it with Compeed or any other blister kit to protect it from abrasion. Popping it can lead to infection. If the skin is broken keep the area clean with antiseptic and cover with a non-adhesive dressing material held in place with tape.

HYPOTHERMIA

Also known as exposure, this occurs when the body can't generate enough heat to maintain its normal temperature, usually as a result of being wet, cold, unprotected from the wind, tired and hungry. It is usually more of a problem in upland areas such as on the moors. Hypothermia is easily avoided by wearing suitable clothing, carrying and eating enough food and drink, being aware of the weather conditions and checking the morale of your companions.

Early signs to watch for are feeling cold and tired with involuntary shivering. Find some shelter as soon as possible and warm the victim up with a hot drink and some chocolate or other high-energy food. If possible give them another warm layer of clothing and allow them to rest until feeling better.

If allowed to worsen, strange behaviour, slurring of speech and poor coordination will become apparent and the victim can quickly progress into unconsciousness, followed by coma and death. Quickly get the victim out of any wind and rain, improvising a shelter if necessary. Rapid restoration of bodily warmth is essential and best achieved by bare-skin contact: someone should get into the same sleeping bag as the patient, both having stripped to their underwear, putting any spare clothing under or over them to build up heat. Send urgently for help.

HYPERTHERMIA

Hyperthermia occurs when the body generates too much heat, eg heat exhaustion and heatstroke. Not ailments that you would normally associate with England, these are serious problems nonetheless.

Symptoms of **heat exhaustion** include thirst, fatigue, giddiness, a rapid pulse, raised body temperature, low urine output and, if not treated, delirium and finally a coma. The best cure is to drink plenty of water. The darker your urine the more you should drink.

Heatstroke is more serious. A high body temperature and an absence of sweating are early indications, followed by symptoms similar to hypothermia (see opposite) such as a lack of coordination, convulsions and coma. Death will follow if treatment is not given instantly. Sponge the victim down, wrap them in wet towels, fan them and get help immediately.

SUNBURN

The sun in the South-West can be very strong. The best way to avoid sunburn – and the extra risk of developing skin cancers that sunburn brings – is to keep your skin covered at all times in light, loose-fitting clothing, and to cover any exposed areas of skin in sunscreen (with a minimum factor of 30). Sunscreen should be applied regularly throughout the day. Don't forget your lips, nose, ears and the back of your neck, and even under your chin to protect you against rays reflected from the ground. Most importantly of all, always wear a hat!

3

THE ENVIRONMENT & NATURE

Conservation

CONSERVATION SCHEMES – WHAT'S AN AONB?

It is perhaps the chief joy of this walk that much of it is spent in either a national park or an Area of Outstanding Natural Beauty (AONB). But what exactly are these designations and what protection do they actually confer?

National Parks

The highest level of landscape protection is the designation of land as a **National Park** (🖥 nationalparks.uk). There are 15 in Britain of which nine are in England (including, of course, Exmoor National Park on this trail). This designation recognises the national importance of an area in terms of landscape, biodiversity and as a recreational resource. It does not signify national ownership and these are not uninhabited wildernesses, making conservation a knife-edged balance between protecting the environment and the rights and livelihoods of those living in the park.

🖵 **CONSERVATION AND CAMPAIGNING ORGANISATIONS**

These voluntary organisations started the conservation movement in the mid-19th century and are still at the forefront of developments. Independent of government and reliant on public support, they can concentrate their resources either on acquiring land which can then be managed purely for conservation purposes, or on influencing political decision-makers by lobbying and campaigning.

Managers and owners of land include well-known bodies such as the **National Trust** (NT; 🖥 nationaltrust.org.uk) that owns over 600 miles of coastline including three sites on the Exmoor coastline (Holnicote, Watersmeet, West Exmoor Coast) and other sites on the Devon coast such as Croyde, Woolacombe and Mortehoe, and Bideford Bay and Hartland; the **Royal Society for the Protection of Birds** (RSPB; 🖥 rspb.org.uk), and the **Council for the Protection of Rural England** (CPRE; 🖥 cpre.org.uk) and **Woodland Trust** (🖥 woodlandtrust.org.uk).

There is also **The Wildlife Trusts** (🖥 wildlifetrusts.org), the umbrella organisation for the 47 wildlife trusts in the UK that manage nature reserves and run marine conservation projects.

Areas of Outstanding Natural Beauty

The second level of protection is **Area of Outstanding Natural Beauty** (AONB; 🖳 landscapesforlife.org.uk); there are 46 AONBs in the UK, 33 wholly in England. Much of the South-West Coast Path crosses land covered by either this designation or its close relative **Heritage Coasts**, of which there are currently 43 in England and Wales.

The primary objective of AONBs is conservation of the natural beauty of a landscape. As there is no statutory administrative framework for their management, this is the responsibility of the local authority within whose boundaries they fall. It is of course one of the joys of this part of the South West Coast Path that much of the last half of the walk is spent in the **North Devon AONB**, which includes the Heritage Coasts of North Devon and Hartland.

Out at sea, **Lundy** is also a heritage coast and it is the only Marine Conservation Zone.

National Nature Reserves and Sites of Special Scientific Interest

The next level of protection includes **National Nature Reserves** (NNRs) and **Sites of Special Scientific Interest** (SSSIs). There are 224 NNRs in England of which three are in Exmoor National Park, with Hawkcombe Wood, near Porlock, the closest to the trail (Dunkery Woods and Tarr Steps are the others in the park). Hawkcombe Wood achieved its status largely because of its insect colonies, including fritillary butterflies. Outside the park and east of Bude lies Dunsdon Farm, which achieved its status due to its Culm grassland pasture that's typical of this region.

There are over 4100 **SSSIs** in England. The **Coastal Heaths of Exmoor** cover an area of 1758 hectares (4343 acres) and boast several rare plants

---

❏ NATIONAL TRAILS

There are 16 national trails in England and Wales, including the as yet uncompleted England Coast Path (see below). According to the National Trail website (🖳 nation altrail.co.uk), the definition of a national trail 'is a long-distance path (or, in one case, bridleway) for walking, cycling and horse-riding through the finest landscapes in the two countries'. (Scotland, by the way, has its own equivalent, called Long Distance Routes, of which there are four.) In total they cover around 2500 miles (4000km) of pathways, of which the SWCP is the longest by far in the UK; the next longest, the Pennine Way, is a mere 268 miles/429km. The Pennine Way was also the first national trail to be opened, back in 1965.

Each national trail has been made by linking existing paths to form one long-distance path, rather than by creating new paths. All of them have a dedicated officer charged with maintaining, improving and promoting the trail. They in turn are helped by the local Highways Authorities, landowners and volunteers who all help in keeping the Trails to a usable standard. Funding comes from Natural England and Natural Resources Wales, as well as local highway authorities and other funding partners.

Work is still ongoing on the England Coast Path which follows the coastline of England. When complete, it will be 2795 miles (4500 kilometres) in length.

including two species of whitebeam. SSSIs are a particularly important designation as they have some legal standing. They are managed in partnership with the owners and occupiers of the land who must give written notice before

❏ THE BEAST OF EXMOOR

Red deer, ponies, otters, badgers... Exmoor isn't short of wildlife to observe and admire. Ask the people of Britain, however, what animal they most associate with the park and the chances are many will mention a creature that only a handful of people have ever seen – and which, officially at least, doesn't even exist.

That creature is the Beast of Exmoor. Sightings of a large, panther-like animal roaming the moors of North Devon were first reported back in the 1970s and reached their peak in 1983 when a sheep farmer in South Molton claimed that over a hundred of his herd had been killed in the space of just three months, their throats in each case having savagely been ripped from them. As speculation about the nature of the beast reached fever-pitch, there were reports of 'copycat' (!) sightings of similar creatures from as far away as Kent and Scotland.

At first the authorities were inclined to take the reports seriously and in response to the attacks on livestock, the Ministry of Agriculture sent in a troop of marines with high-powered rifles to hunt and kill any animal that fitted the description of a large cat between four and eight feet from nose to tail, that tended to crouch low to the ground but which had the ability to leap over six-foot-tall fences, and which was either black, tan or dark grey in colour.

Their mission proved unsuccessful, however, and the commanding officer – possibly with his tongue lodged in his cheek at the time – asserted that, if the creature did exist, it used the surrounding cover of hedges and woods with an almost 'human-like intelligence'.

News that the marines had returned to their barracks clearly reached the creature, for reports of sheep deaths on the moor continued to rise, with 200 sheep killings attributed to the beast in 1987. There was even more good news for the Beast in the mid-1990s when the authorities, growing ever-more sceptical at the lack of any hard evidence of its existence, concluded that there was, in fact, no Beast of Exmoor. In their opinion, all alleged sightings were either the product of mistaken identifications of the more 'mundane' members of Exmoor's animal kingdom (eg domestic cats, dogs and even sheep), or deliberate hoaxes. It was a point of view that was given added credence in 2009 when a carcass washed up on North Devon turned out not to be the body of the beast, but a badly decomposed seal; and again in 2010 when photos of the beast appeared on the front pages of various tabloids – before it was discovered that the photographer had been doctoring his pictures using Photoshop.

Today, the more sober followers of the story have concluded that, if there ever was a Beast of Exmoor, there isn't one now (panthers live for only about 15 years on average). But there remains the distinct possibility that such a creature did once prowl the moors. Experts of 'phantom' or cryptozoological cats (to give them their proper title) point to a fad in the 1960s and 1970s to keep wild cats as pets. Given that in 1976 the Dangerous Wild Animals Act effectively outlawed this practice, it is highly possible that one of these large cats either escaped – or was deliberately released – by its owner into the wild.

But while the creature may not exist anymore, it does, of course, live on in popular memory, folklore – and as a particularly potent concoction of Exmoor Ales Brewery whose Beast of Exmoor Ale weighs in at an impressive 6.6% ABV!

initiating any operation likely to damage the site and who cannot proceed without consent from **Natural England** (⌨ gov.uk/government/organisations/natural-england), the single body responsible for identifying, establishing and managing National Parks, Areas of Outstanding Natural Beauty, National Nature Reserves, Sites of Special Scientific Interest, and Special Areas of Conservation.

Special Area of Conservation (SAC) is an international designation which came into being as a result of the 1992 Earth Summit in Rio de Janeiro, Brazil. This European-wide network of sites is designed to promote the conservation of habitats, wild animals and plants, both on land and at sea. At the time of writing 235 land sites in England had been designated as SACs.

Flora and fauna

With a varied topography that encompasses a full range of landscapes from windblasted moor to wetland marsh, hog's back cliffs to wooded valleys, muddy estuaries to mobile sand dunes, you can begin to appreciate why the South-West can boast such a rich and varied countryside, with several unique species of flora and thriving populations of mammals and birds that, elsewhere in the UK, struggle to survive.

The following is not in any way a comprehensive guide, but merely a brief run-down of the more commonly seen flora and fauna on the trail, together with some of the rarer and more spectacular species.

TREES

For a moorland region Exmoor boasts some surprisingly fine patches of woodland. The most interesting species is the **oak** (family name *Quercus*), which was originally planted as coppice or scrub and supports more kinds of insect than any other tree in Britain. In Exmoor the most prolific species of oak is sessile oak (*Quercus petraea*). Oak woodland is a diverse habitat and not exclusively made up of oak.

❏ OAK LEAVES SHOWING GALLS

Oak trees support more kinds of insects than any other tree in Britain and some affect the oak in unusual ways. The eggs of gall-flies, for example, cause growths known as galls on the leaves. Each of these contains a single insect. Other kinds of gall-flies lay eggs in stalks or flowers, leading to flower galls, growths the size of currants.

THE ENVIRONMENT & NATURE

Other trees that flourish here include **downy birch** (*Betula pubescens*), its relative the **silver birch** (*Betula pendula)*, **holly** (*Ilex aquifolium*) and **hazel** (*Corylus avellana*) which has traditionally been used for coppicing (the periodic cutting of small trees for harvesting).

In addition, Monterey cypress, Scots and Corsican pine, Sitka spruce and Douglas fir are some of the non-native species that have been planted by the landowners of Exmoor down the centuries. Most of the woodland on Exmoor is owned by the Forestry Commission, the Woodland Trust and the National Trust.

Hazel (with flowers)

FLOWERS

There are said to be around 800 species of wild plants within Exmoor National Park. Spring is the time to come and see the spectacular displays of colour on the South West Coast Path, when most of the flowers are in bloom. Alternatively, arrive in August and you'll see the heathers carpeting patches of the moors in a blaze of purple flowers.

Woodland and hedgerows

From March to May, **bluebells** (*Hyacinthoides non-scripta*) proliferate in some of the woods along the trail, providing a wonderful spectacle. The white **wood anemone** (*Anemone nemorosa*) – wide open flowers when sunny, closed and drooping when the weather's dull – and the yellow **primrose** (*Primula vulgaris*) also flower early in spring.

Red campion (*Silene dioica*), which flowers from late April, can be found in hedgebanks along with **rosebay willowherb** (*Epilobium augustifolium*) which also has the name fireweed due to its habit of colonising burnt areas.

❏ **REPORTING WILDLIFE SIGHTINGS**
Report basking shark sightings to the website of the Marine Conservation Society (🖳 mcsuk.org). Remember to note any tags you've spotted. Reports are greatly appreciated.

If you see any of the other larger marine creatures such as dolphins, whales or seals you can report them online through Seaquest Southwest, part of the Devon Biodiversity Records Centre (🖳 dbrc.org.uk). With any report give the location, number and the direction they were heading in.

If you come across a stranded marine animal like a dolphin or porpoise, don't approach it but contact either British Divers' Marine Life Rescue (☎ 01825-765546, 🖳 bdmlr.org.uk) or the RSPCA hotline (☎ 0300-1234 999).

Harebell
Campanula rotundifolia

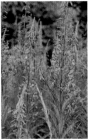

Rosebay Willowherb
Epilobium angustifolium

Foxglove
Digitalis purpurea

Early Purple Orchid
Orchis mascula

Rowan (tree)
Sorbus aucuparia

Dog Rose
Rosa canina

Forget-me-not
Myosotis arvensis

Red Campion
Silene dioica

Scarlet Pimpernel
Anagallis arvensis

Bluebell
Hyacinthoides non-scripta

Germander Speedwell
Veronica chamaedrys

Herb-Robert
Geranium robertianum

Ramsons (Wild Garlic)
Allium ursinum

Meadow Cranesbill
Geranium pratense

Common Dog Violet
Viola riviniana

Common Centaury
Centaurium erythraea

THE ENVIRONMENT & NATURE

Common Ragwort
Senecio jacobaea

Cowslip
Primula veris

Yarrow
Achillea millefolium

Gorse
Ulex europaeus

Bird's-foot trefoil
Lotus corniculatus

Meadow Buttercup
Ranunculus acris

Marsh Marigold
(Kingcup)
Caltha palustris

Yellow Rattle
Rhinanthus minor

Primrose
Primula vulgaris

St John's Wort
*Hypericum
perforatum*

Tormentil
Potentilla erecta

Honeysuckle
*Lonicera
periclymemum*

Ox-eye Daisy
Leucanthemum vulgare

Old Man's Beard
Clematis vitalba

Common Vetch
Vicia sativa

Common Knapweed
Centaurea nigra

In scrubland and on woodland edges you will find **bramble** (*Rubus fruticosus*), a common vigorous shrub responsible for many a ripped jacket thanks to its sharp thorns and prickles. Blackberry fruits ripen from late summer to autumn. Fairly common in scrubland and on woodland edges is the **dog rose** (*Rosa canina*) which has a large pink flower, the fruits of which are used to make rose-hip syrup. Look out, too, on the water in streams or rivers for the white-flowered **water crow-foot** (*Ranunculus penicillatus pseudofluitans*) which, because it needs unpolluted, flowing water, is a good indicator of the cleanliness of the stream.

Other flowering plants to look for in wooded areas and in hedgerows include the tall **foxglove** (*Digitalis purpurea*) with its trumpet-like flowers, **forget-me-not** (*Myosotis arvensis*) with tiny, delicate blue flowers, and **cow parsley** (*Anthriscus sylvestris*), a tall member of the carrot family with a large globe of white flowers which often covers roadside verges and hedgebanks.

Heathland and scrubland

There are three species of heather. The most dominant is **ling** (*Calluna vulgaris*) with tiny flowers on delicate upright stems. The other two species are **bell heather** (*Erica cinera*) with deep purple bell-shaped flowers and **cross-leaved heath** (*Erica tetralix*) with similarly shaped flowers of a lighter pink, almost white colour. Cross-leaved heath prefers wet and boggy ground. As a result, it usually grows away from bell heather which prefers well-drained soils.

Heather is an incredibly versatile plant which is put to many uses. It provides fodder for livestock, fuel for fires, an orange dye and material for bedding, thatching, basketwork and brooms. It is still sometimes used in place of hops to flavour beer and the flower heads can be brewed to make good tea. It is also incredibly hardy and thrives on the denuded hills, preventing other species from flourishing. Indeed, at times highland cattle are brought to certain areas of the moors to graze on the heather, allowing other species a chance to grow.

Not a flower but worthy of mention is the less attractive species **bracken** (*Pteridium aquilinum*), a vigorous non-native fern that has invaded many heathland areas to the detriment of native species.

Grassland

There is much overlap between the hedge/woodland-edge habitat and that of pastures and meadows. You will come across **common birdsfoot-trefoil** (*Lotus*

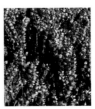

| Sea Holly | Bell Heather | Heather (Ling) | Thrift (Sea Pink) |
| *Eryngium maritimum* | *Erica cinerea* | *Calluna vulgaris* | *Armeria maritima* |

corniculatus), **Germander speedwell** (*Veronica chamaedrys*), **tufted** and **bush vetch** (*Vicia cracca* and *V. sepium*) and **meadow vetchling** (*Lathyrus pratensis*) in both. Often the only species you will see in heavily grazed pastures are the most resilient. Of the thistles, in late summer you should come across the **melancholy thistle** (*Cirsium helenoides*) drooping sadly on roadside verges and hay meadows; unusually, it has no prickles on its stem. The **yellow rattle** is aptly named as its dry seedpods rattle in the wind; this is a good indication for farmers that it is time to harvest the hay.

Other widespread grassland species include **harebell** (*Campanula rotundifolia*), delicate yellow **tormentil** (*Potentilla erecta*) and **devil's-bit scabious** (*Succisa pratensis*). Also keep an eye out for orchids such as the **fragrant orchid** (*Gymnaadenia conopsea*) and **early purple orchid** (*Orchis mascula*).

Dunes

Dunes are formed by wind action creating a fragile, unstable environment. Among the first colonisers is **marram grass** (*Ammophila arenaria*) which is able to withstand drought, exposure to wind and salt spray and has an ability to grow up through new layers of sand that cover it. Other specialist plants are **sea holly** (*Eryngium maritimum*), **sea spurge** (*Euphorbia paralias*) and **sea bindweed** (*Calystegia soldanella*). The one thing that these seemingly indomitable plants can't tolerate is trampling by human feet; stay on the path which is nearly always well marked through dunes.

BUTTERFLIES AND MOTHS

Butterflies are an unexpected treat on the SWCP. Not only are they numerous, but there are several different varieties too. Braunton Burrows (see box p142) plays host to several species including marbled whites, graylings, ringlets and skippers, as well as to **moths**, including ghost, common swift, diamond-back, garden grass veneer and small China mark moths. Butterflies and moths aren't confined to the burrows, however.

The most famous butterfly in the region is the orange and brown heath fritillary, which has declined rapidly over the last 30 years in the UK, but which is thriving in the combes of Exmoor (indeed, Exmoor is one of only four places where they still live, and there are now 15 colonies in the national park).

REPTILES

The **adder** (*Vipera berus*) is the only poisonous snake of the three species found in Britain. They pose very little risk to walkers – indeed, you should consider yourself extremely fortunate to see one, providing you're a safe distance away. They bite only when provoked, preferring to hide instead. The venom is designed to kill small mammals such as mice, voles and shrews, so deaths in humans are very rare but a bite can be extremely unpleasant and occasionally dangerous to children or the elderly. You are most likely to encounter them in spring when they come out of hibernation and during the summer when pregnant females warm themselves in the sun. They are easily identified by the striking

Peacock
Inachis io

Common Blue
Polyommatus icarus

Small
Tortoiseshell *Aglais urticae*

Small Garden/Cabbage
White
Pieris rapae

Silver-washed
Fritillary
*Argynnis
paphia*

Brimstone
*Gonepteryx
rhamni*
(female; male is
bright yellow)

Painted Lady
Cynthia cadui

Large
Garden/
Cabbage White
Pieris brassicae

Small
Copper
*Lycaena
phlaeas*

Small
Heath
*Coenonympha
pamphilus*

Red Admiral *Vanessa atalanta*

White Admiral
Limenitis camilla

Meadow
Brown
*Maniola
jurtina*

Above, clockwise from top left : **1**. Herring gull. **2**. Oystercatchers. **3**. Puffin. **4**. Razorbill.
5. Pied wagtail. **6**. Curlew. **7**. Black headed gull. **8**. Great black-backed gull. (All ©BT).

zigzag pattern on their back. Should you be lucky enough to encounter one, (they enjoy basking on clifftops and on the moors) enjoy it but leave it undisturbed. The **grass snake** (*Natrix natrix*) is the largest British species, growing up to four feet in length. Olive-grey in colour with short black bars down each side and orange or yellow patches just below the head, they are harmless, relying not on venom or biting for defence but instead give off a foul odour if disturbed. It is pretty scarce in the south-west but can be found in damp places on Exmoor.

The **slow-worm** (*Anguis fragilis*) must be one of the more unusual creatures in the British Isles – a reptile that is called a worm, looks like a snake but is actually a legless lizard! Silver-grey with a dark line down the centre of the back and along each side, it is common on Exmoor and in North Devon in general, where it feeds on slugs, worms and insects.

BIRDS

In and around the fishing villages

The wild laugh of the **herring gull** (*Larus argentatus*) is the wake-up call of the coast path. Perched on the rooftops of the stone villages, they are a reminder of the link between people and wildlife, the rocky coast and our stone and concrete towns and cities. Shoreline scavengers, they've adapted to the increasing waste thrown out by human society. Despite their bad reputation it's worth taking a closer look at these fascinating, ubiquitous birds. How do they keep their pale grey and white plumage so beautiful feeding on rubbish?

Nobel-prize-winning animal behaviourist Nikko Tinbergen showed how the young pecking at the red dot on their bright yellow bills triggers the adult to regurgitate food. In August the newly fledged brown young follow their parents begging for food. Over the next three years they'll go through a motley range of plumages, more grey and less brown each year till they reach adulthood. But please don't feed them and do watch your sandwiches and fish & chips – they are quite capable of grabbing food from your hand.

The village harbours are a good place for lunch or an evening drink after a hard day on the cliffs. Look out for the birds which are equally at home on a rocky shore or in villages, such as the beautiful little black-and-white **pied wagtail** (*Motacilla alba*) with its long, bobbing tail.

Also looking black from a distance as they strut the beach are **jackdaws** (*Corvus monedula*). Close up, however, they are beautiful with a grey nape giving them a hooded look and shining blue eyes. They are very sociable: you will often see them high up in the air in pairs or flocks playing tag or performing acrobatic tricks.

Small, dark brown and easy to miss, the **rock pipit** (*Anthus petrosus*) is one of our toughest birds, as it feeds whilst walking on the rocks between the land and the sea. They nest in crevices and caves along the rocky coastline.

Seen on or from the sea cliffs

Walking on the coastal path leads you into a world of rock and sea, high cliffs with bracken-clad slopes, exposed green pasture, dramatic drops and headlands, sweeping sandy beaches and softer country around the estuaries. Stunning

THE ENVIRONMENT & NATURE

stonechats (*Saxicola torquata*) with black, white and orange colouring are common on heath and grassy plains where you may hear their distinctive song, which is not dissimilar to two stones being clacked together. Twittering **linnets** (*Carduelis cannabina*) with their bright red breasts and grey heads fly ahead and perch on gorse and fences. The vertiginous swoops of the path mean it's often possible to be at eye level or even look down on birds and mammals. Watch for **kestrels** (*Falco tinnunculus*), hovering on sharp brown wings, before plummeting onto their prey.

At eye level the black 'moustache' of the powerful slate-grey-backed **peregrine** (*Falco peregrinus*) is sometimes visible. At a glance it can be mistaken for a pigeon, its main prey. But the power and speed of this, the world's fastest bird, soon sets it apart. In the late summer whole families fly over the cliffs. In mid winter look for them over estuaries where they hunt ducks and waders. Despite the remote fastness of the cliffs, peregrine have suffered terribly. Accidental poisoning by the pesticide DDT succeeded where World War II persecution (for fear they would kill carrier pigeons) failed, and they were almost extinct in this region by the end of the 1960s. Its triumphant return means not only a thriving population on its traditional sea cliffs, but more and more nesting in our cities on man-made cliffs, such as tower blocks and cathedrals.

Cliff ledges, a kind of multi-storey block of flats for birds, provide nesting places safe from marauding land predators such as foxes and rats. It's surprising just how close it's possible to get to **fulmars** (*Fulmarus glacialis*), which return to their nesting ledges in February for the start of the long breeding season that goes on into the autumn. Only in the depth of winter are the cliffs quiet. Fulmars are related to albatrosses and like them are masters of the air. You can distinguish them from gulls by their ridged, flat wings as they sail the wind close to the waves with the occasional burst of fast flapping. Fulmars are incredibly tenacious at holding their nesting sites and vomit a stinking oily secretion over any intruders, including rock-climbers! The elegant **kittiwake** (*Rissa tridactyla*), the one true seagull that never feeds on land, is another cliff nester, identified by its 'dipped in ink' black wingtips.

Black above, white below, **manx shearwaters** (*Puffinus puffinus*) make globe-encircling journeys as they sail effortlessly just above even the wildest sea. Small and fast on hard-beating wings black and white **guillemots** (*Uria troile*) and **razorbills** (*Alca torda*) shoot out from their nesting ledges hidden in the cliffs. Guillemot have a long thin bill, razorbill a heavy half circle. There are large colonies of auks, razorbills and guillemots around the Highveer Point to Lynmouth area. **Puffins** (*Fratercula arctica*) with their unmistakable parrot-shaped bills are a rare prize round these coasts. Lundy, once again, is the best place to see these lovely birds.

Less lovely in most people's eyes, though undeniably magnificent, the big, rapacious **great black-backed gulls** (*Larus marinus*) cruise the nesting colonies for prey. Star of the sea show, however, has to be the big, sharp-winged, Persil-white **gannets** (*Morus bassanus*) cruising slowly for fish, then suddenly plunging with folded wings into the sea. Their strengthened skulls protect them from the huge force of the impact with the water.

Two birds more familiar from the artificial cliffs of our cities can be seen here in their natural habitat – **house martins** (*Delichon urbica*), steely-blue backed like a **swallow** (*Hirundo rustica*), but with more V-shaped wings and a distinctive white rump, and **rock doves** (*Columba livia*). These are so mixed with **town pigeons** (*Columba livia domest.*) it's hard to say if any 'pure' wild birds remain, but many individuals with the characteristic grey back, small white rump and two black wing bars can be seen.

Where the path drops steeply to a rocky bay, **oystercatchers** (*Haematopus ostralegus*), with their black and white plumage and spectacular carrot-coloured bill, pipe in panic when they fly off. This is also a good spot to get close to **shags** (*Phalacrocorax aristotelis*) and **cormorants** (*Phalacrocorax pygmeus*), common all round the coast, swimming low and black in the water. Shags are smaller and are always seen on the sea – cormorants are also on rivers and estuaries – and in the summer have a crest whilst cormorants have a white patch near their tail and white face. Close up, these oily birds shine iridescently; shags are green, cormorants are purple. They are a primitive species and since their feathers are not completely waterproof both have to dry their bodies after time in the sea; their heraldic pose, standing upright with half-spread wings on drying rocks is one of the special sights of the coast path.

In pastures, combes and woods

The path rises up onto rich green pasture. **Skylarks** (*Alauda arvensis*) soar tunefully – almost disappearing into the spring sky, while in winter small green-brown **meadow pipits** (*Anthus pratensis*) flit weakly, giving a small high-pitched call. Spring also brings migrant **wheatears** (*Oenanthe oenanthe*): they are beautiful with their grey and black feathers above, buff and white below, and unmistakable when they fly and show their distinctive white rump. **Buzzards** (*Buteo buteo*) soar up with their tilted, broad round wings, giving their high, wild Ke-oow cry. **Ravens** (*Corvus corax*) cronk-cronk over the cliffs and are distinguished from more common **carrion crows** (*Corvus corone*) by their huge size and wedge-shaped tail. In the woods you'll find all three native species of **woodpecker** – **green**, **great** and **lesser spotted** (*Picus viridis* and *Dendrocopos major* and *minor* respectively); the latter two are very much wedded to the woods, while the former, with its laughing call, can often be seen on the moors looking for insects.

In spring familiar birds such as **robins** (*Erithacus rubecula*), **blackbirds** (*Turdus merula*), **blue** and **great tits** (*Parus major* & *caeruleus*), **chaffinches** (*Fringila coelebs*) and **dunnocks** (*Prunella modularis*) are joined by the small green **chiffchaff** (*Phylloscopus collybita*); it's not much to look at but is one of the earliest returning migrants and unmistakably calls its own name in two repeated notes.

In and around estuaries

Descending to the long walk round the estuaries is moving into a different, softer world of shelter and rich farmland. Best for birds in winter, they are a welcome refuge from the ferocity of the worst weather for wildlife and people. There are large flocks of ducks – whistling **wigeon** (*Anas penelope*), a combination of grey and pinky brown, with big white wing patches in flight – and waders like the brown **curlew** (*Numenius arquata*) with its impossibly long, down-curved beak and beautiful sad fluting call, evocative of summer moors. The **redshank** (*Tringa totanus*), **greenshank** (*Tringa nebularia*), golden and grey **plover** (*Pluvialis sp.*) and black-tailed and bar-tailed **godwit** (*Limosa sp.*) can also be seen in winter.

Look out for the big black, white and chestnut **shelduck** (*Tadorna tadorna*), and for the tall grey **heron** (*Ardea cinerea*), hunched at rest or extended to its full 175cm as it slowly, patiently stalks fish in the shallows. A real rarity 10 years ago, another species of heron, the stunning white **little egret** (*Egretta garzetta*) is now unmissable on estuaries. Here the more common gull is the nimble **black-headed gull** (*Larus ridibundus*), with its elegant cap, dark in summer but pale in winter. In summer, terns come: the big **sandwich tern** (*Sterna sandvicensis*) with its shaggy black cap and loud rasping call, and the smaller sleeker aerobatic **common tern** (*Sterna hirundo*).

SEA LIFE

The high cliffs are also a great place from which to look out over the sea. Searching for seals is an enjoyable and essential part of cliff walking. You'll spot lots of grey lobster-pot buoys before your first seal, but it's worth the effort. **Atlantic grey seals** (*Halichoerus grypus*) relax in the water, looking over their big Roman noses with doggy eyes, as interested in you as you are in them. Twice the weight of a red deer, a big bull can be over 200kg. On calm sunny days it's possible to follow them down through the clear water as they dive, as elegant in their element as they are clumsy on land. Seals generally come ashore only to rest, moult their fur, or to breed. The main centre where seals 'haul out' – come up on the rocks – is Lundy Island (see box on p122). Indeed, Devon is a sort of frontier for the seals, as they rarely haul out east of here until you reach Norfolk.

A cliff-top sighting of Britain's largest fish is also a real possibility, but is more chilling than endearing! **Basking sharks** (*Cetorhinus maximus*) can grow to a massive eleven metres and weigh seven tonnes, and their two fins, a large shark-like dorsal fin followed by a notched tail fin, are so far apart it takes a second look to be convinced it's one fish. But these are gentle giants, cruising slowly with open jaws, filtering microscopic plankton from the sea. You are most likely to see one during late spring and summer when they feed at the surface during calm, warm weather. Look out for the coloured or numbered tags, which have been put on for research into this sadly declining species, and report them to the address given in the box on p64.

Taking a longer view and with some good luck, you may see **harbour porpoises** (*Phocoena phocoena*) and **bottlenose dolphins** (*Tursiops truncatus*); the former are particularly prevalent in Ilfracombe. Other cetaceans you may catch a glimpse of are: **Risso's dolphins** (*Grampus griseus*), **common dolphins** (*Delphinus delphis*), **striped dolphins** (*Stenella coeruleoalba*), **orcas** or **killer whales** (*Orcinus orca*) and **pilot whales** (*Globicephala melaena*). However, be warned, they are fiendishly difficult to tell apart: a brief glimpse of a fin is nothing like the 'whole animal' pictures shown in field guides.

MAMMALS

The South-West is blessed with wildlife and three species of mammals are particularly associated with the region. The largest population of **red deer**, *Cervus Elaphus*, lives on Exmoor – one of only three places where the herds are resident in England. Red deer, Britain's biggest wild animal, are nevertheless shy by nature and tend to flee at the approach of people.

There is a very slim chance that a stag may charge during the rutting (mating) season when their behaviour can be unpredictable, though there is no record of this ever happening on Exmoor. They are largely nocturnal and your best chance of seeing them is at dusk when they move out of their woodland coverts to feed. Stags and hinds live separately for most of the year, mingling properly only during the mating season of October and November.

Also at home on the moor are the famous **Exmoor ponies**, a very ancient breed that resembles the miniature breeds of Asia more than any other native British horse. These ponies are hardy and also largely wild or feral, though in the past they were trained to work in mines, on farms or for shepherding. There have never been many of them and during World War II their numbers collapsed to around 50. Today there are more than 500 adult breeding females (most on Exmoor), though a relatively small gene pool – after all, all today's ponies are descended from those 50 – means that they are still on the endangered list.

The third species for which the South-West is renowned is the **otter** (*Lutra lutra*). With Devon the home of the author Henry Williamson – author of *Tarka the Otter* – the county is proud to be associated with this most graceful of British carnivores and even has a Tarka Trail (see box p34). It wasn't always like this, however, and for much of the 20th century (and before) the otter was persecuted because it was (wrongly) believed to have an enormously detrimental effect on fish stocks.

Indeed, the otter was hunted with dogs up until 1977 and the Culmstock Otter Hounds were a regular sight in Exmoor National Park, particularly in the Exe and Barle valleys. Thankfully, today the otter is enjoying something of a renaissance due to some concerted conservation efforts. At home both in saltwater and freshwater, they are a good indicator of an unpolluted environment and Exmoor in particular is enjoying a resurgence in otter numbers; there are now known to be at least 23 residing in Exmoor – a healthy number, given the size of the territory an otter requires. Trivia fans may like to know that the final, climactic scene of the 1979 film version of *Tarka* was set on Instow Beach in North Devon. The author Henry Williamson was taken seriously ill during filming and is said to have died during the filming of the last scene.

Seeing any of these animals requires patience and no little amount of luck. One creature that you will definitely see along the walk, however, is the **rabbit** (*Oryctolagus cuniculus*). Timid by nature, most of the time you'll have to make do with nothing more than a brief and distant glimpse of their white tails as they

THE ENVIRONMENT & NATURE

race for the nearest warren at the sound of your footfall. Because they are so numerous, however, the laws of probability dictate that you will at some stage during your walk get close enough to observe them without being spotted; trying to take a decent photo of one, however, is a different matter.

If you're lucky you may also come across **hares** (*Lepus europaeus*), often mistaken for rabbits but much larger, more elongated and with longer ears and back legs. There are populations of hares all over the arable parts of Exmoor, though nowhere is it common.

Like the otter, the **water vole** (*Arvicola terrestris*) has both been a major character in a well-known work of fiction (in this case 'Ratty' from Kenneth Grahame's classic children's story *Wind in the Willows*), and has suffered a devastating drop in its population. Their numbers had originally declined due to the arrival in the UK countryside of the mink from North America, which successfully adapted to living in the wild after escaping from local fur farms. Unfortunately, the mink not only hunts water voles but is small enough to slip inside their burrows. Thus, with the voles afforded no protection, the mink was able to wipe out an entire riverbank's population in a matter of months. (Incidentally, this is another reason why protecting the otter is important: they kill mink.) A programme is now in place in which the water vole and its habitat is not only protected but the mink are being trapped and killed.

Another native British species that has suffered at the hands of a foreign invader – and indeed has now disappeared altogether from Exmoor and this part of the South-West – is the red squirrel (*Sciurus vulgaris*), a small, tufty-eared native that has been usurped by its larger cousin from North America, the **grey squirrel** (*Sciurus carolinensis*). The nearest place to see the red squirrel is at Poole Harbour – at the very end of the South West Coast Path.

Other creatures you might see include the ubiquitous **fox** (*Vulpes vulpes*), now just as at home in the city as it is in the countryside. While generally considered nocturnal, it's not unusual to encounter a fox during the day too, often lounging in the sun near its den.

Another creature of the night you may *occasionally* see in the late afternoon is the **badger** (*Meles meles*). Relatively common throughout the British Isles, these sociable mammals with their distinctive black-and-white striped muzzles live in large underground burrows called setts, appearing around sunset to root for worms and slugs.

One creature that is strictly nocturnal, however, is the **bat**, of which there are 17 species in Britain, all protected by law. Your best chance of spotting one is at dusk while there's still enough light in the sky to make out their flitting forms as they fly along hedgerows, over rivers and streams and around street lamps in their quest for moths and insects. The commonest species in Britain is the **pipistrelle** (*Pipistrellus pipistrellus*).

In addition to the above, keep a look out for other fairly common but little seen species such as the carnivorous **stoat** (*Mustela erminea*), its diminutive cousin the **weasel** (*Mustela nivalis*), the **hedgehog** (*Erinaceus europaeus*) – these days, alas, most commonly seen as roadkill – and any number of species of **voles**, **mice** and **shrews**.

Using this guide

The route guide has been described from east to west and divided into ten stages. Though each of these roughly corresponds to a day's walk, do not assume that this is the only way to plan your walk. There are so many places to stay en route that you can pretty much divide up the walk wherever you want. However, see the boxes on p30 and p31 for some suggested itineraries.

To provide further help, practical information is presented on the trail maps, including walking times, places to stay, camp and eat, as well as shops where you can buy supplies, and public toilets. Further service details are given in the text under the entry for each settlement. For a condensed overview of this information see the village and town facilities table on pp32-3.

TRAIL MAPS [see key map inside cover; symbols key p208]

Scale and walking times

The trail maps are to a scale of 1:20,000 (1cm = 200m; $3^1/8$ inches = one mile). Walking times are given along the side of each map and the arrow shows the direction to which the time refers. Black triangles indicate the points between which the times have been taken. **See note in the box below on walking times**.

The time-bars are a tool and are not there to judge your walking ability. There are so many variables that affect walking speed, from the weather conditions to how many beers you drank the previous evening. After the first hour or two of walking you will be able to see how your speed relates to the timings on the maps.

Up or down?

On the trail maps in this book, the walking trail is always shown as a **dashed red line**. An arrow across the trail indicates the slope; two

---

❏ **IMPORTANT NOTE – WALKING TIMES**
Unless otherwise specified, **all times in this book refer only to the time spent walking**. You should add 20-30% to allow for rests, photos, checking the map, drinking water etc, not to mention time simply to stop and stare. When planning the day's hike count on 5-7 hours' actual walking.

arrows show that it is steep. Note that the arrow points towards the higher part of the trail. If, for example, you are walking from A (at 80m) to B (at 200m) and the trail between the two is short and steep it would be shown thus: A— — — >> — — – B. Reversed arrow heads indicate a downward gradient.

GPS waypoints
The numbered GPS waypoints refer to the list on pp207-8.

Other features
Features are marked on the map when pertinent to navigation. In order to avoid cluttering the maps and making them unusable not all features have been marked each time they occur.

ACCOMMODATION

Apart from in large towns where some selection of places has been necessary, almost every place to stay that is within easy reach of the trail is marked. Details of each place are given in the accompanying text.

For **B&B-style accommodation** the number and type of rooms is given after each entry: **S** = single room (one single bed), **T** = twin room (two single beds), **D** = double room (one double bed, or two single beds pushed/joined together), **Tr** = triple room and **Qd** = quad. Note that many of the triple/quad rooms have a double bed and either one/two single beds, or bunk beds; thus in a group of three or four, two people would have to share the double bed, but it also means the room can be used as a double or twin. Many places describe these rooms as family rooms.

Rates quoted are **per person (pp)** based on two people sharing a room for a one-night stay; rates are usually discounted for longer stays. Where a single room **(sgl)** is available the rate for that is quoted if different from the rate per person. The rate for single occupancy **(sgl occ)** of a double/twin may be higher and the per person rate for **three/four sharing** a triple/quad may be lower. Unless specified, rates are for bed and breakfast. At some places, generally chain hotels, the only option is a **room rate**; this will be the same whether one or two people (or more if permissible) use the room; this rate generally doesn't include breakfast. See p21 for more information on rates.

The text also mentions whether the rooms are en suite or whether they have private or shared facilities and also if a **bath** (☞) is available in or for at least one room. Also noted is whether premises offer packed lunches (Ⓛ) if requested in advance and if **dogs** (🐾) are welcome. Most places will not take more than one dog in a room and also accept them only subject to prior arrangement. Some make an additional charge (usually per night but occasionally per stay) while others may require a deposit which is refundable if the dog doesn't make a mess. See also p210.

It is safe to assume nowadays that if a place to stay and/or eat has a **website**, it will also have **wi-fi** that is free unless otherwise stated. It can be useful to check the **Facebook page (fb)** before arriving, especially for small or seasonal businesses, as these tend to be kept more up-to-date with changes to opening times than regular websites.

Many places do not accept advance **bookings** for a single-night stay at weekends or in peak holiday periods but they will if someone calls near the actual date or on the day. Whether booking ahead or not, you will almost always get the best rates by booking direct with the accommodation rather than through an agency or price comparison website. Some B&Bs don't accept credit/debit cards but guesthouses and hotels usually do. Booking is sometimes needed at **campsites** in school holidays but is usually not necessary at other times. Always remember to tell campsites that you are walking the coast path when you call ahead. Many campsites will find room for walkers even if they are officially full. You'll also often get a cheaper rate.

The route guide

MINEHEAD   [MAP 1, p77]
Some towns inspire. They have an air of adventure and a sense of urgency. They are mysterious and just a little frightening. You know as soon as you walk into them they are special places. Minehead isn't one of them.
    Mark Wallington, *500 Mile Walkies*

Minehead may not be quite as bad as Mr Wallington would have you believe but there's not much to delay you here. The town's major draw, the huge Butlin's holiday camp on Minehead's eastern fringes, will probably hold little appeal to the average walker. Indeed, Minehead doesn't even have a mine – the name actually derives from the Celtic word, Mynedd, meaning 'hill'.

Nevertheless, Minehead's location, where the flat, former marshlands of Somerset collide with the rolling hills of Exmoor, is a good one, and the town's port was once, during Elizabethan times, a thriving place, built on foundations that date back to Saxon times. Today, however, the place is much sleepier, the biggest thrill in town being the intermittent arrival of the steam trains of **West Somerset Railway** (see box p45) as they puff and chuff into Minehead's centre. Railway enthusiasts can enter the station (£5) to take a closer look at the engine sheds. You can see the **hand-winched railway turntable** in action at various times of the day from both inside the station, and outside beside Turntable Café (p78).

The **Regal Theatre** (☎ 01643 706430, 🖳 regaltheatre.co.uk), on The Avenue, houses a 400-seat auditorium for live performances, and is the venue for the Minehead & Exmoor Music Festival in July (p16).

Despite its relative lack of thrills, as a place to begin a 124½ mile/200km adventure (630 miles if you're hoping to complete the SWCP!), Minehead is pretty good: there are reasonable transport connections (by the standards of the South-West, anyway); plenty of places to stay and eat, should you require them; and with no 'must-sees' in town that demand to be visited, there's little to delay you should you wish to push on with your walking as soon as you arrive.

Services
Minehead Information Centre (☎ 01643-702624, 🖳 visit-exmoor.co.uk/minehead; **fb**; Apr-Oct Tue-Sat 10am-4pm, Sun 11am-4pm, Oct-Apr Sat & Sun noon-3pm) can be found where the main drag meets the sea at The Beach Hotel (see Where to stay). The centre has a decent range of information on the SWCP including bus timetables and is staffed by knowledgeable locals who can also do accommodation booking. There is also a small **museum** (same hours).

For supplies the most central **supermarket** is the Co-op (Mon-Sat 6am-10pm, Sun 10am-4pm), on The Avenue, at the back of which you'll find the **post office**

(Mon-Fri 9am-5.30pm, Sat 9am-1pm). For **outdoor gear**, there's a branch of Trespass (☎ 01643 702686, 🖳 trespass.com; Mon-Sat 9.30am-5pm, Sun 10am-4pm) on The Parade, though there was talk of it closing down, so don't rely on it being open when you get here. For **photography** requirements, Priddy's Photoshop (🖳 priddys.co .uk; Mon-Fri 9am-5.30pm, Sat 9am-5pm) is on Friday St.

The **library** (🖳 somersetlibraries.co .uk; Mon, Tue, Thur & Fri 9am-4pm, Sat 11am-1pm) has a few terminals dedicated to **internet access**. Walkers can access one for free for up to an hour with a temporary membership.

If on the journey here you've already managed to acquire blisters or other ailments, Boots the **chemist** (Mon-Sat 8.30am-5.30pm, Sun 10am-4pm) has a branch on the main drag of The Parade and there are several **banks** with ATMs scattered along it, including HSBC by The Duke of Wellington.

Transport

For details on getting to Minehead, see p45-7 and for local services see pp48-50. For destinations further along the path, the No 10 **bus** service operates between Minehead and Porlock Weir, and the seasonal Exmoor Coaster service runs along the coast to Lynmouth via Porlock. There is also the No 28 service to Taunton. Most services stop on The Avenue.

For a **taxi** call Minehead Taxis (☎ 01643-704123, 🖳 minehead-taxis.co.uk).

Where to stay

For **campers**, the nearest site lies about 1¼ miles from town. *Minehead Camping and Caravanning Club* (☎ 01643-704138, 🖳 campingandcaravanningclub.co.uk; WI-FI £3/day; late Apr to early Oct) is on Hill Rd on North Hill. It's a well-equipped place which boasts wonderful views over the town to the sea. Prices for non-members are around £14-16 for one adult and a tent. Members of the Camping and Caravanning Club (£41 per year) get significant discounts. You may need to stay for a minimum of two nights in the peak summer sea-

son. Getting to the campsite is a bit of a pain, involving a 30-minute walk up a steep hill (though you can cut in from the coast path).

There's an independent hostel, *Base Lodge* (☎ 07731 651536, 🖳 independent hostels.co.uk/members/baselodge; 1 x 5-, 1 x 6-, 1 x 7-bed dorm/2T, shared facilities), at 16 The Parks, just west of the town centre. The genial host is a qualified mountain guide and a mine of information. The rooms are clean, basic and pleasant and the kitchen is well equipped. A dorm bed costs £17.50pp (twin £20pp, sgl occ £25).

YHA Minehead (☎ 0345-371 9033, 🖳 yha.org.uk/hostel/minehead; 2 x 3-, 4 x 4-, 1 x 5-, 1 x 6- bed dorms shared facilities; Ⓛ ; Mar to end Oct) is actually a little way out of town at **Alcombe Combe** – and far from the coast path too – so is not really practical for most people. A dorm bed costs £12.99-24.99pp, private rooms sleeping three to six people £49.99-109.99.

One of the finest **B&Bs** in Minehead, *The Parks* (☎ 01643-703547, 🖳 parksguest house.co.uk; 4D/1T/2Qd, all en suite; Ⓛ; 🐾), 26 Parks Rd, is an elegant Georgian property in a leafy part of town with immaculately maintained rooms. Two of the doubles can also be twins. They charge £41-42.50pp (sgl occ £62). The two family rooms cost from £105/120 for three/four sharing.

Most B&Bs are at the eastern side of town. The first place to look is Tregonwell Rd, where a string of guesthouses and B&Bs stand cheek-by-jowl. *Tregonwell House* (☎ 01643-709287, 🖳 tregonwell house.co.uk; fb; 4D/2T/1D or T, all en suite; Ⓛ; Mar-Oct), at No 1, is fairly typical – it's an unassuming B&B (£40-42.50pp, sgl occ £55-75) with comfy rooms and amiable owners.

Heading south along the road, next door is *Candlelight* (☎ 01643-703977, 🖳 candlelightbb.co.uk; 3D/1T/1Tr, all en suite; Ⓛ) popular with walkers, possibly as packed lunches can be made instead of breakfast; B&B costs £32.50-37.50pp (sgl occ £58-67.50).

Kenella House (☎ 01643-703128, 🖳 kenellahouse.co.uk; 4D/2T, all en suite; Ⓛ; Mar-Oct; 2 nights minimum; no children

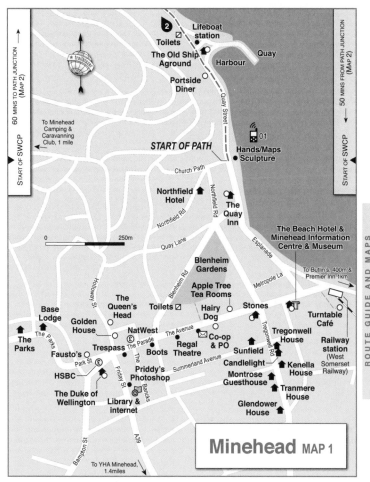

Minehead MAP 1

under 14), at No 7, is slightly smarter than most on this street. The tariff is £40pp (sgl occ full room rate). Across the road at No 14 is *Montrose Guesthouse* (☎ 01643-706473, 🖳 montroseminehead.co.uk; **fb**; 3D/2D or T, all en suite; Ⓛ; Feb-Dec). B&B costs £35-37.50pp (sgl occ room rate); homemade bread and jam are served at breakfast. No children under 14.

Tranmere House (☎ 01643-702647, 🖳 tranmerehouse.co.uk; **fb**; 3D/1T/2Tr, all en suite) is another smart place and decent value (from £36pp, sgl occ from £54).

Finally, on this strip there's *Glendower House* (☎ 01643-707144, 🖳 glendower-house.co.uk; **fb**; 3S/4D/2T/2Tr, all en suite), another large Edwardian place. B&B here costs £37.50-42pp (sgl/sgl occ from

£48/66). Nearby, ***Sunfield*** (☎ 01643-703565, 💻 sunfieldminehead.co.uk; 1S/3D/2T, all en suite; Ⓛ; 🐕), at 83 Summerland Ave, is also popular with walkers. The rates are £36pp (sgl occ £46).

There are some **pubs with rooms** and real character on Quay St, which conveniently is also the street where the SWCP starts. ***The Quay Inn*** (☎ 01643-702839, 💻 thequayinnminehead.co.uk; **fb**; 1D/1T/1Tr, all en suite, 1Qd private bathroom; ▼; Ⓛ; 🐕), the first you come to, is a smart and modern affair with a good kitchen (see Where to eat). They charge £40pp (sgl occ £70).

At the northern edge of town and right on the trail, ***The Old Ship Aground*** (☎ 01643-703516, 💻 theoldshipaground.com; **fb**; 2S/4D/6T, all en suite; 🐕) is not actually as old as it looks, having been built in the 1900s, though it's still got a certain charm, pleasant rooms (£46pp, sgl £47.50, sgl occ full room rate) and, best of all, the finest views in Minehead over the harbour.

Another pub, and one whose origins are significantly older, is ***The Duke of Wellington*** (☎ 01643-701910, 💻 jdwetherspoon.co.uk; **fb**; 5S/2T/13D/5Tr, all en suite; ▼), built in 1820 as a coaching inn but now Wetherspoons-owned and typical of the chain, being functional, central and fair value (room only from £26pp, sgl/sgl occ from £56).

There are several **hotels** in Minehead. On The Avenue is ***Stones*** (☎ 01643-709717, 💻 stonesminehead.co.uk; **fb**; 1S/8D/4T/3Tr/2Qd/1 room sleeps 6, all en suite; ▼; Ⓛ; 🐕). If you're walking with a dog they're definitely worth a call, as they are if you're travelling in a small group as one room has a double bed and four singles. Rates are from £56pp (sgl/sgl occ from £70/86).

A splendid option for your first night away from home is ***The Beach Hotel*** (☎ 01643-704765, 💻 thebeachhotel.org; **fb**; 6D/8D or T, all en suite; ▼; Ⓛ; 🐕). Situated where The Avenue meets the Esplanade, a number of the rooms have sea views and from some you can see the start of the trail. B&B costs £42.50-55pp (sgl occ £60-80). Owned by the YMCA and offering a hospitality training academy for young local apprentices, attached to the hotel are a fine restaurant and café (see Where to eat). Commendably, the hotel opened its doors to the homeless during Covid-19 lockdown periods.

Northfield Hotel (☎ 01643-705155, 💻 www.northfield-hotel.co.uk; **fb**; 3S/5D/22D or T, all en suite; ▼; Ⓛ; 🐕), on Northfield Rd, has a pool, Jacuzzi and some pleasant gardens. B&B costs £52.50-85pp (sgl £75, sgl occ from £90-155).

There is also a ***Premier Inn*** (☎ 0871 622 2313, 💻 www.premierinn.com; 100D or T, all en suite; ▼), though it's about 1km from the centre. If you book off-peak, and in advance, rates can be as low as £29 for a double room, and are still as low as £40 or £60 for a double in peak periods, as long as you book far in advance. However, for last-minute bookings you'll pay closer to £100 in peak periods. Some rooms can also sleep up to two children. Breakfast (continental/cooked £6.99/8.99) is available at ***Brewers Fayre*** (daily 6.30/7-10.30am & 6-10pm) next door.

Where to eat and drink

Perfectly situated a stone's throw away from the start of the path is ***Portside Diner*** (☎ 01643-704100; **fb**; Tue-Sun 9am-3pm), a cute **café** serving all-day breakfasts (£5.75-9.25) and lunches (£6-13) including omelettes, grilled meats, seafood and soups. More centrally located, ***The Beach Café*** at **The Beach Hotel** (see Where to stay; daily 10am-4pm, lunch noon-2pm) uses local suppliers and fresh ingredients, whilst for fine dining in the evening the hotel and café's middle sibling, the ***restaurant*** (Tue-Sat 6.30-8.30pm), has a superb menu. Just up the road, at 29 The Avenue, ***Apple Tree Tea Rooms*** (💻 appletreetearooms.com; **fb**; Wed-Sun & bank-hols 10am-5pm; closed Dec 23 to early Feb) is a friendly little café serving toasted tea cakes, crumpets and cream teas (from £5.40) as well as sandwiches and baguettes (£4-5), toasties and jacket potatoes (£5-7). Beside Minehead train station, ***Turntable Café*** (10am-4pm) has train-platform seating overlooking the station's hand-winched turntable and is good for a bacon bap and a cuppa while you wait for your steam train.

On The Avenue, at No 32, you will find *Hairy Dog* (☎ 01643-706317, 💻 the hairydog.co.uk; **fb**; food daily noon-9pm). A former 'UK Family Pub of the Year' winner, it's been well run by the same family for over 30 years, and has an impressive adventure playground in the back yard. The menu includes fairly standard pub fare (fish & chips, sausage & mash), but the portions are large and the prices are reasonable (most mains cost a tenner). Its sister-establishment *Stones* (see Where to stay) has a restaurant (summer daily 8.30am-9pm, winter hours variable) with its own pizza oven (pizza £12-15) and a similar pub-style menu (mains £11-13) including a range of burgers.

Further up, on Park St, *Fausto's* (☎ 01643-706372, 💻 faustos.co.uk; **fb**; Mon 6.30pm to late, Tue-Sat noon-2.30pm & 6.30pm to late) is a reasonably priced Italian, with pizzas costing from £8.25 to £11.95; while round the corner, on Holloway St, *The Queen's Head Inn* (☎ 01643-702940, 💻 queensheadminehead.co .uk; **fb**; food Mon 6-9pm, Tue & Thur-Sat noon-2.30pm & 6-9pm, Wed & Sun noon-

3pm & 6-9pm) has a good selection of real ales and fairly priced meals, including a number of Thai dishes, many for under £10; it also offers takeaway. Also on Holloway St, *Golden House* (☎ 01643-702723, 💻 www.goldenhouserestaurant.co .uk; **fb**; Wed-Sat noon-2pm & 5-10.30pm, Tue & Sun 5-10.30pm), offers a fairly standard Chinese menu (mains £5.40-7). Nearby, *The Duke of Wellington* (see Where to stay; daily 7am-11pm) boasts a typical and ever-cheap Wetherspoons' menu, including a £4.45 cooked breakfast (served until 11.30am).

The Quay is also a good area for food, with two decent pubs. *The Quay Inn* (see Where to stay; food Mon-Fri noon-2pm, Sat & Sun noon-3pm, daily 6-9pm), just a walking-pole's throw from the start of the coast path, is a smart, well-furnished pub with a large multi-tiered garden and skittle alley. It has a locally sourced menu (most mains less than £10) all prepared by an award-winning chef and serves real ales. *The Old Ship Aground* (see Where to stay; food daily noon-2.30pm & 6-9pm) also serves locally sourced and good value food.

MINEHEAD TO PORLOCK WEIR   [MAPS 1-7]

This **9-mile (14.5km; 3hrs 30 mins, 4hrs 20 mins if taking the rugged alternative route)** first stage of the SWCP offers a taster of much that is wonderful about the Exmoor coast. Beginning with a stroll through ancient, ivy-strangled woodland (Exmoor can, after all, boast some of the most extensive broadleaved coastal woods in Britain), you emerge eventually at North Hill, whereafter the route offers two choices: a gentle pastoral stroll by fields of livestock, or a more rugged alternative that offers a wilder, longer and more remote experience (and, so it is said, a greater chance of spotting native Exmoor wildlife such as red deer) as you contour the coastline on a narrow trail.

The two paths reunite just before the descent to the cream-tea cosiness of Bossington, from where a flat track takes you across farmland, via a turn-off to nearby Porlock and a submerged forest, to the village of Porlock Weir, home to a thousand-year-old port and several thatched grade-II listed cottages.

The route
The South-West Coast Path begins by what has become popularly known either as the '**Hands Sculpture**' or the '**Map Sculpture**', sculpted in bronze by Owen Cunningham and erected in 2001; it is, of course, pretty much obligatory to

ROUTE GUIDE AND MAPS

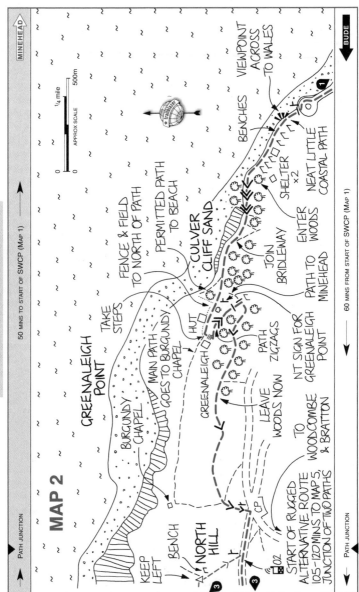

MAP 2

PATH JUNCTION → → 50 MINS TO START OF SWCP (MAP 1) → ← MINEHEAD

APPROX SCALE
¼ mile
500m

GREENALEIGH POINT

KEEP LEFT

BENCH

NORTH HILL

BURGUNDY CHAPEL

TAKE STEPS

MAIN PATH GOES TO BURGUNDY CHAPEL

FENCE & FIELD TO NORTH OF PATH

PERMITTED PATH TO BEACH

VIEWPOINT ACROSS TO WALES

BENCHES

CULVER CLIFF SAND

HUT

GREENALEIGH

PATH ZIGZAGS

JOIN BRIDLEWAY

SHELTER x2

NEAT LITTLE COASTAL PATH

NT SIGN FOR GREENALEIGH POINT

ENTER WOODS

PATH TO MINEHEAD

LEAVE WOODS NOW

TO WOODCOMBE & BRATTON

CP

START OF RUGGED ALTERNATIVE ROUTE 105-120 MINS TO MAP 5, JUNCTION OF TWO PATHS

← 60 MINS FROM START OF SWCP (MAP 1)

← PATH JUNCTION

BUDE

have your photo taken next to it. Photographed, fed, backpacked and booted, it's now time for you to begin. The trail initially sticks to the waterfront as it takes you towards and beyond The Old Ship Aground (see Where to stay/Where to eat) and its neighbouring **lifeboat station**. Leaving the last vestiges of Minehead behind, the trail enters some deep, dark woods scored with numerous paths and bridleways before emerging above the trees below the summit of

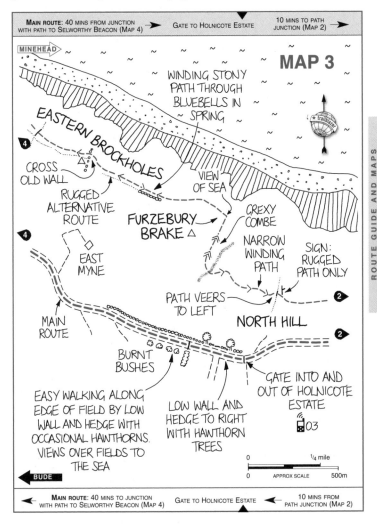

MAIN ROUTE: 40 MINS FROM JUNCTION WITH PATH TO SELWORTHY BEACON (MAP 4) → GATE TO HOLNICOTE ESTATE — 10 MINS TO PATH JUNCTION (MAP 2) →

MINEHEAD

MAP 3

WINDING STONY PATH THROUGH BLUEBELLS IN SPRING

trailblazer

EASTERN BROCKHOLES

4

CROSS OLD WALL

RUGGED ALTERNATIVE ROUTE

VIEW OF SEA

FURZEBURY BRAKE △

GREXY COMBE

4

EAST MYNE

NARROW WINDING PATH

SIGN: RUGGED PATH ONLY

PATH VEERS TO LEFT

NORTH HILL

2

MAIN ROUTE

2

BURNT BUSHES

GATE INTO AND OUT OF HOLNICOTE ESTATE

03

EASY WALKING ALONG EDGE OF FIELD BY LOW WALL AND HEDGE WITH OCCASIONAL HAWTHORNS. VIEWS OVER FIELDS TO THE SEA

LOW WALL AND HEDGE TO RIGHT WITH HAWTHORN TREES

0   ¼ mile
0   APPROX SCALE   500m

BUDE

ROUTE GUIDE AND MAPS

← **MAIN ROUTE:** 40 MINS TO JUNCTION WITH PATH TO SELWORTHY BEACON (MAP 4) ← GATE TO HOLNICOTE ESTATE ← 10 MINS FROM PATH JUNCTION (MAP 2)

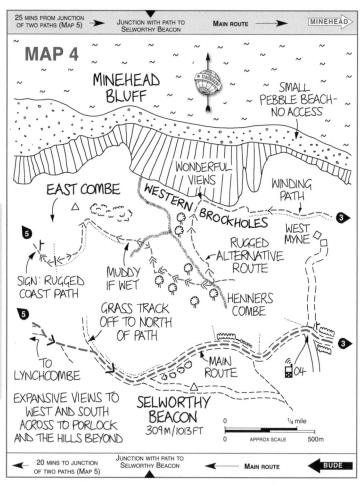

MAP 4

~ ~ ~ ~ ~ ~ ~ ~

MINEHEAD BLUFF

~ SMALL ~ PEBBLE BEACH– NO ACCESS

EAST COMBE

WESTERN BROCKHOLES

WONDERFUL VIEWS

WINDING PATH

3

WEST MYNE

RUGGED ALTERNATIVE ROUTE

5

SIGN: RUGGED COAST PATH

MUDDY IF WET

HENNERS COMBE

GRASS TRACK OFF TO NORTH OF PATH

5

TO LYNCHCOMBE

MAIN ROUTE

3

📱 04

EXPANSIVE VIEWS TO WEST AND SOUTH ACROSS TO PORLOCK AND THE HILLS BEYOND

SELWORTHY BEACON 309M/1013FT

0 ¼ mile
0 APPROX SCALE 500m

❏ **IMPORTANT NOTE – WALKING TIMES**
Unless otherwise specified, **all times in this book refer only to the time spent walking**. You will need to add 20-30% to allow for rests, photography, checking the map, drinking water etc, not to mention time simply to stop and stare. When planning the day's hike count on 5-7 hours' actual walking.

North Hill. (A diversion off the path here takes you down the steep slope to the ruined **Burgundy Chapel** and its accompanying hermitage, a medieval two-roomed construction that dates back over 600 years.) Look out for nightjars and the rare Dartford warbler flitting amongst the western gorse, which itself is a plant that's a bit of a rarity, found only in the West Country and southern Wales.

The path continues westwards a short distance before dividing; the northern path is known as 'the rugged alternative' (see below). Meanwhile the main trail meanders gently, scarcely rising or falling, past fields and flocks, with unbroken views over the sheep to the sea. Wales winks at you across the waves to the north, while Dunkery Beacon – the highest point on Exmoor – glimpses your progress from the south. Passing **Selworthy Beacon** (Map 4; 309m/1013ft), the path descends to a reunion with the alternative trail before descending steeply through **Hurlstone Combe** and on to Bossington.

The rugged alternative route (+ 50 mins)
Do not be put off by the name of this alternative trail – though more testing than the official path this route is not overly difficult and is well worth the **extra 50 minutes** it takes to walk it. **Note that dogs must be kept on a lead on this path**.

The trail runs along a thin and winding path, intermittently following field boundaries and keeping close to the sea, occasionally dipping into miniature combes and crossing streams. The views are tremendous, the path is wilder than the official route and you are less likely to see other people – and far more likely to see red deer. Throughout much of it you are surrounded by gorse although bluebells make for a spectacular display in spring.

Where the regular trail passes near the summit of Selworthy Beacon, the alternative path goes around its lower slopes. Having crossed the upper reaches of **Grexy Combe**, on your left but not visible is the Iron-Age hill fort of **Furzebury Brake**. Further archaeology lies ahead on the path with two medieval settlements, **East Myne** and **West Myne**, while to your right are the **Eastern Brockholes**, which along with **Western Brockholes** are considered to be the places where the stone was quarried to build the two settlements. At **East Combe** you can turn left and climb to the top of Selworthy Beacon, or you can keep on and rejoin the official path after **Hurlstone Combe**.

ROUTE GUIDE AND MAPS

BOSSINGTON   [MAP 5, p85]
Bossington is the kind of blink-and-you-miss-it village that people come to Somerset specifically to see: ancient, cosy, with a gorgeous tearoom and picture-perfect cottages scattered willy-nilly along a single track lane. With its thatched roofs and lack of telegraph wires, it can feel as if you've wandered onto the set of a BBC period drama.

Kitnors Tearooms (☎ 01643-862643, 🖳 www.kitnors.com; **fb**; Easter to Oct daily 11am-4.30pm, Nov to Easter, Sat & Sun 11am-4pm), situated right on the path,

has a splendid little garden at the rear where one can relax to a gentle cacophony of bird-song (the robins are particularly friendly). It's a lovely place to stop and they serve sandwiches, light lunches, speciality coffees and cream teas. There are vegan, gluten-free and dairy-free options, and there are even handmade biscuits for dogs (£1) although your furry friend will have to indulge in such treats outside in the garden.

As for a place to stay, just up the road is *Tudor Cottage* (☎ 01643-862255, 🖳 tudor cottage.net; 1D en suite/2D or T private facilities; ☛; Ⓛ) a 15th-century cottage with a splendid garden and wonderful views across to Porlock Weir. B&B costs £42.50-47.50pp (£65-95 sgl occ).

Bossington sits at the eastern extremity of the wide **Porlock Vale**, an unusually wide, flat valley in comparison with the narrow combes typical of Exmoor. Standing between it and the sea is a natural shingle ridge – a ridge that was breached in 1996 (see box below), causing the farmland to turn into a salt marsh that receives a fresh inundation of salt every high tide. It also led to a rerouting of the SWCP that once followed this ridge but which now takes a more inland course, around the back of the beach. This does mean that the sea will be out of sight for the next few miles – but also that it is much less of a detour to visit the charming village of **Porlock**.

PORLOCK   [see map p89]

Though 10 to 15 minutes from the path, Porlock remains a popular stopover on the SWCP. The plentiful accommodation, amenities, attractions and charming architecture are enough to tempt the tired walker off the trail.

Porlock was mentioned in the Domesday Book of 1086 (as 'Portloc') and several of the village's buildings are only slightly younger. The oldest, **The Chantry**, has parts dating back to the 12th century. The truncated tower on the neighbouring

---

❑ PORLOCK BEACH   [Map 6, p87]

The beach at Porlock Vale is a very dynamic environment. The **shingle bank** that protects the vale from flooding at high tide – and which looks for all the world like a man-made defensive barrier – was actually established about 8000 years ago at the end of the last Ice Age, the rising sea levels piling up the rocks and shingle that had fallen from the nearby cliffs.

Though man may not have built it he has certainly done his best to repair it down the centuries in order to protect the valuable farmland behind, with the last major rebuild occurring in 1990. Man is also responsible for building the WWII **pillboxes** (a type of defensive bunker, usually made from concrete) and the now-ruined **lime kiln** along the beach. Yet in spite of these efforts at preservation, a further breach to the shingle bank in 1996 forced the authorities to rethink their policy and as a result it was decided to allow nature to take its course – meaning that, in years to come, Porlock Vale may well become a lagoon, just as it was around 200 years ago.

The ever-changing landscape of Porlock Vale has exposed some interesting sites and artefacts that had previously lain hidden beneath the seabed. The **submerged forest** that you walk past on the way to Porlock Weir is actually around five or six thousand years old and was first observed only in 1890. In 1998 part of a skeleton of an **auroch**, a giant precursor to modern cattle that roamed these parts about 3500 years ago, was found in the exposed blue clay of an old riverbed. The bones are now on display in Porlock Visitor Centre (see p86). A piece of worked timber from AD900 has also been unearthed embedded in beach clay near the shingle ridge, as have numerous flints.

Perhaps unsurprisingly, the entire beach has been declared a **Site of Special Scientific Interest** (SSSI; see box p61) as it allows scientists to study how such a landscape will develop if left to its own devices, as well as the effect this will have on the flora and fauna of the area, with lapwings, herons, teal, shelduck and egret regular visitors to this rare salt marsh environment.

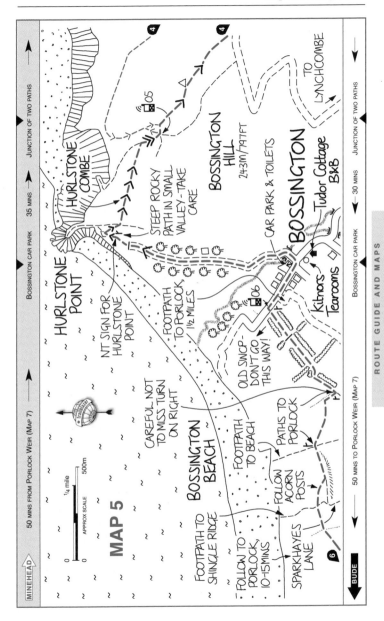

MAP 5

APPROX SCALE
0   500m
0   ¼ mile

MINEHEAD ←
50 MINS FROM PORLOCK WEIR (MAP 7) →
HURLSTONE POINT →
BOSSINGTON CAR PARK →
35 MINS →
JUNCTION OF TWO PATHS ►

HURLSTONE COMBE

HURLSTONE POINT

NT SIGN FOR HURLSTONE POINT

FOOTPATH TO PORLOCK 1½ MILES

STEEP ROCKY PATH IN SMALL VALLEY - TAKE CARE

☐ 05

4

4

BOSSINGTON HILL 243M/797FT

TO LYNCHCOMBE

JUNCTION OF TWO PATHS ►
30 MINS →

CAR PARK & TOILETS

BOSSINGTON

Tudor Cottage B&B

Kitnors Tearooms

☐ 06

OLD SWCP- DON'T GO THIS WAY!

CAREFUL NOT TO MISS TURN ON RIGHT

BOSSINGTON BEACH

FOOTPATH TO SHINGLE RIDGE

FOLLOW TO PORLOCK, 10-15MINS

SPARKHAYES LANE

FOOTPATH TO BEACH

FOLLOW ACORN POSTS

PATHS TO PORLOCK

6

BUDE ↓

50 MINS TO PORLOCK WEIR (MAP 7) →
BOSSINGTON CAR PARK →

ROUTE GUIDE AND MAPS

Church of St Dubricius (named after a 6th-century Welsh saint who, according to legend, crowned King Arthur and later married him to Guinevere) was built only a few decades later; while, inside the church, you'll find fragments of a cross that date back to pre-Norman times.

The main street is also scattered with more old thatched cottages than you can shake a sheaf of straw at, from The Old Rose and Crown Cottage (formerly a pub), opposite the church, to the 13th-century Ship Inn at the western end of the village.

For a more intimate look at one of Porlock's hoary homes, **Dovery Manor Museum** (🖳 doverymanormuseum.org.uk; **fb**; May-Sep Mon-Fri 10am-5pm, Sat 10.30am-4.30pm; free but donation wel-

come) is housed in a 15th-century manor house and has a physic garden based on designs from medieval times.

At the other end of the village, the Visitor Centre boasts a small **village museum** including many of the items discovered on the beach that pre-date even Porlock (see box p84).

See p16 for details of Samphire Festival, an independent music festival.

Services

The **Visitor Centre** (TIC; ☎ 01643-863150, 🖳 porlock.co.uk; **fb**; Easter to Oct Mon-Sat 10am-3.30pm, Nov to Easter Mon-Sat 10am-1.30pm), with its small museum and souvenir shop, lies at the far western end of Porlock and is one of the

---

❏ THE POETS OF PORLOCK

Porlock has long been a favourite place of poets, romantics and dreamers. Robert Southey's friends Samuel Taylor Coleridge and William Wordsworth (who both lived nearby at Nether Stowey and Alfoxden respectively) were frequent visitors and often wandered (as lonely as clouds, presumably) the hills and beaches surrounding the village. Indeed, the regularity of their perambulations and the fact that many of them were undertaken at night aroused suspicions in the locals and rumours began to circulate that they were actually French

Porlock! thy verdant vale so fair to sight,
Thy lofty hills which fern and furze imbrown,
The waters that roll musically down
Thy woody glens, the traveller with delight
Recalls to memory, and the channel grey
Circling its surges in thy level bay.
Porlock! I shall forget thee not,
Here by the unwelcome summer rain confined;
But often shall hereafter call to mind
How here, a patient prisoner, 'twas my lot
To wear the lonely, lingering close of day,
Making my sonnet by the alehouse fire,
Whilst Idleness and Solitude inspire
Dull rhymes to pass the duller hours away.
                                          Robert Southey (1774-1843)

spies. A government agent sent to investigate however, witheringly concluded that they were 'mere poets' and thus no threat to the Crown.

Today, of course, many hikers walk in the footsteps of the Romantic poets along the Coleridge Way (see p34) which ends in the village; a walk that celebrates both the area's associations with the Romantic poets and the wonderful countryside of this part of the world. Yet, ironically, Porlock is perhaps best known not for a poem that it inspired, but one that it prevented: Coleridge was famously interrupted during the composition of his epic *Kubla Khan* by 'a person on business from Porlock', with the result that he forgot the details of the dream on which his poem was to be based and thus never completed the work! The phrase 'a person from Porlock' has since become a synonym for an unwanted visitor; characters named Porlock crop up in works by Arthur Conan Doyle and Alan Bennett amongst others – usually as somebody who arrives unannounced and interrupts the business of others.

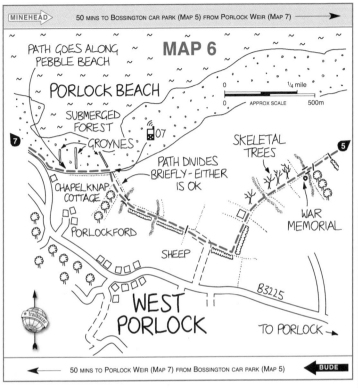

PATH GOES ALONG PEBBLE BEACH

MAP 6

PORLOCK BEACH

SUBMERGED FOREST

07

GROYNES

SKELETAL TREES

7

5

PATH DIVIDES BRIEFLY - EITHER IS OK

CHAPELKNAP COTTAGE

WAR MEMORIAL

PORLOCKFORD

SHEEP

B3225

WEST PORLOCK

TO PORLOCK →

0   ¼ mile
0   APPROX SCALE   500m

50 MINS TO PORLOCK WEIR (MAP 7) FROM BOSSINGTON CAR PARK (MAP 5) BUDE

ROUTE GUIDE AND MAPS

friendliest you'll find. They are happy to do accommodation booking.

The village is big enough for two small **supermarkets**: SPAR (Mon-Thur 7am-7pm, Fri & Sat to 9pm, Sun to 6pm) towards the western end of town is better stocked; One Stop Local Stores (daily 7am-10pm), which has an **ATM** (free), is at the eastern end of the village.

Opposite the SPAR is a shop, **Exmoor Rambler** (☎ 01643-862429, **fb**; Mon-Tue & Thur-Fri 9am-5.30pm, Wed & Sat 9am-6pm, Sun 10am-4pm) selling **outdoor gear**, and also containing the **post office** (same hours as shop).

Nearby on the High St, **Porlock Hardware** (☎ 01643-862427; summer Mon-Sat 9am-5pm, winter Sat to 1pm) also has some camping gear. **Porlock Pharmacy** (Mon-Fri 8.30am-6pm, Sat 9am-1pm) is opposite One Stop.

Transport
[See also pp48-50] **Bus**-wise, the No 10 service calls here en route between Minehead and Porlock Weir; there's also the seasonal Exmoor Coaster service between Minehead and Lynmouth .

For a **taxi** try 1st Call Exmoor Taxis (☎ 07826-212511).

Where to stay
For **campers**, *Sparkhayes Farm Camping Site* (☎ 01643-862470 or 07721 045123, 🖥

www.sparkhayes.co.uk; **fb**; Feb-Dec; 🐾) is on Sparkhayes Lane on the edge of the village and is an excellent choice. There are plenty of flat, grassy pitches (£10/8/3 per adult/student/under-12), laundry facilities, hot showers, a fridge freezer, kettle and microwave, and distant sea views.

Slightly less central, but still close to the village, *Porlock Caravan Park* (☎ 01643-862269, 🖥 porlockcaravanpark.co .uk; 🐾; mid Mar to end Oct), at the High Bank end of the village, also has plenty of space and similar facilities. They charge £10 for a hiker & tent.

If, in this ancient place, a **night above a pub** feels appropriate, *The Ship Inn* (also known as *The 'Top' Ship*; ☎ 01643-862507, 🖥 shipinnporlock.co.uk; **fb**; 4D/1Qd, all en suite; ☜; Ⓛ; 🐾) will not disappoint; B&B here costs £37.50pp (sgl occ £45). A cosy, fascinating, slightly eccentric pub (check out the displays of battle helmets, gas masks and even a 'German officer's uniform', as worn by an extra in the film *The Great Escape*), they also serve up some smashing **food** (see Where to eat).

Note: you may hear The Ship Inn at Porlock referred to locally as the 'Top' Ship; this is because the establishment has a twin at Porlock Weir, also called The Ship Inn, locally referred to as The 'Bottom' Ship. It is an important distinction as the distance between the two is certainly enough to perturb a walker should you have booked a night's accommodation and end up being directed – albeit by a well-meaning local – to the wrong one. It sounds unlikely, but this has happened!

B&B-wise, there are plenty of fine options. In a village with this much thatch it's possible you'll end up sleeping under a roof of straw, such as at *The Gables* (☎ 01643-863432, 🖥 thegablesporlock.co.uk; 2D/1Tr/2Qd, all en suite; ☜; Ⓛ; 🐾; Easter-Sep weekends 2 nights minimum), a gorgeous 17th-century country home on Doverhay Rd, its ancient exterior belying the modern facilities on offer. The triple is a self-contained cottage. They charge £35-37.50pp (sgl occ £50-70).

A more humble, straw-topped, 17th-century dwelling, *Myrtle Cottage* (☎ 01643-

862978, 🖥 myrtleporlock.co.uk; 2D/1Tr/1Qd, all en suite; ☜; Ⓛ; 🐾) has timber-beamed rooms in a central location. B&B costs £37.50pp for two, plus £30 per person for a third or fourth person (sgl occ £55).

Opposite the church, *Reines House* (☎ 01643-862446, 🖥 reineshouse.co.uk; 2D/1Tr, all en suite), is one of the village's cheaper options (from £30pp, sgl occ £45).

High St has two further establishments. *The Cottage* (☎ 01643-862996, 🖥 cottageporlock.co.uk; **fb**; 2D/1D or T/1Tr, all en suite; ☜; Ⓛ) is a gorgeous little place (£37.50-40pp, sgl occ £50-65), and the large and impressive Victorian *Rose Bank Guest House* (☎ 01643-862728, 🖥 rose bankguesthouse.co.uk; 1S/2D/2D or T, all en suite; Ⓛ; 🐾) has a great reputation; from £37.50pp (sgl £50, sgl occ from £60).

Nearby, opposite the Visitor Centre, *Sea View* (☎ 01643-863456, 🖥 seaview porlock.co.uk; 1S/2D/1T, all en suite; ☜; Ⓛ) lives up to its name. B&B costs from £37.50pp (sgl/sgl occ from £40).

Finally, there are three **hotels**. On High St are *The Castle Hotel* (☎ 01643-862504, 🖥 thecastleporlock.co.uk; **fb**; 6D or T/2D/1Qd, all en suite; ☜; WI-FI public areas; 🐾), where rates are from £35pp (sgl occ room rate) and *The Lorna Doone* (☎ 01643-862404, 🖥 lornadoonehotel.co.uk; 5D/5D or T in main building plus Courtyard rooms 1D/2Tr/1Qd, all en suite; ☜; Ⓛ; 🐾) which charges £35-52.50pp (sgl occ room rate).

Where to eat and drink

You certainly won't starve in Porlock, with plenty of tearooms, cafés and restaurants all along the main street.

During the day the pick of the traditional tearooms is *The Whortleberry Tearoom* (☎ 01643-862891, 🖥 www.whor tleberry.co.uk; **fb**; Tue-Sun 10am-4.30pm), which is named after the local blueberry (see box p23). They also have a lovely studio room in the back garden (B&B £42.50pp, sgl occ £75) though there is a three-night minimum stay. *Home Cook Café* (☎ 07790-725357; **fb**; Mon-Sat 10am-3.30pm) isn't quite as quaint, but is very friendly and makes its own soups, cakes and

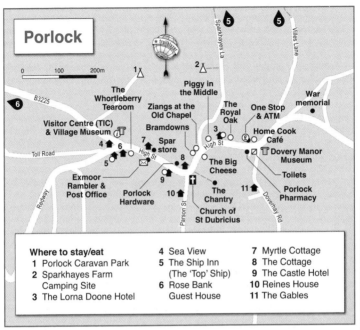

Where to stay/eat
1 Porlock Caravan Park
2 Sparkhayes Farm Camping Site
3 The Lorna Doone Hotel
4 Sea View
5 The Ship Inn (The 'Top' Ship)
6 Rose Bank Guest House
7 Myrtle Cottage
8 The Cottage
9 The Castle Hotel
10 Reines House
11 The Gables

scones, while tiny, family-run *Bramdowns* (☎ 01643-863400, 🖳 bramdowns.co.uk; Fri-Mon 10am-3pm) also serves excellent home-cooked food, including scrumptious crumpets (£1 each) and a range of takeaway sandwiches and pies.

Even if you don't fancy eating here, do take time to visit *The Big Cheese* (☎ 01643-862773, 🖳 thebigcheeseporlock.co .uk; **fb**; Mon-Sat 9am-4.30pm, Wed to 3.30pm), the local champions of cheese (they usually have at least 50 on sale) as well as other locally produced comestibles including wines, jams and vinegars. They also sell locally produced ciders and wine, and serve decent coffee, too.

There's a surprisingly good choice of places to eat in the evening too. On High St, *Piggy in the Middle* (☎ 01643-862647; mid Feb-Dec Mon-Sat 5-9pm) is a fish 'n' chip restaurant which dishes up speciality pies; indeed, there are 32 on offer, including meat, vegetarian, gluten-free and vegan options. Takeaway is also an option here.

Close by, *Ziangs at the Old Chapel* (☎ 01643-8622241 or 07920-409007, 🖳 tc porlock.com; Tue-Sat 5-8pm) is a Chinese restaurant and takeaway housed in a former Methodist chapel, and with a chippy attached.

The restaurant in *The Lorna Doone* (see Where to stay; summer daily 8-9.30am, Mon-Sat noon-2pm, Sun to 2.30pm, Mon-Sat 6-8.30pm, to 8pm in winter) is open to all, and serves good quality pub grub (main meals £10-16), whilst round the corner, *The Castle Hotel* (see Where to stay) also has a restaurant (food daily 9am-10pm) offering standard pub fare at very reasonable prices.

Pub-wise, *The Royal Oak* (☎ 01643-862798; food Mon-Sat noon-3pm & 6-9pm, Sun 3-9pm, slightly reduced hours in winter; 🐾) specialises in real ales and traditional pub grub. Its status as the most popular place in town is rivalled only by

The Ship Inn (see Where to stay; food daily noon-2.30pm, Mon-Thur 6.15-8.30pm, Fri-Sun 6-9pm), where local ales, including the potent 6.6% Exmoor Beast (see box p62), lamb chops (£14.25), Mozzarella Stuffed Meatballs (£11.95) and River Exe Mussels (£12.50) are all on offer.

Continuing on the SWCP, the path plots a flat course between the back of the beach and the farmland before turning sharp right to rejoin the shoreline to **Porlock Weir**.

PORLOCK WEIR

Peaceful Porlock Weir feels like the type of place where you could quite easily sit back and forget that you're supposed to be walking, as you opt instead to while away your time listening to the sea and staring wearily out towards Wales. The boats rock lazily in the weir's small harbour and the waves lap somnolently onto the pebbles and shingle of the millennia-old harbour arm.

The one-room **Boatshed Museum** (Easter-Oct daily 10am-5pm; free but donations welcome) features interesting displays about the settlement's seafaring heritage.

Harbour Stores (☎ 01643-863033; summer Mon-Fri 10am-5pm, Sat & Sun 9am-5pm, winter 10am-1pm) sells souvenirs and snacks as well as takeaway hot drinks.

The No 10 **bus** service operates between here and Minehead (see pp48-50 for details).

There are three **B&B** options in Porlock Weir, all with restaurants. *The Ship Inn* (also known as *The Bottom Ship*, see p88; ☎ 01643-863288, 🖳 ship innporlockweir.co .uk; 2D/1T, all en suite; ✆; Ⓛ; 🐾) is the best-value choice, and best suited to passing walkers, with three comfortable rooms (£37.50pp, sgl occ from £45), real ales on tap and hearty pub **food** (daily noon-2.30pm & 6-8.30pm); (mains £11-13).

The other two choices are much more top-end, and don't usually accept single-night stays. *Porlock Weir Hotel* (☎ 01643-800400, 🖳 porlock weirhotel.co.uk; **fb**; 17D, all en suite; ✆; Ⓛ; 🐾), formerly known as Millers at the Anchor,

had a complete revamp in 2019 and re-opened as a wellness hotel with 17 luxurious en-suite rooms (from £57.50pp, sgl occ from £103) and a secluded garden for yoga and meditation. The main restaurant (8am-11am, noon-3pm & 6-9pm) is run by owner and head chef Miguel Tenreiro and serves the likes of slow roasted pork belly or leek and Devon blue risotto, while the terrace bar (11.30am-9pm) offers pizzas from their wood-fired pizza oven.

Formerly known as The Café, *Locanda on the Weir* (☎ 01643-863300, 🖳 locandaontheweir.co.uk, 4D/1D or T, all en suite; ✆; WI-FI downstairs; Ⓛ sandwiches; 🐾) has five sumptuous rooms and sits in a slightly elevated position with good views across the harbour and beyond from all but one of the rooms. B&B starts at a whopping £87.50pp (sgl occ full room rate). Its Italian restaurant offers a daily changing set three-course menu. There are also bar snacks such as paninis (£10) and sandwiches (£12.50).

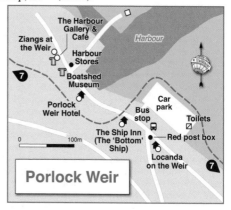

Porlock Weir

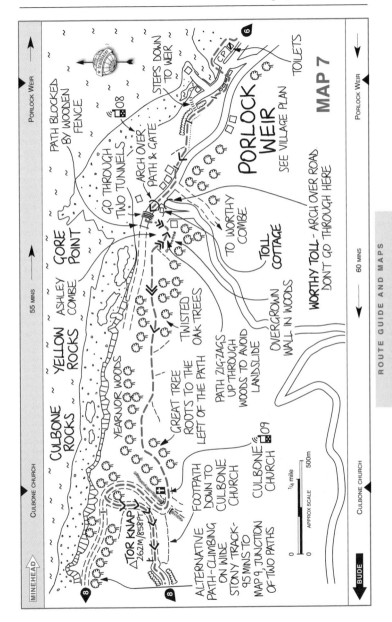

CULBONE ROCKS

YELLOW ROCKS

ASHLEY COMBE

GORE POINT

PATH BLOCKED BY WOODEN FENCE

GO THROUGH TWO TUNNELS

ARCH OVER PATH & GATE

STEPS DOWN TO WEIR

PORLOCK WEIR
SEE VILLAGE PLAN

MAP 7

TOILETS

TO WORTHY COMBE

TOLL COTTAGE

WORTHY TOLL - ARCH OVER ROAD DON'T GO THROUGH HERE

OVERGROWN WALL IN WOODS

TWISTED OAK TREES

PATH ZIG-ZAGS UP THROUGH WOODS TO AVOID LANDSLIDE

GREAT TREE ROOTS TO THE LEFT OF THE PATH

YEARNOR WOODS

FOOTPATH DOWN TO CULBONE CHURCH

CULBONE CHURCH

TOR KNAP
262M /858FT

ALTERNATIVE PATH - CLIMBING ON MILE STONY TRACK - 95 MINS TO MAP 9, JUNCTION OF TWO PATHS

¼ mile   500m
APPROX SCALE

MINEHEAD

CULBONE CHURCH

55 MINS

PORLOCK WEIR

BUDE

CULBONE CHURCH

60 MINS

PORLOCK WEIR

ROUTE GUIDE AND MAPS

Lunches can be found at the popular *Harbour Gallery and Café* (☎ 01643-863514, 🖥 harbourgalleryandcafe.co.uk; **fb**; Apr-Oct daily 10am-5pm, winter Fri-Tue 10.30am-3pm but hours can vary), which also has work by local artists on the walls. Note the lunch menu is only served until 3.30pm. Next door *Ziangs at the Weir* (☎ 01643-863215, 🖥 ziangsworkshop .com; Mon noon-5pm, Tue-Sun noon-7pm) serves east Asian food, including individually tailored noodle dishes (£8.95). They also do takeaway.

PORLOCK WEIR TO LYNTON [MAPS 7-12]

This **12½-mile (20.1km; 6hrs, 5¾hrs on alternative route)** stage will come as something of an unpleasant surprise for those who were hoping for a gentle few days at the start of the walk to ease themselves into the trip. While not as tough as the final two stages on this walk – nor indeed even as tough as the next one – this hike to the conjoined villages of Lynmouth and Lynton is still fairly taxing and makes for a surprisingly long day. Furthermore, with **no cafés or pubs** (save for The Blue Ball Inn at Countisbury, just a short distance from Lynmouth), you'll need to be self-sufficient or this long day is going to feel even longer!

Thankfully there are enough distractions on this stage – including Culbone Church – to help you ignore the quiet screaming coming from your calf muscles. There are also the rare whitebeams of Culbone Wood, dotted here and there with the remains of several humble leper huts; while a short deviation off the trail will take you to Foreland Point – Devon's most northerly extremity.

Furthermore, you can also take pride in the fact that during the day you march across the border into Devon. As such, you will have already achieved

---

❑ ASHLEY COMBE

Just past Worthy Toll the trail passes through a couple of tunnels which were once an integral part of the gorgeous gardens of Ashley Combe house. The **home of Ada Byron** (the only legitimate daughter of the poet, Lord Byron), later Countess Lovelace, the house was originally built in 1799 but improved significantly by Lord King, the first Lord Lovelace and Ada's husband who, influenced by the fairy-tale castles of Italy, decided in 1835 to lavish a huge sum in adapting Ashley Combe to please his wife. The tunnels from the road led to the house's tradesman's entrance and were built so that Ada and the other inhabitants didn't have their views of the ornate terraced gardens interrupted by the comings and goings of commoners. Towers, turrets, archways and other follies decorated the terraces, which were walled on three sides but opened out onto the sea, while spiral staircases led between the different levels.

A team of Swiss engineers was even brought in to lay a network of carriageways throughout the grounds. The house fell into disrepair soon after the Countess's death in 1852. Though it found a use as a home for orphans during WWII, it soon became uninhabitable and in 1974 it was pulled down for safety reasons. While its true glory has long since faded, it's still fascinating to pick out some of the original features of the gardens – the twisting paths, and the stone benches set into the garden walls – as you walk along the trail from Worthy Toll.

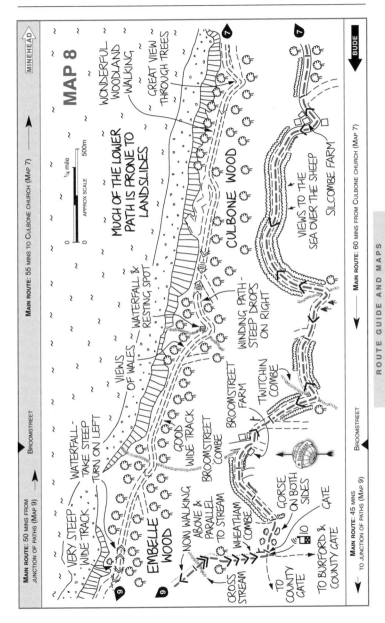

MAP 8

MINEHEAD →

BUDE →

MAIN ROUTE: 55 MINS TO CULBONE CHURCH (MAP 7)

¼ mile

500m

APPROX SCALE

0

0

WONDERFUL WOODLAND WALKING

GREAT VIEW THROUGH TREES

MUCH OF THE LOWER PATH IS PRONE TO LANDSLIDES

CULBONE WOOD

7

7

VIEWS TO THE SEA OVER THE SHEEP

SILCOMBE FARM

MAIN ROUTE: 60 MINS FROM CULBONE CHURCH (MAP 7)

WINDING PATH – STEEP DROPS ON RIGHT

TWITCHIN COMBE

BROOMSTREET FARM

BROOMSTREET COMBE

GOOD WIDE TRACK

WATERFALL & RESTING SPOT

VIEWS OF WALES

WATERFALL – TAKE STEEP TURN ON LEFT

BROOMSTREET ▲

MAIN ROUTE: 50 MINS FROM JUNCTION OF PATHS (MAP 9)

VERY STEEP WIDE TRACK

EMBELLE WOOD

NOW WALKING ABOVE & PARALLEL TO STREAM

CROSS STREAM

9

9

WHEATHAM COMBE

TO COUNTY GATE

GORSE ON BOTH SIDES

GATE

TO BURFORD & COUNTY GATE

BROOMSTREET ▲

MAIN ROUTE: 45 MINS TO JUNCTION OF PATHS (MAP 9)

ROUTE GUIDE AND MAPS

❑ CULBONE CHURCH

The small church at Culbone is one of the hidden gems of the South-West Coast Path. England's smallest complete parish church, it measures 35ft (10.66m) and seats a congregation of around 30. However, Culbone church is not just tiny – its origins are also extremely old. It is one of the few buildings that also features in the *Domesday Book*. At Culbone Stables a Bronze Age stone marker – one of many which were believed to have lined the way between Lynmouth and Porlock – was discovered in 1940. Celtic missionaries from Wales and Ireland travelled to the West Country along this path from about the late 6th century onwards, leading to a revival of the Christian faith in England. One of these missionaries was the patron saint of Culbone, **St Beuno**. Though his link with the church is unclear, it is believed that Culbone became a place of reverence in his day; and the wheeled cross on the Bronze Age standing stone marker acted as a signpost, pointing the faithful to Culbone as an important place of pilgrimage.

The Saxons are believed to have been the first to build a church here, made of wood, which in time was replaced by a stone edifice by the Normans. The oldest part of the church today is probably the sandstone window on the northern side of the chancel (the space around the altar), which is thought to be at least a thousand years old, though many other features are only slightly younger: the font, for example, is believed to be around 800 years old, as is the arch that separates the chancel from the nave (where the congregation sits). The tiny window on the north side of the nave is known as a leper squint – where lepers, who were banned from entering the church, could still watch the services.

One of the most noticeable features of the church is the number of gravestones dedicated to people with the surname 'Red'. Nicholas Red was churchwarden in 1856 (he is responsible for the Ten Commandments on one of the walls of the church) and it is his descendants who populate much of the graveyard. It is believed that the name provided the inspiration for the Ridds in the novel *Lorna Doone*. While you're in the graveyard, look at the church steeple: it was erected in around 1810, though locals swear that it is actually the missing top part of the truncated steeple of the Church of St Dubricius (see p86) in Porlock.

The church is still in use, though there is no tarmac leading to it; instead, worshippers have to take either the precarious 4WD track down to the church, or do as you have just done and walk here!

the feat of completing Somerset's entire contribution to the SWCP – and you're still only on the second day!

The route

The trail out of Porlock Weir begins between the houses behind Porlock Weir Hotel, climbing up behind the village and onto the thatched and rather decorative **Worthy Toll**; has a toll gate ever been so ornate? Keeping **Toll Cottage** on your left, pass through the more northerly of the two arches then follow the path as it twists its way, under, over and through the overgrown terraces of **Ashley Combe** (see box on p92).

A lazy meander along a gently undulating path past the **twisted oak trees** of Yearnor Woods soon brings you out onto a better track that winds its way down to **Culbone Church** (see box above) – an essential stop on the SWCP.

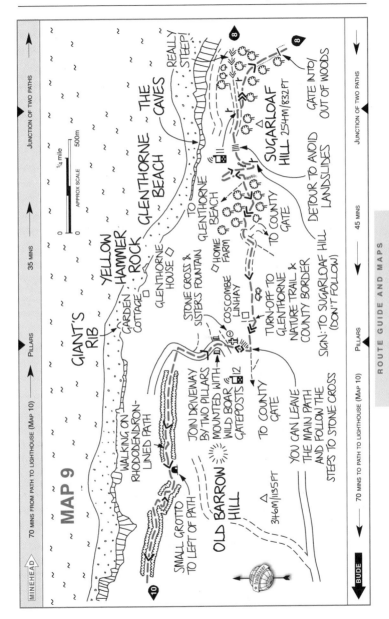

MAP 9

70 MINS FROM PATH TO LIGHTHOUSE (MAP 10) ——▶ ▶ PILLARS ▲ 35 MINS ◀ JUNCTION OF TWO PATHS

GIANT'S RIB

YELLOW HAMMER ROCK

WALKING ON RHODODENDRON-LINED PATH

SMALL GROTTO TO LEFT OF PATH

OLD BARROW HILL

△ 346M/1135FT

JOIN DRIVEWAY BY TWO PILLARS MOUNTED WITH WILD BOAR GATEPOSTS

TO COUNTY GATE

YOU CAN LEAVE THE MAIN PATH AND FOLLOW THE STEPS TO STONE CROSS

GARDEN COTTAGE ◇

GLENTHORNE HOUSE ◇

STONE CROSS & SISTERS FOUNTAIN

◇ HOME FARM

COSCOMBE LINHAY

TURN-OFF TO GLENTHORNE NATURE TRAIL & COUNTY BORDER

SIGN: TO SUGARLOAF HILL (DON'T FOLLOW)

GLENTHORNE BEACH ~ THE CAVES

REALLY STEEP!

TO GLENTHORNE BEACH

TO COUNTY GATE

DETOUR TO AVOID LANDSLIDES

SUGARLOAF HILL 254M/832FT

GATE INTO/OUT OF WOODS

⑧

⑧

500m

¼ mile

APPROX SCALE

⑩

ROUTE GUIDE AND MAPS

BUDE ◀—— 70 MINS TO PATH TO LIGHTHOUSE (MAP 10) PILLARS 45 MINS JUNCTION OF TWO PATHS

The path divides after Culbone Church (Map 7). The main (southern) trail from here heads up the hill, out of the trees, into farmland and from there onto a road – though we use the term loosely, for cars are something of a rarity around here and easily outnumbered by livestock to left and right. It's difficult to lose your way – just keep heading west past Silcombe Farm and Broomstreet Farm, the track eventually dwindling to a footpath. Soon after, it takes a sharp right down **Wheatham Combe** and back into the woods on the lower northern slopes of **Sugarloaf Hill**, where it is reunited with the alternative (northern) route (see below).

Alternative route between Culbone Church and Sugarloaf Hill

This alternative (northern) path is at times rugged and should be trodden carefully but the woodlands it passes through make for a wonderful alternative to the fields above. The areas that you walk through have interesting histories, too.

Splendidly isolated **Culbone Wood** has throughout the ages been home to many deemed too dangerous to remain in mainstream society – from the 'mentally insane' in the 13th century to lepers in the 16th. Meanwhile, **Embelle Wood** and its stony pathways are known to have been used by smugglers carrying their ill-gotten gains away from Embelle Wood Beach. Presumably chosen for its remoteness – despite the presence of a limekiln – the beach is thought to be the most remote in Somerset. Indeed, so remote is it that David Burgess, a self-styled 21st-century Robinson Crusoe, built himself a driftwood shack here in 1985. He managed to remain almost undetected until he became the focus of the national press briefly in 2011 after the park authorities finally told him to leave, although they then reportedly reached a 'mutually satisfactory arrangement' allowing him to continue 'occasional use' of the shack.

A note of caution: be wary of landslides. Although generally well signed, landslips are a common occurrence on this section and the diversions made necessary because of them can be sudden, especially around **Broomstreet Combe**. Between there and the reunion with the official path the trail is also particularly steep.

The path continues parallel to the coast now under the woodland canopy, sometimes climbing the slopes to avoid the occasional landslip, then passing through deciduous woodland and coniferous plantations, parts of which have been cleared. You soon cross the **Somerset–Devon border** (which isn't marked on the trail, though occurs at Coscombe Linhay, Map 9), near the signposted turn-off to Glenthorne Nature Trail, before the path deviates off the large track to visit the 19th-century **stone cross** that marks the Sister's Fountain. The name comes from one of the nieces of the original owner of nearby Glenthorne House who liked to play at this spot. In local legend, the well, or spring, was created by Joseph of Arimathea by striking his staff on the ground, thus providing much-needed refreshment on his journey to Glastonbury.

Passing through the **wild boar gateposts** (the entrance to 19th-century Woodland Lodge as well as to Glenthorne House), the route follows the driveway down the hill before taking a narrow trail off to the left just before the driveway also turns left. The path is now brightly embroidered to left and right with vivid rhododendron and gorse. The way is more exposed now too, a pleas-

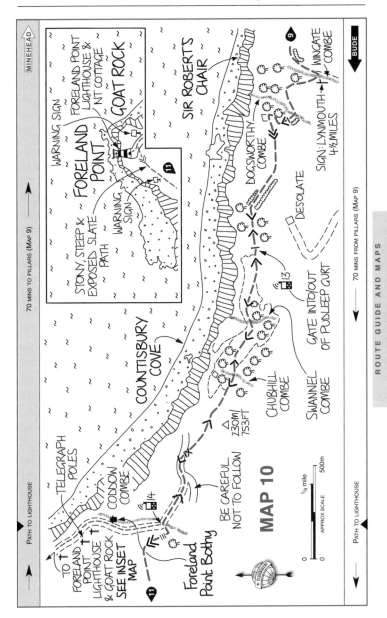

MINEHEAD

PATH TO LIGHTHOUSE

70 MINS TO PILLARS (MAP 9)

WARNING SIGN

FORELAND POINT LIGHTHOUSE & NT COTTAGE

GOAT ROCK

FORELAND POINT

STONY, STEEP & EXPOSED SLATE PATH

WARNING SIGN

11

SIR ROBERT'S CHAIR

9

DOGSWORTHY COMBE

WINCATE COMBE

SIGN: LYNMOUTH 4½ MILES

BUDE

DESOLATE

13

GATE INTO/OUT OF PUDLEEP GURT

SWANNEL COMBE

CHUBHILL COMBE

△ 230M/ 753FT

COUNTISBURY COVE

TELEGRAPH POLES

CODSON COMBE

14

BE CAREFUL NOT TO FOLLOW

MAP 10

APPROX SCALE

500m

¼ mile

0

0

PATH TO LIGHTHOUSE

70 MINS FROM PILLARS (MAP 9)

TO LIGHTHOUSE

FORELAND POINT LIGHTHOUSE & GOAT ROCK SEE INSET MAP

Foreland Point Bothy

11

ROUTE GUIDE AND MAPS

ant change after so long in the shade of trees, though patches of woodland still punctuate the trail, particularly when passing the several **combes** (Map 10) on the way: Wingate, Dogsworthy, Pudleep Gurt, Swannel and Chubhill. Eventually, with limbs wearying and feet aching, tarmac is reached before **Coddow Combe**, at which point those with enough fortitude can follow the road down to Foreland Point (see p97) and the lighthouse that marks the north-ernmost tip of Devon, while the rest take the path off left up the slope, the reward for one's efforts being a clear view of Lynmouth.

The path to Foreland Point

For those wishing to see Devon's most northerly point, a short walk down the road on your right will take you to the **lighthouse** at Foreland Point, built in 1900. From here, you can either return on the same path or, if you would like to stick as close to the coast as possible and not retrace your steps, there is also a path that continues around The Foreland and rejoins the official coastal path. Note that much of it is exposed and it does involve walking on scree. It is a beautiful if challenging walk (especially if you are carrying a pack) but there is a need for caution. There is the option of spending a night here: *Foreland Point Bothy* (Map 10, p97; ☎ 0344-335 1296, 🖳 nationaltrust.org.uk/holi-days/foreland-bothy-devon; 🐾; open year-round) sleeps four (1D & 2S on bunk platforms; £21-28 for the whole place). Note that booking is essential. There is a sink and cold water tap and loo outside (for which you will be given a code when you book), but no cooking facilities; bedding is not provided, nor is there heating or lighting in the bothy, so you will need to be prepared for your night in the wild. To book a night here contact the National Trust.

COUNTISBURY   [Map 11]

The fairly uninteresting church of St John the Baptist at Countisbury marks the start of the drop down to the harbour, though at this late stage you would be for-given for calling in first at *The Blue Ball Inn* (☎ 01598-741263, 🖳 blueballinn.com; 11D/3Tr, all en suite; 🕳; (Ⓛ); 🐾), in parts dating back to 13th century. B&B costs from £37.50pp (sgl occ from £65); each room boasts a bath (though, curiously, not all have a shower!). The **food** (noon-2.30pm & 5.30-8.30pm) is quite 'bistro-esque', with a few pub classics too (mains £12-14).

Just along the road *Berry Lawn Linhay Bothy* (☎ 0344-335 1296, 🖳 nationaltrust.org.uk/holidays/berry-lawn-linhay-bothy; 🐾; open year-round; booking essential) is another National Trust-run bothy, which sleeps four people (2D & 2S wood-en platforms; £22-28 for the whole place). Like Foreland Point Bothy (see above), it's basic, with just a cold-water sink (not drinking water), and an outdoor compost toilet. No heating. No electricity. No bed-ding.

The seasonal Exmoor Coaster **bus** service stops outside the pub; see pp48-50.

Returning to the trail, the stagger down to **Lynmouth** seems long and it's a rare person who isn't exhausted by the time they've walked through the patch of woodland to emerge at the back of Lynmouth Manor House. If you, too, feel exhausted, spare a thought for the brave lifeboatmen (see p100) of Lynmouth who in 1899 *carried* their craft overland all the way to Porlock Weir to rescue a nearby ship in distress – a journey that took some 10 hours in total!

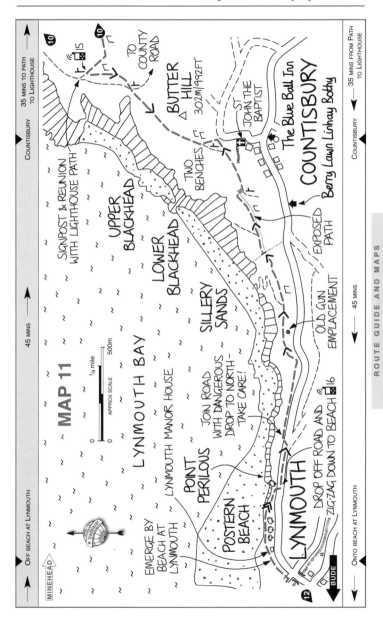

MAP 11

LYNMOUTH BAY

MINEHEAD

OFF BEACH AT LYNMOUTH ← 45 MINS → ▶ COUNTISBURY ← 35 MINS TO PATH TO LIGHTHOUSE →

SIGNPOST & REUNION WITH LIGHTHOUSE PATH

UPPER BLACKHEAD

LOWER BLACKHEAD

SILLERY SANDS

TWO BENCHES

BUTTER HILL △ 302M/992FT

TO COUNTY ROAD

ST JOHN THE BAPTIST

The Blue Ball Inn

COUNTISBURY

Berry Lawn Linhay Bothy

¼ mile

0 500m

APPROX SCALE

LYNMOUTH MANOR HOUSE

POINT PERILOUS

JOIN ROAD WITH DANGEROUS DROP TO NORTH— TAKE CARE!

EXPOSED PATH

OLD GUN EMPLACEMENT

← 45 MINS →

EMERGE BY BEACH AT LYNMOUTH

POSTERN BEACH

LYNMOUTH

DROP OFF ROAD AND ZIG-ZAG DOWN TO BEACH

BUDE ▼

ONTO BEACH AT LYNMOUTH → ◀ COUNTISBURY ← 35 MINS FROM PATH TO LIGHTHOUSE →

LYNMOUTH   [see map p103]

'My walk to Ilfracombe led me through Lynmouth, the finest spot, except Cintra and the Arrabida, which I have ever seen.'
                                   Robert Southey

Lynmouth and its neighbour up the hill, Lynton, combine to form the biggest settlement in the whole of Exmoor National Park. Nicknamed 'Little Switzerland' by the Victorians (who popularised these twin towns as a tourist resort in the 19th century) owing to the beauty, tranquillity and steep gradients of its surrounding countryside, the two villages act as a hub for a plethora of paths, with the Two Moors Way, Samaritans Way and Tarka Trail (see box p34) all joining the Coast Path in passing through or terminating here. Between them, the two villages have ample facilities, though things like supermarkets and banks are all located up the hill in Lynton.

Two events dominate Lynmouth's history. The first is the famous **Overland Launch** of 1899, when Lynmouth's heroic lifeboat crew, wishing to rescue a boat in the Bristol Channel but unable to set sail from Lynmouth due to a force-eight gale, opted instead to drag their lifeboat *The Louisa* over Countisbury Hill and down to Porlock Weir. The second event occurred on Friday 15 August 1952 when, following almost a fortnight of torrential downpours, a cloudburst unleashed 9 inches of rain on Exmoor that sent a wall of water cascading towards the unsuspecting village, dispersing boulders from the surrounding countryside onto the streets. Thirty-four people lost their lives that day and sixty buildings were destroyed entirely. **Lynmouth Flood Memorial Hall** (10am-6pm; free entrance), down near the harbour, exists as a lasting reminder of the tragedy.

Rhenish Tower, located at the end of the pier and one of only two buildings to have been reconstructed since the flood, was originally built in 1832 by wealthy local landowner, General Rawdon. The General returned from his grand tour of Europe in the early 19th century and had the tower built as an imitation of those that he had admired on the Rhine. Once used for pilchard spotting by the local fisherman, the tower has recovered since the flood – much like Lynmouth itself – and has become a sort of symbol of the town.

Services

Exmoor National Park Centre at **Lynmouth Pavilion** (☎ 01598-752509, 🖥 exmoor-nationalpark.gov.uk; daily 10am-5pm; free) has a wealth of **information** on the park. The advisors are connoisseurs of all things Exmoor and also know a thing or two about the SWCP. Inside you'll find Exmoor-related exhibitions and short informative films about the local area. For tourist information see Lynton (see p104).

For a post office, ATMs and supermarkets, you need to head up the hill to Lynton.

Transport

[See also pp48-50] The No 309/310 **bus** operates in the early morning and evening to Barnstaple. Additional seasonal services are provided by the No 300 to Ilfracombe, and the Exmoor Coaster to Minehead. Buses stop by the car park near the road bridge at the back of the village.

For a **taxi** try Riverside Taxis (☎ 01598-753442, 🖥 riversidetaxis-lynton.co.uk).

Where to stay

The nearest **camping** option to either Lynmouth or Lynton is *Sunny Lyn Holiday Park* (☎ 01598-753384, 🖥 sunnylyn.co.uk; fb; 🐾; pay as you go WI-FI; Easter-Oct) which has a **shop** (Easter-Oct daily 9am-5pm) and a *café* (Easter-Sep 8.30-10.15am) that serves breakfasts. The rate (£10 for a hiker and tent) includes use of the shower facilities; laundry facilities are also available. The site can be accessed from either village. From Lynmouth walk up the very steep B3234 (Lynbridge Rd) for approximately three-quarters of a mile and it will be on your left by the river.

Lynmouth's **B&Bs** are primarily found beyond the road bridge towards the back of town (ie furthest from the sea). Along Watersmeet Rd you will find several places with pleasant riverside settings. These include: ***Orchard House Hotel*** (☎ 01598-753247, 🖳 orchardhousehotel.co.uk; **fb**; 1D/1T/3Tr all en suite, 1D private bathroom; 🛁; Ⓛ; 🐕) which charges £32.50-40pp (sgl occ £48-50) and has a free hot tub in the garden; ***Hillside House*** (☎ 01598-753836, 🖳 hillside-lynmouth.co.uk; 1S/4D/1T all with private facilities; 🛁; Ⓛ; 🐕), an 18th-century house though with parts that date back to the 1400s (B&B rates are from £42.50pp, sgl/sgl occ from £45/55); and ***East Lyn House*** (☎ 01598-752540, 🖳 eastlynhouse.co.uk; 7D/1T, all en suite; Ⓛ) where rates are £57.50-68pp (sgl occ from £30, if booked direct), but under-18s are not welcome, and there is a two-night minimum stay from April to October.

On the other side of the East Lyn River there is ***Lorna Doone House*** (☎ 01598-753354, 🖳 lornadoonehouse.co.uk; **fb**; 4D/2D or T, all en suite; 🛁; Ⓛ; 🐕; Feb-Nov), the landlords of which have been working in the hospitality industry for over a quarter of a century. B&B costs from £32.50pp (sgl occ from £45); dinner, bed and breakfast rates also available.

Also by the river is the flower-filled ***Ye Olde Sea Captain's House*** (☎ 01598-753369, 🖳 thecaptainshouseinlynmouth.co.uk; 1S/6D or T/2Tr, most en suite, others share facilities; 🛁; Ⓛ; 🐕); rates here are £50-65pp (sgl £55).

Back in the heart of Lynmouth – and thus nearer the trail – ***The Village Inn*** (☎ 01598-752354, 🖳 thevillageinnexmoor.co.uk; **fb**; 2D/1Tr, en suite; 🛁; Ⓛ; 🐕), on Lynmouth's small pedestrianised strip, provides B&B (from £35pp, sgl occ from £45) above a 'traditional' Free House. It's a bit run down these days, but staff are friendly and helpful.

Riverside Cottage (☎ 01598-752390, 🖳 riversidecottage.co.uk; 7D/1T, all en suite; 🛁; Ⓛ; well-behaved 🐕), is virtually opposite and has two floors of balcony-fronted rooms overlooking the harbour and river. B&B costs £32.50-45pp (sgl occ rates on request).

There are quite a few **hotels** in Lynmouth (though note that they all require a two-night minimum stay). On the harbour itself, ***Rock House Hotel*** (☎ 01598-752251, 🖳 rockhouselynmouth.co.uk; **fb**; 1S/5D/2D or T, all en suite; Ⓛ; 🐕) peers out to sea and charges from £49.50pp (sgl from £60, sgl occ rates on request). On the opposite side of the harbour and dating back to the 14th century, ***The Rising Sun*** (☎ 01598-753223, 🖳 risingsunlynmouth.co.uk; **fb**; 11D/2T, all en suite; 🛁; Ⓛ; 🐕) is an olde-worlde thatched-roofed place with modern facilities. R D Blackmore is said to have written some of *Lorna Doone* within its walls. Rates are from £67pp (sgl rates on request). They also have Shelley's Cottage (1D; 🛁; 🐕; from £100pp, sgl rates on request), a detached cottage where the poet, Percy Bysshe Shelley, is reputed to have stayed in 1812, though Shelley's Hotel (see p102) makes the same claim.

Further back from the sea is ***The Bath Hotel*** (☎ 01598-752238, 🖳 bathhotellynmouth.co.uk; **fb**; 11D/7T/3Qd, all en suite; 🛁; Ⓛ; 🐕; mid Feb to early Jan), an unpretentious place in a great location; the name comes from the fact that it is built on the site of an old inn that used to have its bath-water delivered by horse and cart from a well beneath Rhenish Tower (see p100). B&B costs from £45pp (sgl occ rates on request).

By the West Lyn river is ***The Lyn Valley Guest House*** (☎ 01598-753300, 🖳

❑ WHERE TO STAY: THE DETAILS

In the descriptions of accommodation in this book: 🛁 means at least one room has a bath; Ⓛ means a packed lunch can be prepared if arranged in advance; 🐕 signifies that dogs are welcome in at least one room but also subject to prior arrangement, an additional charge may also be payable; **fb** indicates a Facebook page. See also p74.

lynvalleyguesthouse.com; **fb**; 3D/1Qd, all en suite; ☞; Ⓛ; Mar-Dec; may accept one-night bookings), where the hosts are amiable and the food (see Where to eat) is good; they charge £50-60pp (sgl occ £90-110).

Overlooking the West Lyn River is *Bonnicott House Hotel* (☎ 01598-753346, 🖥 bonnicott.com; **fb**; 6D/1T, all en suite; Ⓛ), a grade-II listed former rectory dating back to 1809. B&B costs from £32.50pp (sgl occ from £60). They are happy to do evening meals (Apr-Dec Mon, Tue & Thur-Sat 6.30-8.15pm) if arranged in advance; there is also a log burner in the front room should you be an intrepid winter walker.

The most famous hotel is *Shelley's* (☎ 01598-753219, 🖥 www.shelleyshotel.co.uk), a sophisticated place where the Romantic poet chose to honeymoon in the summer of 1812. The hotel has been closed for some time for major renovations, but is planning to reopen again, possibly in 2022, so try calling ahead to catch up with developments.

Where to eat and drink
There's a fair selection of places to eat in Lynmouth catering for all budgets. *The Lyn Valley Guest House* (see Where to stay) was temporarily closed to non-residents at the time of research but was previously a great place to come for an early-morning full English breakfast. The evening menu was good too, so it's worth checking the current situation with them.

Another central option for breakfast, which was also temporarily closed to non-residents, is the café at *Riverside Cottage* (see Where to stay; daily 10am-4pm) where you could get a locally sourced fry-up washed down with coffee potent enough to thoroughly energise you before you set off up the sharp hill to Lynton.

Near the B&Bs on Watersmeet Rd are some fine places to eat: *Lyndale Tearooms* (☎ 01598-753553; **fb**; summer daily 8am-4.30pm, winter hours variable) provides cheap and decent breakfasts and lunches, as well as cream teas. Staff are friendly, and

can tell you about the bus services that run by.

Across the water and with wonderful views over the river, *Ye Olde Sea Captain's House* (see Where to stay; daily 10am-6pm) offers cream teas and light snacks in its flower-filled garden.

For evening grub, *The Rising Sun* (see Where to stay; daily noon-2.30pm & 6-9pm) is one of the more sophisticated pubs on the trail. The restaurant-standard evening menu includes Devon crab (£25), steak cuts from Exmoor National Park Beef (£24-18), grilled Wye Valley asparagus (£19) and Exmoor caviar *blinis* (mini caviar pancakes served with clotted cream; £30). The lunchtime menu is more affordable (dishes £6-12).

There's a more typical pub-food menu at *Rock House Hotel* (see Where to stay; food daily noon-3/4pm, restaurant 6.30-9pm), where mains cost from £11 to £15, and lunchtime sandwiches £6 to £8. Afternoon cream teas are also available. More down to earth is *The Village Inn* (see Where to stay; food daily noon-8.45pm) which does good honest pub grub (mains from £10.95) in big portions.

Great fish dishes, such as local ale-battered cod and chips (£13.50) can be caught at *The Bath Hotel* (see Where to stay; daily 10-11.30am, noon-4pm & 5.30-9pm), where there are also some mouth-watering desserts (£6-9). They open for breakfast too (full English £8.95).

For less formal fish, *Esplanade Fish Bar* (☎ 01598-753798; **fb**; daily noon-8pm depending on weather and season) is one of the best chippies on the trail, and does takeaway as well as eat-in.

About one kilometre out of town, up a very steep hill, *Nartnapa's Kitchen* (☎ 01598-753496, 🖥 nartnapa.co.uk; food Mon-Sat 3-9pm), is a riverside pub-restaurant serving the best Thai food in the area (the chef is from Thailand), and local beers from its own **micro-brewery**, FatBelly Brewery. Mains cost from £13-15, and they do takeaways – ideal if you're camping at nearby Sunny Lyn.

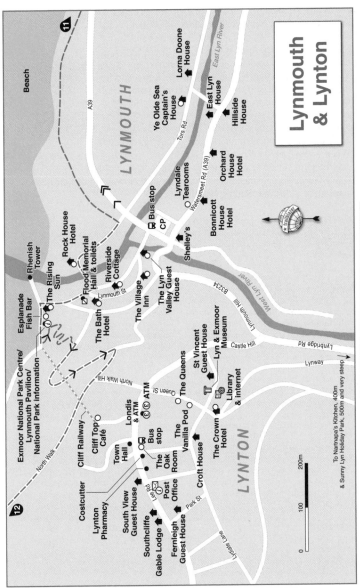

While the sight of Lynmouth and its pubs is undoubtedly welcome, for many walkers there's one more effort required before the day is out: the zig-zag trail shadowing the direct path of the **Cliff Railway** (☎ 01598-753486, 🖳 cliffrailwaylynton.co.uk; mid Feb to early Nov daily 11am-5pm depending on the season, check website for details; adult/child single £3/2; 🐾 £1) to **Lynton**. This railway dates back to the late 19th century; prior to its construction holidaymakers were transported between Lynmouth and Lynton by pony. The two carriages are connected by a cable that runs around pullies at each end.

© BT

When water from the West Lyn River fills the 700-gallon tanks of the upper car – at the same time that water empties out of the tanks of the lower carriage – the heavier carriage starts to descend along the 862ft railway, pulling the bottom carriage up as it does so. Simple, but effective!

LYNTON   [see map p103]

Though not as attractive, perhaps, Lynton certainly has more amenities than Lynmouth.

The **library** (☎ 01598-752505; Tue 2-4pm, Fri & Sat 10am-noon), on Market St, offers internet access (£1/15 mins).

The **post office** (Mon-Fri 8am-5.30pm) is on Lee Rd and houses a small **tourist information point** with a few maps and leaflets, while nearby lies Lynton **pharmacy** (Mon-Fri 8am-1pm & 2-6.30pm, Sat 9am-noon) and a Costcutter **supermarket** (daily 7am-7pm). A few doors down, there's also a Londis supermarket (Mon-Sat 8am-9pm, Sun 8.30am-8pm) which has a free **ATM**, and another free ATM outside the building next to it.

Lyn and Exmoor Museum (Easter-Oct Tue-Thur & Sat 10.30am-1.30pm & 2-5pm; admission £2) has a fairly small collection of farm tools; of more interest, perhaps, is the building in which it is housed, the oldest dwelling in Lynton and perhaps the only museum in Devon which is said to be haunted!

Transport

[See also pp48-50] Filers' No 309 & 310 **bus** services stop here en route from Lynmouth to Barnstaple. To return to Lynmouth, Porlock or Minehead in the school summer holidays take the No 300

bus service. Buses stop along Lee Rd.

For a **taxi** try Riverside Taxis (☎ 01598-753442, 🖳 riversidetaxis-lynton.co.uk).

Where to stay

For **camping**, see Lynmouth, p100. To reach the campsite from Lynton, having arrived at the top of North Walk Hill, cross the road to descend Queen St then turn left onto Lynway and continue to the bottom of the hill.

Finding **B&B** accommodation in Lynton for a single-night stay in a peak period may be difficult. Contacting proprietors direct is generally the best way to book for one night and for single occupancy.

The main area for accommodation is Lee Rd, where an almost unbroken line of B&Bs borders one side of the road.

South View Guest House (☎ 01598-753728, 🖳 southviewguesthouselynton.co.uk; **fb**; 2D/1T/2Tr, all en suite; ▼; Ⓛ; 🐾), at 23 Lee Rd, charges from £37.50pp (sgl occ from £65). *Southcliffe* (☎ 01598-753328, 🖳 southcliffe.co.uk; **fb**; 6D/1T, all en suite; ▼; Ⓛ) is a grand Victorian property where two rooms have a balcony (rates are £37-45pp, sgl occ £48-86), *Gable Lodge* (☎ 01598-752367, 🖳 gablelodge lynton.com; 5D/1Tr, all en suite; ▼; Ⓛ)

charges from £35pp (sgl occ from £55).

Away from Lee Rd, on Park St is a walker-friendly option, *Fernleigh Guest House* (☎ 01598-752666, 🖳 fernleigh.net; **fb**; 3D/3Qd, all en suite; ✎) where rates for two/three/four people are £75/90/105 per room (sgl occ from £50).

On Lydiate Lane, *Croft House* (☎ 01598-752391, 🖳 lyntonbandb.co.uk; **fb**; 4D/1D or T/1T, all en suite; ✎) is a Georgian property, originally built in 1828 for a local sea captain but now welcoming walkers to their individually styled rooms. The house also boasts a lovely little walled garden that's a bit of a sun trap. B&B costs from £41pp (sgl occ from £55), though two-night stays are usually required.

Two options on Market St are *St Vincent Guest House* (☎ 01598-752720, 🖳 stvincentlynton.co.uk; **fb**; 1S private facilities, 5D/1T, all en suite; ✎; (ℒ)), which charges from £37.50pp (sgl £50, sgl occ from £70), and *The Crown Hotel* (☎ 01598-752253, 🖳 thecrownlynton.co.uk; **fb**; 1S/4D/1T/4Qd, all en suite; ✎; (ℒ); 🐾). B&B here costs from £37.50pp (sgl occ from £55) and walkers leaving early can have a packed lunch instead of breakfast. There's also some great food (see Where to eat).

Where to eat and drink
The choice of food is quite good. Among the different cuisines served in town, there's all-things Mediterranean at *The Oak Room* (☎ 01598-753838, 🖳 theoakroom lynton.co.uk; **fb**; food Fri-Mon noon-2pm & daily 6-9pm), which can be highly recommended and serves evening dishes (£15-22) such as Spanish-style meatballs, as well as lunchtime tapas some days.

Serving more local fare, at the top of the funicular railway is *Cliff Top Café* (☎ 01598-753486; Apr-Sep daily 9am-6pm or later, rest of year hours vary).

The Vanilla Pod (☎ 01598-753706, 🖳 thevanillapodlynton.co.uk; **fb**; Apr-Oct daily 10am-4pm & from 6pm; Nov-Mar daily 10am-4pm, Fri-Sun from 6pm; 🐾 café part only), at 10-12 Queen St, is a lovely café-restaurant with great food (Middle Eastern fare and local English dishes) and they welcome walkers.

The best place for **pub food** is *The Crown Hotel* (see Where to stay; food Mon-Thur 11am-3pm & 4.30-9pm, Fri-Sun 11am-9pm). There's traditional pub-grub, from jacket potatoes (£4.80) to daily specials (£8-12) as well as real ales to wash it all down.

Another place serving real ales and typical pub-fare is *The Queens* (☎ 01598-752075; **fb**; food daily noon-9pm; 🐾), an old pub but one with a modern 'bistro' feel and some huge portions of grub including delicious home-made curries.

LYNTON TO COMBE MARTIN   [MAPS 12-17]

This **13½-mile (21.7km; 6¼hrs)** stage is the longest of the three spent within Exmoor and as your last day in the park it certainly does not disappoint. Including both the weird and mysterious landscape of the Valley of Rocks and the SWCP's highest point, Great Hangman, it is a day of both varied terrain and spectacular scenery: superlatives include Great Hangman itself (see p113) and one of Britain's biggest waterfalls, Hollow Brook, as well as one of its steepest valleys, Heddon. Then, finally, having conquered all that the path can throw at you, you end the day with a slow descent to the village that, purportedly, has the longest high street in England: Combe Martin. But even without these record breakers this stage would still make for a fascinating day's walking, with ancient abbeys, wild woodland and grazing goats to occupy your attention.

Being the longest stage in Exmoor, and one of the more remote sections of the SWCP, you won't be surprised to find that we recommend you plan your day carefully. There are, after all, only two places where you can get food – one on the path (the tearooms at Lee Abbey, though they are not open every day), and one a short walk off it (The Hunters Inn at Heddon) – so if you don't intend to stop at either of these you must **carry your own refreshments**; Heddon Valley is a fine and timely place to stop and see if you can spot any of the local wildlife while scoffing your sandwiches, or watching the waves from the shelter of the reconstructed lime kiln.

The route

The day begins simply enough by following **North Walk** across the cliff railway and out of town along a path skirting **Hollerday Hill**. There are tremendous views out to sea and along the shoreline. Indeed, so distracting can this prove that it usually comes as something of a surprise when you round a corner and are confronted by the **Valley of Rocks** (see below) with the appropriately named **Castle Rock** ahead of you, its silhouette like a hilltop fortress overlooking the sea. There now follows a short but pleasant-enough road walk with **Lee Abbey** on your right. Built in 1850, and an evacuated boys' school during

❏ THE VALLEY OF ROCKS

'*...covered with huge stones ... the very bones and skeletons of the earth; rock reeling upon rock, stone piled upon stone, a huge terrific mass.*'   **Robert Southey**

The Valley of Rocks is a group of peculiarly weathered rock formations, most with equally unusual names, that was formed by the last Ice Age. Unlike other combes in Exmoor and North Devon, the Valley of Rocks runs parallel with the sea instead of towards it. As a result, this valley is unlike any other in the South-West and, possibly as a result, many myths and legends have grown up around the area.

The names given to many of the rock formations hint at some of these myths. The formations known as **Devil's Cheesewring** and **Ragged Jack**, for example, could refer to a local legend that suggests that the Devil (also known as 'Jack' in local mythology) built a castle here for some of his wives. On returning to the castle one day, the Devil was enraged to discover that they had been indulging in a drunken orgy with a neighbour, an act of betrayal that compelled the Devil, in a fit of temper, to destroy the castle and turn the women into rock – which is the scene that confronts us today.

Since the Devil's residency there have been several other inhabitants in the valley. Evidence of both Iron and Bronze Age settlements have been discovered and amongst the bracken there are the faint remains of stone circles, possibly once used by Druids. Probably the best-known tenant, however, is a fictional one: Mother Melldrum, the soothsayer in RD Blackmore's *Lorna Doone*, who 'kept her winter' here.

Today, the most famous residents are the huge birds of prey that soar and swoop above the valley, along with the Exmoor ponies that graze in the area and the feral goats who clip-clop amongst the rocky outcrops. The current curly-horned inhabitants have occupied the valley since the 1970s, though there are thought to have been goats living here as far back as Neolithic times, making them almost as much a part of the valley as the rocks themselves.

The path through the valley passes between Castle Rock and Ragged Jack. Having joined the road to Lee Abbey, Devil's Cheesewring will be on your left.

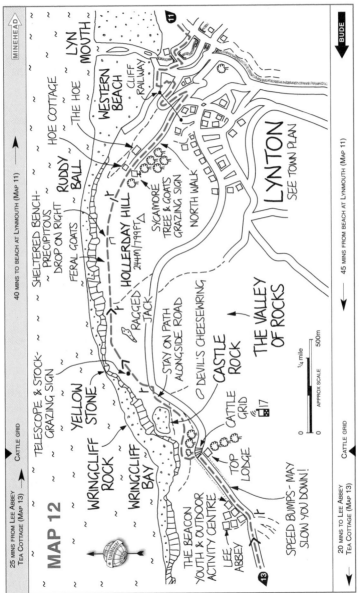

MINEHEAD

MAP 12

25 MINS FROM LEE ABBEY
TEA COTTAGE (MAP 13) →

CATTLE GRID

40 MINS TO BEACH AT LYNMOUTH (MAP 11) →

LYN MOUTH

THE HOE

WESTERN BEACH

CLIFF RAILWAY

HOE COTTAGE

RUDDY BALL

SHELTERED BENCH-
PRECIPITOUS
DROP ON RIGHT

FERAL GOATS

HOLLERDAY HILL
244M/799FT △

RAGGED JACK

TELESCOPE & STOCK-
GRAZING SIGN

YELLOW STONE

WRINGCLIFF ROCK

WRINGCLIFF BAY

THE BEACON
YOUTH & OUTDOOR
ACTIVITY CENTRE

LEE ABBEY

SPEED BUMPS- MAY
SLOW YOU DOWN!

TOP LODGE

CATTLE GRID

CASTLE ROCK

DEVIL'S CHEESEWRING

STAY ON PATH
ALONGSIDE ROAD

THE VALLEY
OF ROCKS

LYNTON
SEE TOWN PLAN

SYCAMORE
TREE & GOATS
GRAZING SIGN

NORTH WALK

20 MINS TO LEE ABBEY
TEA COTTAGE (MAP 13)

CATTLE GRID

45 MINS FROM BEACH AT LYNMOUTH (MAP 11) →

BUDE →

APPROX SCALE

0   ¼ mile
0   500m

ROUTE GUIDE AND MAPS

WWII, the abbey is now a Christian conference centre. There are some tea-rooms a little further down the road from the abbey itself. *Lee Abbey Tea Cottage* (summer Wed-Sat 10.30am-5pm) serves a lot of homemade and Fairtrade produce including some delicious cakes and, of course, cream teas.

Shortly after the tearooms you have the option of continuing up the steep and wooded road route, or you can choose the more off-piste **Woody Bay Alternative Route** around Crock Point.

The Woody Bay alternative route

This route is a delight for those who believe that the Coast Path should stick as close to the shoreline as possible; others, however, will wonder exactly what the point of this short diversion is. There's nothing wrong with it, of course, though on first viewing it doesn't seem to add much to the overall experience, being a simple ramble along field edges bookended by a stroll through woodland. Nor do you even get a good view of the bay after which it is named due to the thick vegetation you pass through (a clear case of not being able to see the Woody for the trees).

Less than 30 minutes after setting off, you are reunited with the main trail.

The two paths do not stay apart for too long and, having reconnected on the road, the SWCP continues through attractive woodland. **Hollow Brook Waterfall** (Map 14) presents an impressive distraction, though perhaps not as impressive as you were hoping if it hasn't rained recently: while it is one of the biggest waterfalls in the UK, dropping 200m (656ft) in total, it does so over a total horizontal distance of 400m. That said, there are some 50m drops (off the path) which will have you reaching for your camera.

The path leaves the woods and takes to the cliffs again, with the views back along the coast little short of extraordinary. **Beacon Roman Fortlet**, excavated in the 1960s and capable of holding around 80 soldiers, still watches the Welsh tribes from the hill above you but the path remains virtually horizontal as far as rocky **Highveer Point**, from where the descent to **Heddon's Mouth** begins.

Despite feeling far from civilisation, it's only a short jaunt (10-15 mins) from the path to *The Hunters Inn* (off Map 14; ☎ 01598-763230, 🖥 the-huntersinnexmoor.co.uk; **fb**; 7D/1T/2Qd, all en suite; ☛; (Ⓛ); 🐾), full of charm (some rooms have a four-poster bed) and a good place to stay – if only to delay your exit from Exmoor! B&B costs from £40 (sgl occ full room rates). They also have a self-contained apartment (2D; £105-150pp, sgl occ £150). The **food** (daily noon-3pm & 6-9pm) is good too, with baguettes and filling cream teas (3-6pm) in the afternoon and hearty mains (£13-18) served in the evenings; just watch out for the peacocks!

Heddon Valley is actually one of the steepest in England, a fact you'll realise soon enough as the path continues by climbing sharply up a wooded hill-side, from where deer can often be seen on the hills opposite while birds of prey circle above. There are good views back down the combe with the roof of the inn emerging through the trees.

(cont'd on p113)

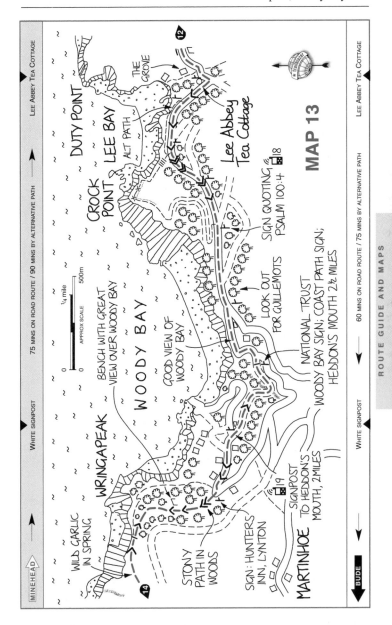

LEE ABBEY TEA COTTAGE

DUTY POINT

LEE BAY

THE GROVE

CROCK POINT

ALT PATH

Lee Abbey Tea Cottage

MAP 13

SIGN QUOTING PSALM 100:4

LOOK OUT FOR GUILLEMOTS

NATIONAL TRUST WOODY BAY SIGN; COAST PATH SIGN; HEDDON'S MOUTH 2½ MILES

WRINGAPEAK

WOODY BAY

BENCH WITH GREAT VIEW OVER WOODY BAY

GOOD VIEW OF WOODY BAY

WILD GARLIC IN SPRING

STONY PATH IN WOODS

SIGN: HUNTERS INN, LYNTON

SIGNPOST TO HEDDON'S MOUTH, 2 MILES

MARTINHOE

¼ mile
APPROX SCALE
500m

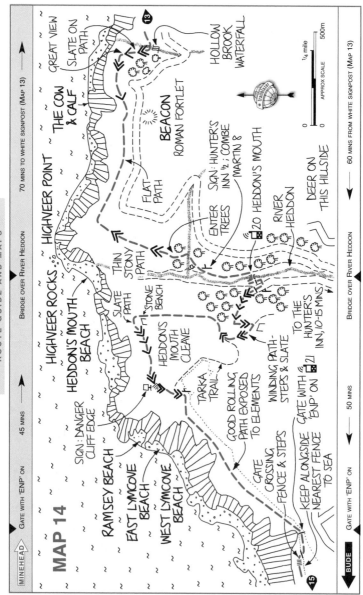

MAP 14

MINEHEAD

GATE WITH 'ENP' ON — 45 MINS — BRIDGE OVER RIVER HEDDON — 70 MINS TO WHITE SIGNPOST (MAP 13)

RAMSEY BEACH

EAST LYMCOVE BEACH

WEST LYMCOVE BEACH

SIGN: DANGER CLIFF EDGE

HIGHVEER ROCKS

HEDDON'S MOUTH BEACH

HIGHVEER POINT

THE COW & CALF

GREAT VIEW

SLATE ON PATH

13

SLATE PATH

HEDDON'S MOUTH CLEAVE

STONE BENCH

THIN STONY PATH

FLAT PATH

BEACON
Roman Fortlet

HOLLOW BROOK WATERFALL

ENTER TREES

SGN: HUNTER'S INN ½; COMBE MARTIN 8

20 HEDDON'S MOUTH

RIVER HEDDON

DEER ON THIS HILLSIDE

TARKA TRAIL

GOOD ROLLING PATH EXPOSED TO ELEMENTS

WINDING PATH · STEPS & SLATE

TO THE HUNTER'S INN, 10-15 MINS

GATE CROSSING FENCE & STEPS

KEEP ALONGSIDE NEAREST FENCE TO SEA

GATE WITH 'ENP' ON 21

15

BUDE — GATE WITH 'ENP' ON — 50 MINS — BRIDGE OVER RIVER HEDDON — 60 MINS FROM WHITE SIGNPOST (MAP 13)

APPROX SCALE

0 — 500m

0 — ¼ mile

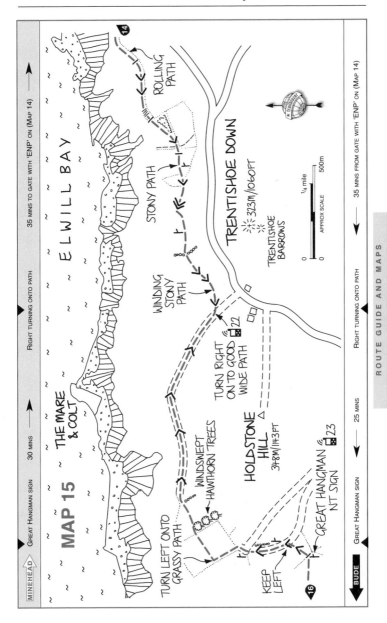

MINEHEAD

GREAT HANGMAN SIGN — 30 MINS — THE MARE & COLT — RIGHT TURNING ONTO PATH — 35 MINS TO GATE WITH 'ENP' ON (MAP 14)

MAP 15

E L W I L L B A Y

14

ROLLING PATH

STONY PATH

WINDING STONY PATH

TRENTISHOE DOWN

313m/1060FT

TRENTISHOE BARROWS

TURN LEFT ONTO GRASSY PATH

WINDSWEPT HAWTHORN TREES

TURN RIGHT ONTO GOOD WIDE PATH

22

HOLDSTONE HILL
348m/1143FT

KEEP LEFT

16

GREAT HANGMAN NT SIGN

23

0 ¼ mile
APPROX SCALE
0 500m

BUDE — GREAT HANGMAN SIGN — 25 MINS — RIGHT TURNING ONTO PATH — 35 MINS FROM GATE WITH 'ENP' ON (MAP 14)

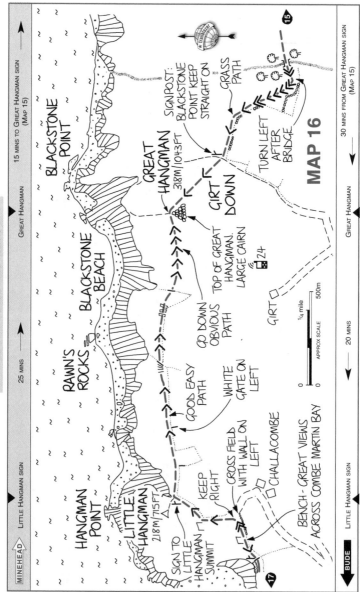

MINEHEAD ▷ LITTLE HANGMAN SIGN ◀ 25 MINS ▲ GREAT HANGMAN ▲ 15 MINS TO GREAT HANGMAN SIGN (MAP 15) →

BLACKSTONE POINT

BLACKSTONE BEACH

RAWN'S ROCKS

HANGMAN POINT

LITTLE HANGMAN
218M/715FT △

SIGN TO LITTLE HANGMAN SUMMIT

KEEP RIGHT

CROSS FIELD WITH WALL ON LEFT

CHALLACOMBE

BENCH- GREAT VIEWS ACROSS COMBE MARTIN BAY

GOOD EASY PATH

WHITE GATE ON LEFT

GO DOWN OBVIOUS PATH

TOP OF GREAT HANGMAN. LARGE CAIRN

GREAT HANGMAN
318M/1043FT

GIRT DOWN

SIGNPOST: BLACKSTONE POINT KEEP STRAIGHT ON

GRASS PATH

TURN LEFT AFTER BRIDGE

MAP 16

GIRT

¼ mile
APPROX SCALE
0 ————— 500m

15

BUDE ◁ LITTLE HANGMAN SIGN ◀ 20 MINS ▲ GREAT HANGMAN ▲ 30 MINS FROM GREAT HANGMAN SIGN (MAP 15) →

24

17

(cont'd from p108) Continuing on the path, magnificent cliff-top walking leads you onto bare, scrubby **Trentishoe Down** (Map 15), before a slow descent brings you to the foot of Great Hangman. **Great Hangman** (Map 16) is the highest point on the SWCP at 318m or 1043ft (though bear in mind, of course, that you won't be starting your ascent from sea-level but a point approximately 140m above sea level at Sherrycombe – which is a small mercy). On its northern side it also happens to be mainland Britain's highest sea cliff, with a vertical face of around 250m (around 800ft).

The initial climb will certainly get the heart pounding but you'll also be pleasantly surprised at how brief (hopefully!) the assault is; what's more, the huge **cairn** at the top of Great Hangman is a great spot to survey the land, take photos and enjoy a rest – safe in the knowledge that your day's walking is almost at an end.

The path now has only one way to go and the long, slow walk downwards begins. The path passes by **Little Hangman** (218m/715ft), visitable off to the right of the trail; non-masochists, however, should continue downwards where, shortly afterwards, there are splendid views down to your destination for this stage: **Combe Martin Bay**.

COMBE MARTIN   [map p115]

Combe Martin, anciently Marhuscombe, which lieth low as the name implies, and near the sea, having a cove for boats to land, a place noted for yielding the best hemp in all the County of Devon, and that in great abundance, but in former times famous for mines of tin, and, that which is better merchandise, silver, though Cicero denieth that there is any in Britain.

Tristram Risdon, 1640

Today the hemp fields and mines of tin and silver have all disappeared and if Combe Martin is known for anything now, it is its high street which, so it is said, is the longest in England. (It's a claim that is dubious at best, especially given that much of the street is residential rather than commercial; though it is true that they once featured in *Guinness World Records* for holding the longest street party.)

The town is perhaps not as attractive as some on the route though it's not without some points of interest including the small **Combe Martin Museum** (☎ 01271-889031, 🖳 combemartinmuseum.co.uk; **fb**; Apr-Oct Mon-Fri 10.30am-5pm, Sat & Sun 11am-3pm, Nov-Mar Tue-Thur 10.30am-3pm; £2.50) on Cross St. With displays on the industrial, maritime and

natural history of the village a visit is worthwhile. There's also the **Pack o' Cards** pub (see Where to stay) built in 1690 by a local dignitary following a particularly large win whilst gambling, an event that led to his decision to construct the inn with 52 stairs and 52 windows (52 being the number of cards in a pack), 4 floors (ie the number of suits in a pack), and with 13 doors on every floor and 13 fireplaces throughout (representing the number of cards in a suit)!

See p16 for details of festivals and events here.

Services

The museum is home to the **tourist information point** (same details as museum); the staff have information about accommodation but can't do bookings; there is free WI-FI as well as **internet access** (donations welcome).

The village also boasts a **post office** (Mon-Sat 9am-5pm); Premier **shop** (Mon-Sat 7.30am-10pm) which has a free **ATM**; Central **supermarket** (daily 7am-10pm), also with an ATM inside; **launderette** (daily 8am-8pm); Boots **pharmacy** (Mon-Fri 9am-6pm, Sat 9am-1pm) and a **walking/camping outlet**, The Outdoor Shop (daily 10am-5pm). The **library** (Tue & Sat 10am-noon, Thur 1-3pm) is about half a mile from the centre, along King's St.

Transport

[See also pp48-50] The No 301 **bus** service to Barnstaple via Ilfracombe calls here as do the seasonal No 300 and No 302 services in the school summer holidays. Buses run along the main street and stop at several places including by the beach.

For a **taxi**, try Andy Cabs (☎ 01271-889200, 🖳 andycab.co.uk).

Where to stay

By the standards of this path there's not a great choice of places to stay in Combe Martin, though most are OK.

There are two large holiday parks on the outskirts of Combe Martin but the best option for **campers** is friendly *Newberry Valley Camping and Caravanning Park* (☎ 01271-882334 or 07835 521850, 🖳 newberryvalleypark.co.uk; **fb**; adult/child £12/6; 🐾; ➥; Mar-Oct). The facilities are excellent, with extremely spacious showers and even a bathtub in one of the bathrooms! There's also a little **shop** (daily 8.30am-6.30pm in high season, limited hours in low season) that sells a few basics. The site is abundant in wildlife (they have their own alpaca field) and has won the David Bellamy Conservation & Nature Gold Award numerous times! It is located a short distance out of the town on the bend a little way up Newberry Hill.

If you feel you have a few more miles in you it is worth considering continuing to Watermouth (see p116) where there are some campsites, including a couple that are better value for hikers.

There is a huddle of **B&Bs** on Woodlands, up the hill on the way out of town. The best, perhaps, is *Mellstock House* (☎ 01271-882592, 🖳 mellstockhouse.co.uk; 3D/1D or T/1Qd, all en suite; Ⓛ) with a licensed bar and the offer of evening meals. There's a decent breakfast menu including smoked salmon and eggs, and a drying room too – little wonder that this place is popular with walkers. They

also offer a pick-up and drop-off service from/to Lynton/Lynmouth and Woolacombe should you book for two nights. B&B costs from £45pp (sgl occ from £72).

Providing close competition is *Fontenay* (☎ 01271-889368; 1D/1T shared bathroom; ➥; Ⓛ; ➥), just before the bend in the road near the top of the hill; it's a large family house with a nice sideline in selling crafts made from locally sourced driftwood. The bread and other food at breakfast is home cooked and organic where possible; the eggs are from their own chickens. They charge £28pp (sgl occ £28).

Back down the hill, *Acorns Guest House* (☎ 01271-882769, 🖳 acorns-guesthouse.co.uk; **fb**; 5D/1Qd all en suite/1T private facilities; Ⓛ; ➥) is a huge late-Victorian terrace with friendly owners who charge from £37.50pp (£60 sgl occ), while *Channel Vista* (☎ 01271-883514, 🖳 channelvista.co.uk; 1S/1T/4D/1Tr, all en suite; ➥; Ⓛ; ➥) has a licensed honesty bar in their pleasant Victorian conservatory. B&B costs from £41pp (sgl £50, sgl occ £50).

There are also some B&Bs in the centre of town. The very welcoming *Blair Lodge* (☎ 01271-882294, 🖳 blairlodge.org.uk; 1S private bathroom, 2T/5D/1Qd, all en suite; ➥; Feb-Oct), at the top of Moory Meadow, just off the main street, is licensed to sell alcohol and provides evening meals. They charge £36-39pp (sgl £39, sgl occ £51-54).

On King St, but away from the traffic, up some steps, *Saffron House* (☎ 01271-883521, 🖳 saffronhousebandb.co.uk; 3D/2Tr/1Qd, all en suite; ➥; Ⓛ; ➥; mid Feb-end Oct) is a large former farmhouse with its own outdoor swimming pool (May-Sep). Expect to pay from £39pp (from £60 sgl occ).

Combe Martin also has two **pubs** in which you could spend the night: *The Fo'c's'le Inn* (☎ 01271-883354, 🖳 focsleinn.co.uk; 5D/1Qd, all en suite; ➥; ➥; Easter-Nov) is perfectly located for walkers where the path enters Combe Martin, and charges from £37.50pp (sgl occ from £40).

Less convenient, but full of character,

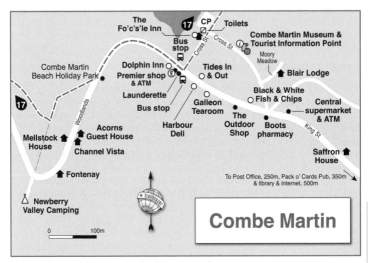

Combe Martin

Pack o' Cards (☎ 01271-882300, 🖥 pack ocards.co.uk; **fb**; 3D/3Tr, all en suite; WI-FI intermittent in rooms; Ⓛ) is a listed building (see p113) in use as an inn since the early 19th century. Their rooms are amongst the smartest in town, with one featuring a four-poster bed. Rates are from £47.50pp (sgl occ room rate).

If you want a **hotel**, you'll need to continue about half a mile along the coast path beyond Combe Martin to *Sandy Cove Hotel* (Map 17; ☎ 01271-882243, 🖥 sandycove-hotel.co.uk; **fb**; 37 rooms, all en suite; ➤; 🐾), which commands wonderful views and has attractive terraced gardens leading down towards the coastline. B&B costs £90-157pp (sgl occ £124-182). Food is available, for non-residents too, at the hotel's Seacliffe Restaurant (7am-9pm; mains £14-19) and the less formal Cove Restaurant (noon-9pm; most mains £9-15).

Where to eat and drink
A splendid option for breakfast is *Harbour Deli* (☎ 01271-883688; **fb**; Apr-Nov Mon-Sat 9am-5pm, Sun 10am-4pm, winter hours variable), where you'll get a large full English for £7.50. Staff are very friendly

and they do decent lunches (the baguettes are excellent) and great cakes too.

Also on Borough Rd is *Galleon Tearoom* (☎ 01271-883732; **fb**; Mar-Oct daily 10am-5pm; 🐾), which has a great little roof terrace: a delight on a sunny day. Dogs are also welcome in this family-run establishment with breakfasts and cream teas a speciality.

Central and cheap, but not particularly attractive, is the diner-lookalike café and takeaway *Tides In & Out* (☎ 01271-882918; 10am-8pm) where you can get fry-ups, jacket potatoes, quiches, cakes and cream teas.

By the beach, **pub food** can be found at *The Fo'c's'le Inn* (see Where to stay; food Easter-Nov daily noon-3pm & 6-8.30pm) – where you'll get a decent meal for £10-17 – and also at *The Dolphin Inn* (☎ 01271-883424; **fb**; food Easter-Sep daily noon-3pm & 5-9pm, winter hours variable) which serves bar-meals and a carvery on a Sunday (£10). Further out of town, *Pack o' Cards* (see Where to stay) also serves food (mains £14-19; summer holidays daily noon-9pm, rest of year Mon-Sat noon-3pm & 5.30-9pm, Sun noon-

8pm), has a big garden and does a Sunday carvery for £12.95.

For top-notch **takeaway** look no further than *Black & White Fish & Chips* (☎ 01271-883548; Mon-Thur noon-2pm & 5-8.30pm, Fri & Sat noon-2pm & 5-9pm) on Borough Rd.

COMBE MARTIN TO WOOLACOMBE [MAPS 17-22]

For this **14¼-mile (23km; 6hrs 35 mins)** stage, and the one after it, the landscape is no longer dominated by the high rolling hills, hanging woodlands, steep-sided canyons and soaring cliffs prevalent in Exmoor. The scenery instead is one of sand and seals, smugglers' coves and surfers, broad beige beaches and bleach-blonde hair. This stage still provides a fairly strenuous workout for your calf muscles, with some stiff climbs, though generally the gradients are kind. That said, the start of the walk is punctuated by some fairly mundane road walking, but this is more than made up for by some great cliff-top walking and some wonderful views of Lundy Island and Ilfracombe – a tourist hot-spot with plenty of amenities. Refreshments are also available at several spots along the way.

After Ilfracombe the path meanders through the greenery of Torrs Park before following a wonderfully undulating route around Morte Point from where you will be treated to your first views of Woolacombe and its long, gorgeous expanse of sand. Seals, dolphins and basking sharks are frequently spotted from the cliffs around Morte Point (with Rockham Bay being an especially good spot for seals). Whether you'll see one of those exotic British creatures is largely a matter of luck, of course – though one mammal you definitely will see bobbing up and down in Morte Bay as you stroll/stagger into Woolacombe are the local surfers, a largely migratory creature that populates the coastline from Woolacombe to Saunton in huge numbers, particularly in summertime.

The route

There is a need for caution when leaving Combe Martin: both that you take great care whilst walking along the road and that you do not miss the sign that directs you off it. Accompanied by some rather pleasant woodland the path initially takes a rather haphazard route before arriving at **Watermouth Bay**.

WATERMOUTH [MAP 17]

There's not much to Watermouth other than a small, pretty harbour, the old Victorian **Watermouth Castle**, now a theme park (🖳 watermouthcastle.com; admission £15.50) and several decent **campsites**.

In the school summer holidays the No 300 **bus** service stops here en route between Lynmouth and Ilfracombe; see pp48-50.

Watermouth Valley Camping Park (☎ 01271-862282 or 07564-214336, 🖳 water mouthpark.co.uk; **fb**; 🐾; May-Sep) is a cheap and lovely campsite, perfectly situated on the path and near a pub and a café. The rate for hikers (£6pp) is for a one-night stay only. (Please note: don't get confused between this campsite and Watermouth Cove Holiday Park next-door.)

Across the road and up the hill from the pub, *Mill Park* (☎ 01271-882647, 🖳 mill-park.com; **fb**; WI-FI main bldg; 🐾; Mar-Oct) is a smarter affair whose chief recommendation for hikers may be their '**tent cocoon**' (£30-45) – a two-person wooden hut with electricity that makes a great alternative to sleeping in a tent, particularly if

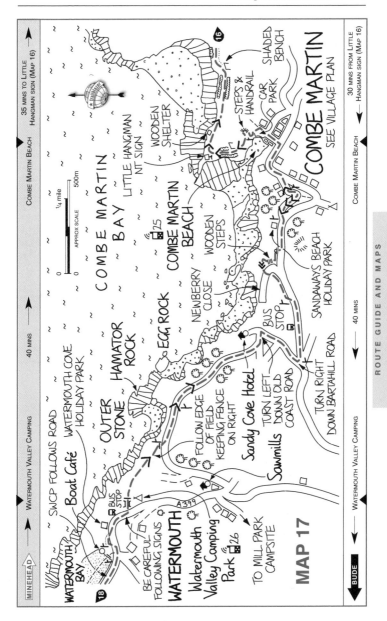

MINEHEAD ▷

WATERMOUTH VALLEY CAMPING ⟶ 40 MINS ⟶ WATERMOUTH VALLEY CAMPING ⟶ COMBE MARTIN BEACH ⟶ 35 MINS TO LITTLE HANGMAN SIGN (MAP 16)

16

COMBE MARTIN
SEE VILLAGE PLAN

SHADED BENCH

CAR PARK

STEPS & HANDRAIL

WOODEN SHELTER

LITTLE HANGMAN NT SIGN

COMBE MARTIN BAY

¼ mile
500m
0
APPROX SCALE

COMBE MARTIN BEACH

WOODEN STEPS

NEWBERRY CLOSE

SANDAWAYS BEACH HOLIDAY PARK

BUS STOP

TURN LEFT DOWN OLD COAST ROAD

TURN RIGHT DOWN BARTAHILL ROAD

Sandy Cove Hotel

FOLLOW EDGE OF FIELD KEEPING FENCE ON RIGHT

Sawmills

EGG ROCK

HAMATOR ROCK

OUTER STONE

WATERMOUTH COVE HOLIDAY PARK

SWCP FOLLOWS ROAD

Boat Café

BUS STOP

BE CAREFUL FOLLOWING SIGNS

WATERMOUTH BAY

18

WATERMOUTH
Watermouth Valley Camping Park

A399

TO MILL PARK CAMPSITE

MAP 17

25

26

COMBE MARTIN BEACH ⟶ 30 MINS FROM LITTLE HANGMAN SIGN (MAP 16)

40 MINS

ROUTE GUIDE AND MAPS

BUDE ▽

the weather doesn't look too friendly. Alternatively they have three **bell tents** and three '**glampods**' each of which costs £40-65; however, there is a minimum two-night stay for these. For all three options you will need your own sleeping bag and mat. For a normal **tent** and up to two people they charge £15-22.

About 500m west of Watermouth and on the left up the hill is *Little Meadow Campsite* (Map 18; ☎ 01271-866862, 🖳 littlemeadow.co.uk; 🐾; Mar-Sep), part of Lydford Farm. The rate for a hiker and a tent is £5.

The local **pub** is *Sawmills* (☎ 01271-883388, 🖳 sawmillsfreehouse.co.uk; **fb**; 4D or T; 🐾), which has four smart rooms

for **B&B** from £45pp and serves **food** all day (daily 8/9am till 10pm); the menu (mains £12-15) includes burgers, loaded fries and nachos.

Right by the coast path, and opening out onto the pretty little harbour of Watermouth Bay, *Boat Café* (☎ 07846-496069, 🖳 boatcafeilfracombenorthdevon .co.uk; **fb**; Tue-Sun 10am-4.30pm; 🐾), also known as 'Storm in a Teacup', is a quirky choice for breakfast, lunch, or just a spot of cream tea. Food is served from a converted boat, and tables are strewn across the shingle beach as well as on decking beside the boat. There is some seating inside the boat too.

As tranquil and sleepy as Watermouth Harbour may seem now, it played an integral part in the allies' Operation Pluto (an acronym for Pipelines Under The Ocean) during WWII. The idea was to lay pipes under the Channel to supply fuel to allied forces, and to test the plan a 51½-mile (83km) pipe was laid between Watermouth and Swansea across the Bristol Channel. It proved a success and the first pipe was laid under the English Channel to France in 1944 – with further pipes installed for the remainder of the war as the fighting moved closer to Germany.

Some woodland cliff-side walking to **Widmouth Head** follows, from where, sadly, you will get your last good views of Great Hangman. Your eyes will not remain unoccupied for long, however, as from **Rillage Point** another magical spectre arrives on the horizon – that of Lundy Island (see box p122).

Next comes **Hele**.

HELE   [MAP 18]

The beach here has been a popular bathing spot since Victorian times but whether stopping for a paddle or you just need a quick snack to spur you on to Ilfracombe, you may be glad to see the Premier **shop** (daily 7am-9pm).

In the school summer holidays the No 300 **bus** service calls here; see pp48-50.

If you'd rather sit down for your lunch, there are two options for **food** before you navigate Beacon Point to Ilfracombe. *Hele Bay Pub* (☎ 01271-867795; 🖳 helebay pub.co.uk; **fb**; 🐾; food Apr-Oct Mon-Sat noon-3pm & 5-9pm, Sun noon-8pm, Oct-Apr closed Mon, Sun noon-5pm), 39 Beach Rd, produces award-winning traditional homemade pub grub (mains £12-14), including homemade pies in shortcrust pastry, 'chased chorizo chicken' and 'trawlerman's pasta' with mussels, cod and prawns. Good selection of real ales too.

By the roundabout and beach, *Snacking Kraken* (☎ 01271-863911, 🖳 snackingkraken.com; **fb**; late Mar-June & Sep daily 9am-5pm, July & Aug Sun-Thur 9am-6pm, Fri-Sun to 9pm, may close in bad weather) serves breakfasts (£3.95-8.45), light bites and lunches. Their regular specials' board features locally sourced fish tacos and there is pizza to eat in or takeaway. Also does beer and cider.

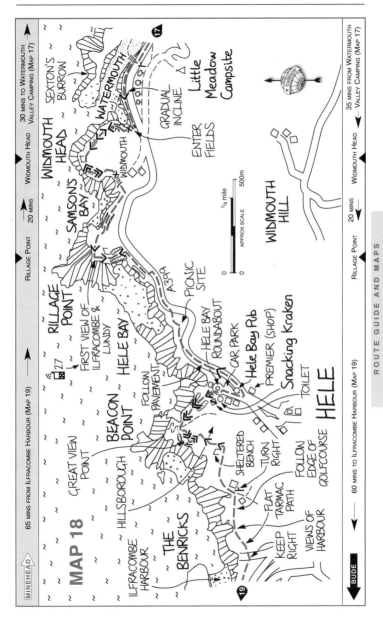

MAP 18

65 MINS FROM ILFRACOMBE HARBOUR (MAP 19) ⟶   RILLAGE POINT   20 MINS ⟶ WIDMOUTH HEAD   30 MINS TO WATERMOUTH VALLEY CAMPING (MAP 17) ⟶

ILFRACOMBE HARBOUR

THE BENRICKS

HILLSBOROUGH

GREAT VIEW POINT

BEACON POINT

FOLLOW PAVEMENT

FIRST VIEW OF ILFRACOMBE & LUNDY

RILLAGE POINT

HELE BAY

SAMSON'S BAY

WIDMOUTH HEAD

WATERMOUTH

SEXTON'S BURROW

17

27

A399

PICNIC SITE

HELE BAY ROUNDABOUT

CAR PARK

Hele Bay Pub

PREMIER (SHOP)

Snacking Kraken

TOILET

HELE

WIDMOUTH

ENTER FIELDS

GRADUAL INCLINE

Little Meadow Campsite

SHELTERED BENCH

TURN RIGHT

FOLLOW EDGE OF GOLFCOURSE

FLAT TARMAC PATH

KEEP RIGHT

VIEWS OF HARBOUR

19

0   ¼ mile
APPROX SCALE
0   500m

WIDMOUTH HILL

BUDE

ROUTE GUIDE AND MAPS

Having passed the edge of **Hele** the path navigates the (very steep) wooded slopes and fields of **Hillsborough**, from where fabulous views of **Ilfracombe** and its harbour (since 2012 featuring Damien Hirst's *Verity* statue; see box below) greet you.

ILFRACOMBE   [see map p125]

'The situation of Ilfracombe is by nature lovely'   **S Baring-Gould** *Devon* (1907)

The first part of Ilfracombe that's visible as you stroll around Beacon Point is the town's harbour. Whether *MS Oldenburg*, the boat to Lundy (see box p122), is in dock or not, it's difficult not to be struck by the natural beauty of this little haven. Sheltered between the hills of Capstone and Hillsborough, it's little wonder there's been a harbour here since the 12th century, though, as with just about every resort on the North Devon coastline, the town owes its prosperity largely to the Victorians, whose decision to route the steamships and railways here bought the crowds to Ilfracombe en masse.

Today, the town can be divided into four distinct areas. The **harbour** is the largest in North Devon and, somewhat surprisingly given its rather homely aspect, experiences the world's second highest tidal rise and fall. It is also the place from which to embark on a coastal cruise or sealife safari. **Fore St** is the oldest part of Ilfracombe and used to be the town's social and business hub. It's quieter now, but strolling up or down the steep cobbled street it is easy to envisage the seafaring residents of old staggering out of the George and Dragon, the town's oldest pub, dating from 1360.

The third area is **High St**, the continuation of Fore St (there's a large metal arch separating the two) and a town-centre of sorts. Just after the divide you will find **Ilfracombe Chocolate Emporium** (☎

❏ **VERITY**

Mention Ilfracombe's controversial steel and bronze resident to a local and many will proudly inform you that British artist Damien Hirst's *Verity* is the tallest statue in the United Kingdom, standing 25cm (10") taller than Antony Gormley's *Angel of the North* (which peers down over the A1 near Gateshead).

When approaching Ilfracombe from Hillsborough *Verity* can be difficult to spot in the harbour, which can lead one to question this claim regarding the statue's stature. It is, however, true. Unless directly beneath *Verity* you generally don't appreciate the sculpture's scale. (*Angel of the North* you always gaze up at.) A great deal of *Verity*'s height of 20.25 metres (66.43ft) is made up of her sword but it won't be this aspect of the sculpture that makes you wonder what it's all about. The torso and head of the 25-tonne statue have been truly controversial as they depict half of *Verity*'s body skinless with her skull and womb (including a developing foetus) revealed. Standing on a pile of legal books, in her sword-free hand you'll also spot a set of scales. So … what is it all about? Well, a verity (*Veritas*), is 'the quality or state of being true' and Hirst describes the statue as a 'modern allegory of truth and justice.' Whilst the sword and scales represent the traditional symbols of Justice, *Verity*'s stance is based on the sculpture *Little Dancer of Fourteen Years* (c.1881) by French artist Edgar Degas (1834-1917).

Verity took two years to plan and produce, and was erected over a week in October 2012. Weather and lightning proof, it appears she'll be dividing opinion in the town for at least the next two decades: that being the span of time for which Hirst has kindly (depending on your opinion on it) loaned the sculpture to Ilfracombe.

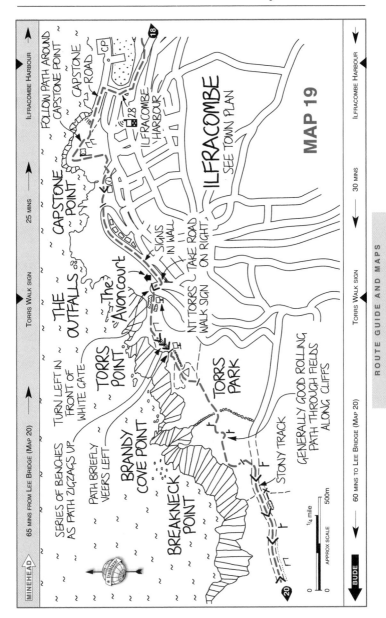

MAP 19

ILFRACOMBE
SEE TOWN PLAN

MINEHEAD

ILFRACOMBE HARBOUR

TORRS WALK SIGN

25 MINS

30 MINS

BUDE

ILFRACOMBE HARBOUR

TORRS WALK SIGN

65 MINS FROM LEE BRIDGE (Map 20)

60 MINS TO LEE BRIDGE (Map 20)

FOLLOW PATH AROUND
CAPSTONE POINT

CAPSTONE
ROAD

CP

18

28

ILFRACOMBE
HARBOUR

CAPSTONE
POINT

SIGNS
IN WALL

NT TORRS TAKE ROAD
WALK SIGN ON RIGHT

THE
OUTFALLS

The
Avoncourt

TURN LEFT IN
FRONT OF
WHITE GATE

TORRS
POINT

TORRS
PARK

PATH BRIEFLY
VEERS LEFT

BRANDY
COVE POINT

BREAKNECK
POINT

SERIES OF BENCHES
AS PATH ZIGZAGS UP

STONY TRACK

GENERALLY GOOD ROLLING
PATH THROUGH FIELDS
ALONG CLIFFS

20

0   ¼ mile
APPROX SCALE
0   500m

Trailblazer

01271-867193 or ☎ 07774-411954, 🖳 ilfracombechocolateemporium.co.uk; **fb**; Easter-Oct Mon-Sat 10am-5pm, Aug Sun 10am-4pm, Oct-Easter Tue-Sat 10am-4pm; free), a museum dedicated to the humble cocoa bean and all its derivatives; with luck you will be here on a day when they are making chocolate so you can watch it.

The fourth and final area, the **seafront and The Promenade**, is pretty enough, and the large conical buildings that greet you as you circle Capstone Hill are certainly striking. This is the home of the TIC, a gallery and **Landmark Theatre** (🖳 landmark-ilfracombe.com). Nearby is **Ilfracombe Museum** (☎ 01271-863541, 🖳 ilfracombe museum.co.uk; **fb**; Easter-Oct Mon-Sat 10am-5pm, Nov-Easter Tue-Fri 10am-1pm; £5, £4 concs); it has five rooms, with sections dedicated to sailing, Lundy and the harbour, and makes for a diverting half-hour or so.

❏ LUNDY ISLAND

Lying 11 miles off the coast of North Devon, where the Bristol Channel meets the Atlantic Ocean, Lundy Island is an extraordinary place in a wonderful location. It is also one that, with careful planning, can be reached by the intrepid pedestrian – and its coastline walked – in just one day.

Measuring 3½ miles long and just a mile wide, the island is renowned for its **wildlife**: approximately 35 species of bird breed on the island annually including puffins ('Lund-ey' means Puffin Island in Norse) and many other seabirds such as razorbills and guillemots. Amongst the landlubbers there are sika deer and Lundy ponies, while out at sea you may glimpse basking sharks and dolphins.

Standing on the clifftops amongst wildflowers – possibly even next to a famous Lundy cabbage – the walker can stare out across the water and easily imagine why for many centuries Lundy was a favoured hiding place for **pirates**, its remoteness and proximity to two coastlines and Bristol Channel's bustling shipping lane making it the perfect hideout. **Marisco Castle** is named after a famous family of swashbuckling criminals including William de Marisco, who met a most unfortunate end – in 1242 he was charged with conspiring to kill King Henry III and it is thought that he was the first man to have been hung, drawn and quartered.

Taking less than two hours, *MS Oldenburg* (late Mar to late Oct; 3-4 sailings per week; day return £42/22 adults/children, open return £74/38) carries passengers to the car-free island from Ilfracombe and Bideford. Alternatively, in winter a helicopter service (return fare £131/70 adult/child) runs on Mondays and Fridays from Hartland Point (see p189).

If a single day on Lundy seems inadequate – which it will if you wish both to walk the whole coastline and have time to investigate all its other attractions – there are 23 restored historic buildings on the island in which you can stay, including the castle and a **lighthouse**. The cost varies greatly depending on the size of the property and the season in which you visit, and be aware that some can be rented only on a weekly basis over the school summer holidays. **Camping** (£20pp for two nights; late Mar to early Oct) is also an option in a field near the island's pub and **shop** (hours vary but generally 9am-4.30pm). All accommodation booking must be done in advance as even the campsite is very popular in the summer months. *Marisco Tavern* (food daily 8.30-10am, noon-2/3pm & 6-8.30/9pm) serves food to suit all budgets.

For more information in regards to sailings, helicopter flights and the island in general you should contact **Lundy Shore Office** (☎ 01271-863636, 🖳 lundyis land.co.uk; Mon-Fri 9am-5pm, Sat 9am-1pm) in Ilfracombe or, for accommodation, The Landmark Trust (🖳 landmarktrust.org.uk). For Lundy Island itself call ☎ 01237-431831.

St Nicholas Chapel, on Lantern Hill, guards the harbour's entrance. Built in 1321, the chapel's use has changed down the centuries from place of worship to lighthouse to family home; currently it's maintained by Ilfracombe Rotary Club and you can look around (free, although donations are welcome).

See p16 for details of festivals and events held here.

Services

The **tourist information centre** (☎ 01271-863001, 🖳 visitilfracombe.co.uk; Easter to Oct Mon-Fri 9.30am-4.30pm, Sat & Sun 10.30am-4.30pm, Nov to Easter Mon-Sat 10am-4pm) shares one of the conical buildings with the theatre; they do accommodation booking (see box p42).

Internet access can be found at **Ilfracombe Library** (☎ 01271-862388; Mon & Sat 9am-1pm, Tue & Fri to 5pm, Thur to 6pm; £2/hr, free if you join the library), on Sommers Crescent between The Promenade and Fore St.

Also on the High St there is: the **post office** (Mon-Fri 9am-5.30pm, Sat to 12.30pm), part of the **general store** McColls (daily 7am-11pm); the **Co-op** (daily 7am-9pm), which is the best place for food supplies in the centre, and has an ATM outside; the **chemists** Superdrug (Mon-Sat 8.30am-5.30pm, Sun 10am-4.30pm) and **banks** with **ATMs** including NatWest and Lloyds.

Ilfracombe **Laundrette** (daily 10am-8pm) is at 15 Wilder Rd. Another shop selling general necessities, though nearer the harbour on St James Place, is St James **Newsagents** & Minimarket (daily 8.30am-9pm).

Transport

[See also pp48-50] Ilfracombe is well-served with **bus** services including Nos 21, 21A, 31 and 301, plus the seasonal 300 & 302 to and from several other destinations along the path.

For a **taxi** try A Taxis (☎ 01271-865321, 🖳 ataxiilfracombe.co.uk), or Filers Taxis (☎ 01271-862575, 🖳 filers taxis.com).

Where to stay

There's no campsite in Ilfracombe, but there is a good **hostel** here: *Ocean Backpackers* (☎ 01271-867835, 🖳 ocean-backpackers.co.uk; **fb**; 3 x 6-, 1 x 8- dorm beds, 1S/2D/3Qd/2 x family rooms sleeping 5, most en suite, rest share facilities;✉; 🐾 in private room only; Mar-Nov), at 29 St James Place. It is a comfortable place (dorm beds £20pp, sgl £35, 2-5 sharing private room £20-30pp) right in the centre of town and provides free tea and coffee for its guests. It also has self-catering facilities and a drying room.

There are a few **B&Bs** in town, though not many are particularly central. Two exceptions are *Acorn Lodge* (☎ 01271-862505, 🖳 theacornlodge.co.uk; 2S share facilities, 4D/1D or T/1Tr, all en suite; Ⓛ), at 4 St James Place, which charges from £33.50pp (sgl from £48, sgl occ from £57), but they usually only accept bookings for a minimum of two nights, and *The Olive Branch Guest House* (☎ 01271-879005, 🖳 olivebranchguesthouse.co.uk; **fb**; 3D/1T, all en suite; ✉), a Georgian Grade-II listed building on Fore St. Newly renovated with very comfortable rooms, they charge from £47.50pp (sgl occ from £70).

A little out of town there is a whole stretch of B&Bs. Along St Brannock's Rd are: *Burnside* (☎ 01271-863097, 🖳 burn side-ilfracombe.co.uk; 2D/1D or T, all en suite), No 34, which charges £32.50-40pp (sgl occ from £55) and has a room with a four-poster bed; *The Dorchester* (☎ 01271-865472, 🖳 the-dorchester.com; **fb**; 6D/ 1Tr, all en suite; Ⓛ; Mar-Nov), No 59, which charges £30-37.50pp (sgl occ £45-55) and is licensed; and *Strathmore* (☎ 01271-862248, 🖳 the-strathmore.co.uk; 2S/4D/1T/1Tr, all en suite; ✉; Ⓛ; 🐾 half of the charge goes to a charity, the Dogs Trust), No 57, which is also licensed and charges from £39pp (sgl £47, sgl occ from £45). At No 56 *Lyncott House* (☎ 01271-862425, 🖳 lyn cotthouse.co.uk; 4D/1Tr, all en suite; ✉) is an elegant Victorian property; rates here are from £40pp (sgl occ from £50).

Close to where the path leaves the town, at 6 Torrs Walk Ave, *The Avoncourt* (Map 19; ☎ 01271-862543, 🖳 avoncourt ilfracombe.co.uk; 2S/6D/1T/1Tr, all en suite; ☛; Ⓛ; 🐾) is a fairly standard guest-house charging from £40pp (sgl £50, sgl occ from £60) but has its own honesty bar and three rooms have balconies.

In addition to the B&Bs there are plenty of **hotels**. On Wilder Rd, close to the Promenade, is *The Imperial* (☎ 01271-862536, 🖳 leisureplex.co.uk; 16S/40D/41T /7Tr, all en suite; ☛; WI-FI in public areas) which charges from £32pp (sgl occ from £32). Note that in the winter months (end Oct/early Nov to Mar) accommodation is only available Monday to Friday.

The Royal Britannia (☎ 01271-862939, 🖳 royalbritannia.co.uk; fb; 10D/ 2T/2Tr/6Qd, all en suite; ☛; 🐾) is well sited, actually overlooking the boats from its location on Broad St. Rates here are from £30pp (sgl occ from £46). Back on Fore St there is *Harcourt Hotel* (☎ 01271-862931, 🖳 harcourthotel.co.uk; fb; 2S/3D/ 1T/2D or T, all en suite; ☛; Ⓛ; 🐾); B&B rates are from £40pp (sgl from £40, sgl occ from £60). They have drying facilities.

Where to eat and drink
Tearooms and cafés A short stroll along Wilder Rd will present you with numerous tearooms and cafés, most of which also provide breakfasts and lunches. Particularly good are *Dolly's Café* (☎ 01271 863661; daily 9.30am-4.30pm, summer to late; 🐾 outside only) and *The Naked Cake* (☎ 01271-864641, 🖳 the nakedcake.business.site; fb; 🐾 outside only; Mar-Oct 10am-4pm). There's plenty of types of food including – at the latter – a range of toast with different toppings (from £6.25) as well as lots of cakes (!).

Also worth a look on St James Place is *Curiosity Cottage* (☎ 01271-863510; 🐾 garden only; Easter-Oct daily 9.30am-4.30pm) which does mini cream teas for those who are watching their waistline; whilst up on the High St is a more typical English tea room, *Swiss Cottage Café* (☎ 01271-864433, 🖳 swisscottagecafe.com; fb; Mon-Sat 9am-4pm, summer later if busy).

Down by the harbour, vegetarian and gluten-free options are available close to

the path on the corner of Hiern's Lane and Broad St at pint-sized *Adele's Café* (☎ 01271-863268; fb; Mar-Dec daily 7.30am-4pm; 🐾), plus wine, cider, real ale and, of course, cream teas.

Pubs Good pub-grub can be found at *Prince of Wales* (☎ 01271-866391; food Wed-Sun noon-9pm & bank hol Mons; 🐾) on Fore St. An old-fashioned boozer and the menu includes homemade curries.

Also on Fore St, Ilfracombe's oldest pub, dating from 1360, the *George & Dragon* (☎ 01271-863851, 🖳 georgeand dragonilfracombe.co.uk; fb; food daily noon-3pm & 6.30-9pm) has a selection of real ales, a no mobile phones policy and a menu that includes boozy beef braised in real ale (£9.50).

The Smugglers (☎ 01271-863620; fb; food Easter to Nov daily 10am-late, winter hours variable), on The Quay, is a quirky place with red leather alcoves, fish tanks set in the wall and seafaring antiquities hanging from the ceiling. The menu is huge and includes steaks and fish.

The Ship and Pilot (☎ 01271-863562; Mon-Sat 11am-midnight, Sun 11.30am-11.30pm) doesn't do food, but may interest those with a thirst for cider: there's up to 40 different types here.

Restaurants For smarter dining, on Fore St is the highly recommended, *Seventy-one Bistro* (☎ 01271-863632, 🖳 seventyone .biz; fb; school summer holidays Mon-Sat 6.30pm to late; mid Mar/Easter to July Tue-Sat 6.30pm to late, rest of year Fri & Sat 6.30pm to late, Thur if enough bookings) is great; a mouth-watering surf 'n' turf (west country rump steak and local lobster) costs £17.95, while 2-/3-course set menus cost £24/29.

Right on the harbour, *The Pier Brewery Tap & Grill* (☎ 01271-865516; fb; 11am-11pm) is a modern tap and grill serving the likes of pulled pork burgers (£9.95) and pork-and-porter sausage and mash (£10).

Spanish food is available at *The Terrace* (☎ 01271-863482, 🖳 terracetapas bar.co.uk; fb; summer daily from 6pm;

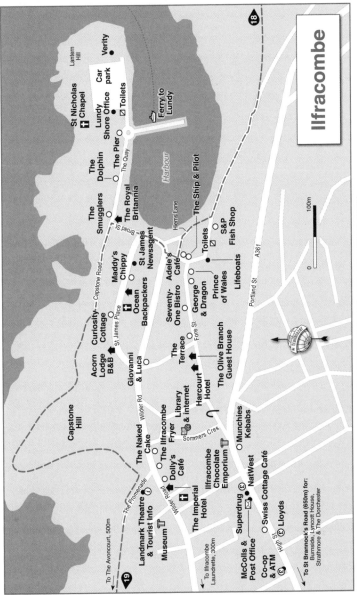

Ilfracombe

Lantern Hill

Verity

St Nicholas Chapel

Lundy Shore Office

Car park

Toilets

Ferry to Lundy

The Dolphin

The Pier

The Quay

Harbour

The Royal Britannia

The Smugglers

Broad St

The Ship & Pilot

Maddy's Chippy

St James Newsagent

Heins Lane

Toilets

S&P Fish Shop

Capstone Road

Ocean Backpackers

Seventy-One Bistro

Adele's Café

George & Dragon

Prince of Wales

Lifeboats

Curiosity Cottage

St James Place

Portland St

A361

Acorn Lodge B&B

Giovanni & Luca

The Terrace

Fore St

The Olive Branch Guest House

Capstone Hill

The Naked Cake

Wilder Rd

The Ilfracombe Fryer

Library & internet

Harcourt Hotel

Sommers Cres

Munchies Kebabs

Dolly's Café

Ilfracombe Chocolate Emporium

NatWest

The Promenade

Landmark Theatre & Tourist Info

Wilder Road

The Imperial Hotel

Museum

Superdrug

Swiss Cottage Café

High St

Co-op & ATM

Lloyds

McColls & Post Office

To The Avoncourt, 500m

To Ilfracombe Laundrette, 300m

To St Brannock's Road (650m) for: Burnside, Lyncott House, Strathmore & The Dorchester

0   100m

Trailblazer

winter Tue-Sat only) on Fore St, an award-winning tapas and wine bar. There is a gin menu to supplement the tapas (£3.75-7.95 per dish).

For authentic Italian at reasonable prices head to Wilder Rd and *Giovanni & Luca* (☎ 01271-879394, ☐ giovanniandluca.co.uk; **fb**; Mar-Oct Tue-Sun noon-2.30pm & 6-9.30pm, winter to 9pm).

Takeaways For fish 'n' chips, there is *The Ilfracombe Fryer* (☎ 01271-865003, ☐ ilfracombefryer.co.uk; **fb**; Tue-Sat noon-2pm & 5-7pm) on Wilder Rd; *Maddy's Chippy* (☎ 01271-863351; **fb**; daily noon-9pm), at 25 St James Place; or, on The Quay, *The Dolphin* (☎ 01271-879297, ☐ thedolphinilfracombe.co.uk;

fb; daily 10.30am-9.30pm). The last two are also sit-down restaurants, and Maddy's is licensed so you can enjoy a beer with your cod and chips.

If you fancy your fish straight off the trawler *S & P Fish Shop* (☎ 01271-865923, ☐ sandpfish.co.uk; **fb**; Tue-Sat 10am-3pm or later depending on demand, winter opening hours may vary) is on the harbour itself and as well as supplying takeaway, the fully-licensed café is well worth a visit! Check out their Facebook page where they regularly post their catch of the day.

High St favourite *Munchies Kebabs* (☎ 01271-855666, ☐ munchieskebab.co.uk; **fb**; Sun-Thur 4pm-midnight, Fri & Sat 4pm-3.30am) is your best option if you're all fish 'n' chipped-out!

Leaving Ilfracombe the path ventures along the hills and cliffs of **Torrs Park** before heading down to **Lee Bay**. The vale in which the nearby village of **Lee** sits is known locally as 'Fuchsia Valley' due to the abundance of the scarlet flower blossoming in the area's hedgerows at certain times of year.

There's no longer anywhere to stay in the village of Lee, but if you're in need of refreshments *The Grampus Inn* (Map 20: ☎ 01271-862906, ☐ the grampusinn.co.uk; **fb**; **food** Mon-Sat noon-3pm & 6-9pm, Sun noon-4pm) serves real ales and tasty sandwiches/ploughmans (£6-10) as well as a more hearty pub classics (mains £8.50-12.50) including ham, egg and chips (£10.50). Ilfracombe Community Transport's No 35 **bus** service calls here on a Tuesday and Friday; see pp48-50.

Becoming a little more testing, the path now makes its way along **Damage Cliffs**, a National Trust site. The trail then passes by 19th-century **Bull Point Lighthouse** (Map 21) housed in its own secure compound (the Bull Point Pen?), before following the cliff-tops to **Morte Point**, a place so wild it was once referred to locally as 'the place God made last and the Devil will take first'.

Notice that despite all this natural splendour many of the cliffs and peninsulas have such morbid names: Damage Cliffs, Breakneck Point, 'Morte' (French for 'Death') Point; shipwrecks were common here in the 19th century and many of the geological culprits were named appropriately. Indeed, Morte Point was said to be responsible for five shipwrecks in 1852 alone, while **Grunta Beach** is so named because after one unlucky ship ran aground the cargo of pigs she was carrying ran into the cove – grunting.

As you coax and tease your legs into the final stretch around Morte Point, take time to admire Baggy Point across the bay and stare in awe at the golden sands of Woolacombe's blue-flag beach: surf's up!

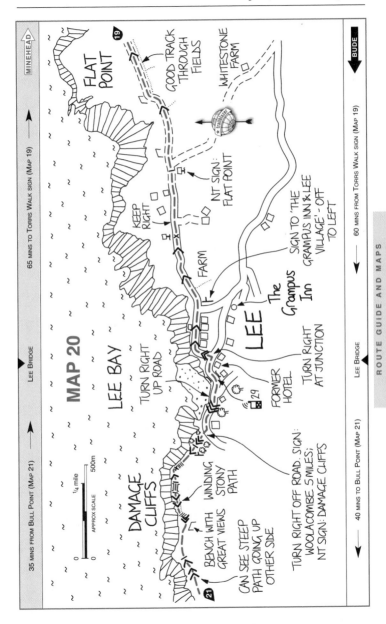

MINEHEAD

FLAT POINT

19

GOOD TRACK THROUGH FIELDS

WHITESTONE FARM

60 MINS FROM TORRS WALK SIGN (MAP 19)

BUDE

NT SIGN: FLAT POINT

65 MINS TO TORRS WALK SIGN (MAP 19)

LEE BRIDGE

KEEP RIGHT

FARM

SIGN TO 'THE GRAMPUS INN & LEE VILLAGE' - OFF TO LEFT

MAP 20

LEE BAY

TURN RIGHT UP ROAD

The Grampus Inn

LEE

TURN RIGHT AT JUNCTION

FORMER HOTEL

TURN RIGHT OFF ROAD SIGN: WOOLACOMBE 5 MILES; NT SIGN: DAMAGE CLIFFS

WINDING STONY PATH

DAMAGE CLIFFS

BENCH WITH GREAT VIEWS

CAN SEE STEEP PATH GOING UP OTHER SIDE

21

¼ mile

500m

0

0

APPROX SCALE

35 MINS FROM BULL POINT (MAP 21)

LEE BRIDGE

40 MINS TO BULL POINT (MAP 21)

ROUTE GUIDE AND MAPS

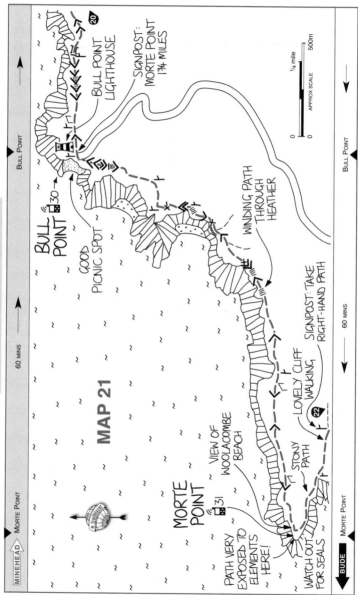

MINEHEAD ▷ MORTE POINT

← 60 MINS →

MAP 21

BULL POINT ▶ BULL POINT

20

BULL POINT LIGHTHOUSE

SIGNPOST: MORTE POINT 1¾ MILES

¼ mile

APPROX SCALE 500m

0 0

BULL POINT 30

GOOD PICNIC SPOT

WINDING PATH THROUGH HEATHER

SIGNPOST: TAKE RIGHT-HAND PATH

60 MINS

LOVELY CLIFF WALKING

22

STONY PATH

MORTE POINT 31

VIEW OF WOOLACOMBE BEACH

PATH VERY EXPOSED TO ELEMENTS HERE!

WATCH OUT FOR SEALS

MORTE POINT

BUDE ◁

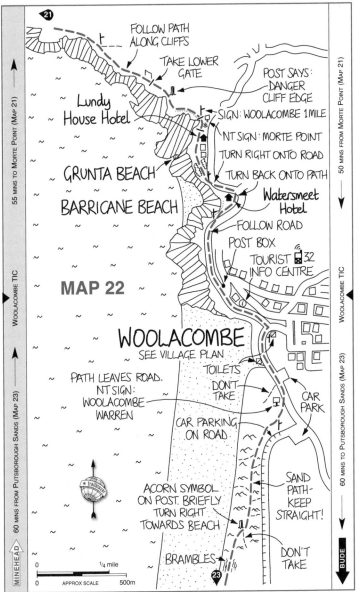

FOLLOW PATH ALONG CLIFFS

TAKE LOWER GATE

POST SAYS: DANGER CLIFF EDGE

Lundy House Hotel

SIGN: WOOLACOMBE 1 MILE

NT SIGN: MORTE POINT

TURN RIGHT ONTO ROAD

GRUNTA BEACH

TURN BACK ONTO PATH

BARRICANE BEACH

Watersmeet Hotel

FOLLOW ROAD

POST BOX

TOURIST INFO CENTRE 32

MAP 22

WOOLACOMBE
SEE VILLAGE PLAN

TOILETS

PATH LEAVES ROAD. NT SIGN: WOOLACOMBE WARREN

DON'T TAKE

CAR PARK

CAR PARKING ON ROAD

SAND PATH – KEEP STRAIGHT!

ACORN SYMBOL ON POST. BRIEFLY TURN RIGHT TOWARDS BEACH

DON'T TAKE

BRAMBLES

0   1/4 mile
0   APPROX SCALE   500m

55 MINS TO MORTE POINT (MAP 21)

WOOLACOMBE TIC

60 MINS FROM PUTSBOROUGH SANDS (MAP 23)

MINEHEAD

50 MINS FROM MORTE POINT (MAP 21)

WOOLACOMBE TIC

60 MINS TO PUTSBOROUGH SANDS (MAP 23)

BUDE

ROUTE GUIDE AND MAPS

WOOLACOMBE

Nestling at the eastern end of Morte Bay, the village of Woolacombe has a friendly and pleasant atmosphere. Stretching out to the south, its vast beach, which accompanies the path for approximately two miles (3.2km), is often granted the title of 'Britain's best beach' by traveller surveys and magazines. The view of the golden expanse as you enter the village certainly acts as a fine welcome.

The village remained pretty much untouched until a fashion for sea bathing took the country by storm in the early 19th century, leading to the village's slow conversion into a resort. Bustling now with surfers in summer, it also has all the amenities a coastal-path walker needs.

Oddly, the name 'Woolacombe' is said to have nothing to do with the large sheep population that lives hereabouts, but actually comes from Wolmecoma, or 'Wolves Valley', referring to the large wolf population that presumably lived in the woods that existed around here at one time!

Services

The helpful **tourist information centre** (☎ 01271-870553, 🖳 woolacombetourism.co .uk; Easter-Oct daily 10am-4pm, Oct-Easter Mon-Sat 10am-1/4pm weather dependent) also boasts free **internet access** and **wi-fi**: they've even got iPads for customers to use. They are also happy to book accommodation and sell tickets for Lundy. And they sell souvenirs.

You can take money out for free at the **ATM** on South St or at the one outside Barton **Pharmacy** (Mon-Fri 9am-1pm & 2-6pm, Sat 9am-4pm, Sun 10am-4pm).

The well-stocked Londis **supermarket** (daily 8.30am-8pm) on West Rd also houses the **post office** (daily 8.30am-5.30pm except Wed from 9.30am). The

newsagent, Shirley's (Mon & Tue 6.45am-7pm, Wed-Fri 6.45am-7.30pm, Sat 7am-7.30pm, Sun 7am-6.30pm), is also well stocked and sells OS maps.

Back up on South St is a **launderette** (daily 8am-6pm).

Transport

[See also pp48-50] As is usual for this path, Woolacombe is not well served by public transport. The No 31 **bus** operates to Ilfracombe while the No 303 goes to Braunton and Barnstaple. In the summer season the No 302 goes as far as Combe Martin. There are bus stops on Barton Rd and The Esplanade.

The local **taxi** firm is E Zee cabs (☎ 07966 548303 or 01271-871000, 🖳 ezeecabs.co.uk).

Where to stay

Campers will be pleased with the excellent facilities (restaurant, bar, mini supermarket, outdoor and indoor swimming pools) at *Woolacombe Sands Holiday Park* (☎ 01271-870569, 🖳 woolacombe-sands.co .uk; **fb**; £7-23pp; WI-FI free in the club house; 🐾; late Mar to Oct) on Beach Rd, though less pleased with the prices – during peak periods you'll have to pay upwards of £20 per person to sleep in your own tent! It's a 15-minute walk from the village centre; the footpath leading to it from the end of South St is preferable to the walk along busy Beach Rd.

There's a **hostel** of sorts at 3 West Rd. *The Beach House Hostel* (☎ 07500-701982, 🖳 thebeachhousedevon.co.uk; **fb**; 1T/2Tr, plus 2x4-bed dorms and 1x2-bed dorm, shared facilities; Mar-Dec) is more of a boutique hostel, with smart, comfortable rooms, but no self-catering facilities or breakfast. There is an attached restaurant

---

❑ **DOGS ON WOOLACOMBE BEACH**

Dogs are allowed on the beach but only to the south of the stream which lies a couple of hundred metres south of town (ie the main entrance to the beach) – and even then only on a lead. You can release them, however, beyond the large Mill Rock that lies at the back of the beach. There are no restrictions between December and March.

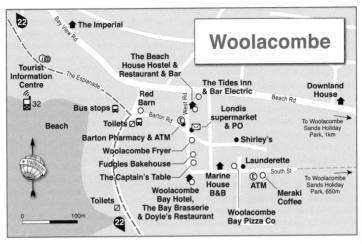

and bar, though (see Where to Eat). Rates are £38-42pp for the private rooms. Dorm beds cost £37.50-40.50.

There is some **B&B-style accommodation** too, though once again finding places suitable for walkers – ie that don't mind muddy boots and, most importantly, are willing to accept one-night bookings (see box on p132) – is surprisingly difficult.

Before you even reach the town, with private steps leading up from the path, there's *Lundy House Hotel* (Map 22; ☎ 01271-870372, ☐ lundyhousehotel.co.uk; **fb**; 6D/2D or T, all en suite; ☛; 🐾; Mar/Easter to end Oct). They charge £45-67.50pp (sgl occ room rate), but only accept advance bookings for a minimum of two nights.

Entering the village you also pass the large *Watersmeet Hotel* (Map 22; ☎ 01271-870333, ☐ watersmeethotel.co.uk; **fb**; 1S/13D/9D or T/1T/4Tr, all en suite; ☛), originally built in 1907 as an Edwardian 'Gentleman's residence' and now charging from £85pp (sgl occ full room rate). All rooms bar three have wonderful sea views.

More typical B&B accommodation can be found tucked away on South St: *Marine House* (☎ 01271-870972, ☐ marinehouse.co.uk; **fb**; 1D/1D or T, both en suite; no children) which charges £47.50pp with breakfast (sgl occ £85) and £40pp (sgl occ £72) for room only. On Bay View Rd, *The Imperial* (☎ 01271-870594, ☐ theimperialwoolacombe.co.uk; 3D/1Qd, all en suite, 1T private facilities; ☛; small 🐾; Mar-early July & Sep-end Oct) is more family-friendly (and dog-friendly) and a decent place with some lovely sea-view rooms and even a free-to-use hot tub which faces the sea. Rates here are £40-45pp (sgl occ £75). The four-person room is an annexe with one double room, one bunk-bed room and a living area. Rates for three or four people sharing a room are very reasonable at just £85 and £95 respectively. They also have some self-catering accommodation which they rent for single-night stays outside peak season (one-/two-bed apartment £85/100).

Further along Beach Rd, *Downland House* (☎ 01271-870426, ☐ downland house.co.uk; 2D both en suite/1D private bathroom; ☛; late Mar-end Oct) has three south-facing rooms with private balconies from which you can see Baggy Point and Lundy. It was temporarily closed at the time of research so call them for information about reopening and current rates.

By far the grandest place in the village is *Woolacombe Bay Hotel* (☎ 01271-870388, ☐ woolacombe-bay-hotel.co.uk;

ROUTE GUIDE AND MAPS

64 rooms inc 26D/4T, rest can be adapted for three/four sharing, all en suite; ☛; Feb-Dec), with a wellness spa, a beautiful outdoor swimming pool complex and even its own cinema! All the rooms are stylish and some are nothing short of huge. They charge from £62.50pp (sgl occ from £105) but note that one-night bookings are rarely accepted.

Where to eat and drink

There is a decent range of places to eat in Woolacombe. For the best coffee in town, head to *Meraki Coffee* (**fb**; daily 8.30am-3pm), a small, modern café on South St, which also does cakes, pastries and a few breakfasts – try the eggs Benedict, or the pancakes. For a more substantial morning fry-up head to *The Captain's Table* (☎ 01271-870618; **fb**; food Mar-Oct daily 8.30am-6pm, summer up to 9pm but weather/business dependent; well-behaved 🐾). The menu includes a number of breakfasts, as well as sandwiches, jacket potatoes, pasta and burgers.

The Beach House Restaurant & Bar (☎ 07817-127916, ☐ thebeachhousedevon .co.uk; **fb**; Mon, Tue & Thur-Sat noon-10pm, Wed 5.30-10pm, Sun noon-6pm) is one of Woolacombe's better restaurants, and has a menu (mains £13-25) that includes Devon crab, slow braised pork belly, and linguini pasta with tiger prawns and mussels. The terrace is a great spot for wine and sunsets.

Next door is *The Tides Inn* (☎ 01271-871420, ☐ tidesinnwoolacombe.co.uk; **fb**; food daily summer holidays noon-2.30pm & 6-9pm, winter evenings only; 🐾), another bar and bistro with a large sun terrace and a menu including seafood chowder (£16) and pork ribs (£17.50). Below it and part of the same building, *Bar Electric* (☎ 01271-870429, ☐ barelectric.co.uk; **fb**; food summer daily 9am-9pm, rest of year Fri-Sun 9am-9pm; 🐾) produces gastro-pub style food including stone-baked pizzas (£10-13).

By the main junction in town and with good views of the sea, family friendly *Red Barn* (☎ 01271-870264, ☐ redbarnwoola combe.co.uk; **fb**; food daily noon-8pm) is one of Woolacombe's livelier places, complemented by surfers watching for waves and live music on Fridays (Mar-Dec). The menu includes mussels in cider and wild mushroom risotto. There are also well-priced burgers, sandwiches and pasties.

The Bay Brasserie is one of two fine eateries at Woolacombe Bay Hotel (see Where to stay; daily noon-3pm & 6-9pm), where the menu includes pizza and pasta (£10.50-12.50) as well as a fish of the day. More upmarket, *Doyle's Restaurant* (daily 7-9pm; mains £14-24) serves the likes of lamb neck fillet with minted new potatoes, and charred and roasted whole aubergine with garlic and basil couscous.

Takeaway can be found at *Woolacombe Bay Pizza Company* (☎ 01271-871222, ☐ woolacombepizza.co.uk; **fb**; Apr-Sep daily noon-11pm, Oct-Mar hours variable), which serves pizzas with standard toppings from £6.50, and at *Woolacombe Fryer* (☎ 01271-870752, ☐ woolacombefryer.com; **fb**; summer daily noon-9pm, out of season Thur-Sat noon-3pm & 5-8pm, Sun noon-5pm), 1 Barton Rd, where you'll discover fabulous fish 'n' chips.

For supreme pasties, made-to-order baguettes and other baked goodies, swing by *Fudgies Bakehouse* (☎ 01271-870622; **fb**; daily 10am-4pm) on West Rd.

❏ WHERE TO STAY: THE DETAILS

In the descriptions of accommodation in this book: ☛ means at least one room has a bath; Ⓛ means a packed lunch can be prepared if arranged in advance; 🐾 signifies that dogs are welcome in at least one room but also subject to prior arrangement. Note that virtually everywhere only accepts advance bookings for a minimum stay of two nights at peak periods such as weekends, bank holidays and school holiday periods.

Above: The Lynton & Lynmouth Cliff Railway connects these two villages and is the steepest and highest water-powered railway in the world. Opened in 1890 it's still fully operational. See p104.

Left: Sublime walking on top of the forested cliffs near Foreland Point (Map 10; bottom photo © Yoyo McCrohan). **Above**: Culbone Church (see p94). **Bottom**: Hawker's Hut (see p198).

Above: There's a lot to carry if you want to camp but the rewards are many. **Below**: Bringing a stove (**left**) guarantees lunch with a view (© S McCrohan). Camping above Croyde beach (**right**).

Above: Colourful beach huts at Crooklets Beach (Map 54). **Below**: Ilfracombe (see p120).

Above and right: The unique village of Clovelly, famed for its cobblestone street that leads down to the harbour but is too steep for vehicles. Instead, deliveries are made by wooden sled! (See p180).

Top: Barefoot across Croyde Beach (Map 25). **Middle**: There are several open-air seawater pools on this walk, such as this one at Westward Ho! (Map 39). **Bottom**: The golden sands of Northam Burrows Country Park (Map 38; photo © Joel Newton).

WOOLACOMBE TO BRAUNTON [MAPS 22-28]

This **14¾-mile (23.8km; 6½hrs inc 10 mins from Velator Bridge to Braunton)** stage is the most diverse in this book. From the cliffs and beaches surrounding Woolacombe and Croyde to the more easygoing terrain through Braunton Burrows – the focal point of the North Devon UNESCO Biosphere Reserve (see box p142) – this is a fulfilling although physically undemanding day's walk.

Magnificent, sweeping views from Baggy Point across the busy sands of Woolacombe and Croyde contrast sharply with the bleaker beauty of Braunton Burrows and the lonely Taw Estuary, where the only sounds are the slap of rope against mast or the shrill whistle of an oystercatcher on the wing.

Diverse though the landscape may be on this stage, there can be no doubt that the predominant features are the beaches. There are in fact three vast stretches of golden sand, each separated by a single grassy promontory. The first, Woolacombe, has of course been visible since you rounded Morte Point on the previous stage and is one of the bigger beaches on the entire path – a vast flat bronze plain that stretches for almost two miles from the village to Baggy Point.

Take a stroll around this promontory and you'll then be greeted by the sight of Croyde, Woolacombe's trendier, more glamorous neighbour and rival and a favourite with surfers and families, even though the beach is considerably smaller. Then less than an hour's walk from the end of Croyde beach lies the even vaster beach at Saunton.

Indeed, the only disappointment with these beaches is that, officially, the SWCP doesn't cross any of them, preferring instead to pick its way between the sand dunes at the back of the beach – though only the most pedantic of coastal walkers will choose to stick to the path rather than kick their boots off and stroll along the flats. The exception to this is Saunton Sands, parts of which are used by the army for training practice and thus access is limited. But even here the coastal walker is well compensated as the dunes at the back of Saunton form Braunton Burrows Nature Reserve, the largest sand dune system in England and home to rare lizards and snails.

There are numerous places to stop for refreshments along the way including both Croyde and Saunton, though Saunton itself can be bypassed via an alternative path which, if taken, will be the last gradient of any description you'll encounter until Westward Ho!, over two days away. Stick to the main trail, however, and you'll be forced instead to walk along the busy, pavementless Saunton Rd – the worst bit of walking on this path.

Continuing on through the Burrows, and along the banks of the Taw – the favoured home of egrets, godwits, herons and oystercatchers – you pass Horsey Island and follow the River Caen, eventually finding yourself on the outskirts of Braunton and the end of this stage.

(cont'd on p136)

ROUTE GUIDE AND MAPS

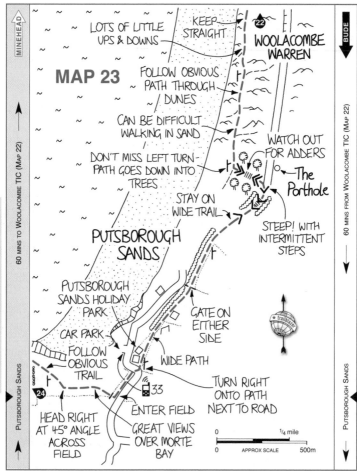

MINEHEAD

LOTS OF LITTLE UPS & DOWNS

KEEP STRAIGHT

22 WOOLACOMBE WARREN

BUDE

MAP 23

FOLLOW OBVIOUS PATH THROUGH DUNES

60 MINS TO WOOLACOMBE TIC (MAP 22)

CAN BE DIFFICULT WALKING IN SAND

DON'T MISS LEFT TURN - PATH GOES DOWN INTO TREES

WATCH OUT FOR ADDERS

The Porthole

60 MINS FROM WOOLACOMBE TIC (MAP 22)

STAY ON WIDE TRAIL

PUTSBOROUGH SANDS

STEEP! WITH INTERMITTENT STEPS

ROUTE GUIDE AND MAPS

PUTSBOROUGH SANDS HOLIDAY PARK

CAR PARK

FOLLOW OBVIOUS TRAIL

GATE ON EITHER SIDE

WIDE PATH

33

TURN RIGHT ONTO PATH NEXT TO ROAD

24

PUTSBOROUGH SANDS

HEAD RIGHT AT 45° ANGLE ACROSS FIELD

ENTER FIELD

GREAT VIEWS OVER MORTE BAY

0   1/4 mile

0   APPROX SCALE   500m

PUTSBOROUGH SANDS

☐ **IMPORTANT NOTE – WALKING TIMES**
Unless otherwise specified, **all times in this book refer only to the time spent walk-ing**. You will need to add 20-30% to allow for rests, photography, checking the map, drinking water etc, not to mention time simply to stop and stare at the beautiful scenery. When planning the day's hike count on 5-7 hours' actual walking.

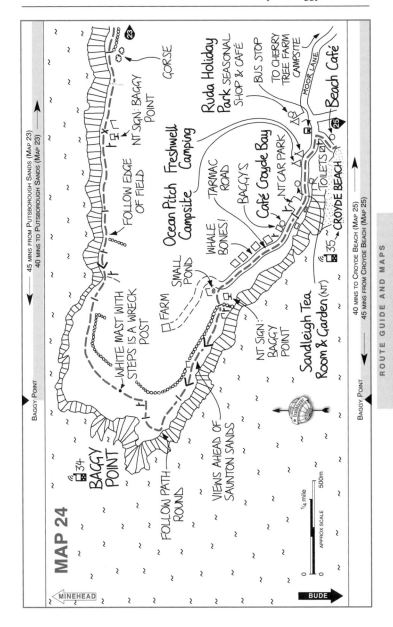

MAP 24

BAGGY POINT

45 MINS FROM PUTSBOROUGH SANDS (MAP 23)
40 MINS TO PUTSBOROUGH SANDS (MAP 23)

23

GORSE

NT SIGN: BAGGY POINT

FOLLOW EDGE OF FIELD

Ruda Holiday Park SEASONAL SHOP & CAFÉ

BUS STOP

TO CHERRY TREE FARM CAMPSITE

MOOR LANE

Beach Café

25

Ocean Pitch Campsite

Freshwell Camping

TARMAC ROAD

Café Croyde Bay

BAGGY'S

NT CAR PARK

WHALE BONES!

TOILETS

35

CROYDE BEACH

40 MINS TO CROYDE BEACH (MAP 25)
45 MINS FROM CROYDE BEACH (MAP 25)

WHITE MAST WITH STEPS IS A WRECK POST

SMALL POND

FARM

NT SIGN: BAGGY POINT

Sandleigh Tea Room & Garden (NT)

BAGGY POINT

VIEWS AHEAD OF SAUNTON SANDS

34

BAGGY POINT

FOLLOW PATH ROUND

¼ mile

500m

APPROX SCALE

0

0

MINEHEAD

BUDE

The route

The day starts simply enough with a walk through the sand dunes of **Woolacombe Warren** (Map 23) where, if you're in need of a pick-me-up, *The Porthole* (☎ 07533 333976 or 07507-906005; **fb**; daily 10am-5pm) can deliver coffee, cake and sandwiches from its wood-cabin perch above **Putsborough Sands**. From there you start the haul to Baggy Point. Note, if the tide allows, you can just walk straight along the beach cutting through the car park at the beach's southern end to rejoin the main trail.

A splendid stroll leads to **Baggy Point**. Owned by the National Trust and a popular spot with climbers, it is also part of an SSSI (see p61) – of scientific interest due to its mixture of Devonian Age (417-354 million years ago) stone. The **white mast** is a 'wreck post' – a spot where, if the sea was too rough to launch a lifeboat but a shipwreck was close enough to the shore, a pulley system would be set up (using a cannon to fire one end of the rope out to the ship) between the point and the ship's mast in order to rescue the stranded sailors. There are tremendous views of Lundy and along the coast to Croyde Bay and Saunton Sands from here.

The clusters of buildings that you can see in the far distance are Westward Ho!, Clovelly and Hartland Point. As you walk around the point admire the views south and imagine the American troops practising for D-day on the sands below you as you stroll into Croyde. General Eisenhower and the Allied leaders decided that the beaches of Woolacombe, Croyde and Saunton most closely resembled those on France's Normandy coast, thus they were used for rehearsing for the big day. WWII pillboxes on Croydehoe Farm can still be seen.

On your way into **Croyde** and slightly before the National Trust car park for Baggy Point is *Café Croyde Bay* (see Map 24; ☎ 0800-1884860, 🖥 cafecroyde bay.co.uk; **fb**; summer Mon-Wed 9am-4pm, Thur-Sun 8.30am-10pm) serving an all-day brunch menu plus hot drinks and alcoholic beverages. Also here, the former Baggy Lodge hostel has been completely refurbished as a 'boutique hostel' and rebranded **Baggy's** (🖥 baggys.co.uk), but with a minimum stay of seven nights in the peak season and three nights off-peak, it's aimed squarely at beach-loving families rather than coast path walkers wanting a bed for just one night.

Sandleigh Tea Room and Garden (☎ 01271-890930, 🖥 nationaltrust .org.uk/baggy-point; **fb**; Feb-Oct daily 10am-4pm, main season to 5pm), just beyond the car park, is a glorious place. Run by the National Trust, it serves delights such as homity pie, crab sandwiches and cream teas with strawberries. Cake and coffee, too. On the path leading down to the beach, *Beach Café* (10am-4.30pm) keeps surfers happy with breakfast baps, burgers and the like.

CROYDE   [see map p139]

Croyde can feel as if its sole purpose is to serve its beach and its world-class surf. However, people were aware of the bay way before surfing took off in Cornwall in the 1960s. The village actually has an ancient heart which you can see if you look amongst the noisy bars of the village centre (which is about 15 minutes back from the beach that has earned Croyde its popularity). Indeed, some of the B&Bs and pubs

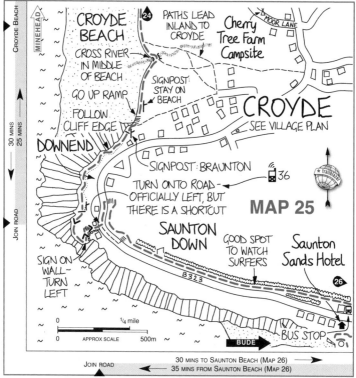

CROYDE BEACH

MINEHEAD

CROYDE BEACH

CROSS RIVER IN MIDDLE OF BEACH

GO UP RAMP

FOLLOW CLIFF EDGE

DOWNEND

30 MINS

25 MINS

JOIN ROAD

PATHS LEAD INLAND TO CROYDE

SIGNPOST: STAY ON BEACH

SIGNPOST: BRAUNTON

TURN ONTO ROAD - OFFICIALLY LEFT, BUT THERE IS A SHORTCUT

SAUNTON DOWN

SIGN ON WALL~ TURN LEFT

Cherry Tree Farm Campsite

MOOR LANE

CROYDE

SEE VILLAGE PLAN

36

MAP 25

GOOD SPOT TO WATCH SURFERS

Saunton Sands Hotel

B323

26

0   1/4 mile
0   APPROX SCALE   500m

BUS STOP

BUDE

JOIN ROAD

30 MINS TO SAUNTON BEACH (MAP 26)
35 MINS FROM SAUNTON BEACH (MAP 26)

ROUTE GUIDE AND MAPS

are housed in buildings that are over 300 years old. But if you're not planning on staying in Croyde, you can forego them altogether, for the coast path continues to hug the beach.

The **post office** (Mon, Tue, Thur & Fri 8am-5.30pm, Wed & Sat 8am-12.30pm) has a **shop** (Mon-Sat 8am-5.30pm, Sun 8am-1pm) and an **ATM**, as does Billy Budd's (see Where to eat), though both charge a small fee for their use. Debit/credit cards are readily accepted throughout the village but if you're desperate for money free of charge you will have to go to the big Tesco supermarket outside Braunton.

See p16 for details of the GoldCoast Oceanfest.

Transport

[See also pp48-50] Stagecoach's 21C **bus** runs regularly to Barnstaple.

If you wish to go north to Woolacombe or Ilfracombe you will need to change in either Braunton or Barnstaple.

There are **bus stops** near Billy Budd's in the centre of the village as well as nearer the beach close to Ruda Holiday Park.

For a **taxi** try Croyde Coastal (☎ 07788-703188, ☐ croydecoastal.co.uk).

Where to stay

Croyde has a number of **campsites**. There's a cluster of informal ones at the northern end of the beach that are favourites for surfers, including *Ocean Pitch Campsite*

(Map 24; ☎ 07581 024348, 🖳 ocean
pitch.co.uk; **fb**; £15pp; Easter-Oct) and
Freshwell Camping (Map 24; ☎ 07376
497637, 🖳 croydefreshwellcamping.co.uk;
fb; adult/child £15/7.50; Easter-Oct), both
of which have free-to-use portacabin shower blocks and a laidback vibe. Freshwell
Camping is listed as an 'Accommodation
Way Maker' on the SW Coast Path, offering single night pitches to walkers, as well
as the option of luggage transfer (separate
charge applies).

Nearby, *Ruda Holiday Park* (Map 24;
☎ 0330-1234850 or 0333-2076863, 🖳
parkdeanresorts.co.uk/location/devon/ruda;
£14-50 per pitch; mid Mar to end Oct) is a
behemoth with its own Costcutter **supermarket** (daily 8am-6pm) and *café* (daily
10am-6pm, later if resident), both of which
are open when the park is open. You usually have to book for at least two nights,
though, and peak-season prices are extor-
tionate.

Smaller and cheaper than Ruda are *Bay
View Farm Campsite* (☎ 01271-890501, 🖳
bayviewfarm.co.uk; **fb**; Easter-Sep; £26-31
per pitch) and *Cherry Tree Farm Campsite*
(☎ 01271-890495, 🖳 cherrytreecamping
croyde.co.uk; **fb**; adult/child £14/7; May
half-term & mid July to late Aug); the latter,
despite advertising a minimum three-night
stay policy, will often allow walkers to stay
for only one night.

In central Croyde, *The Orchard
Campsite* (☎ 07779-371195, 🖳 theorchard
campsitecroyde.co.uk; adult/child £14/8;
🐾) is a small site run by the same family
who own Bridge Farm B&B (see below).
They always try to squeeze hikers in but
booking is recommended, particularly for
Bank holiday weekends.

For **B&Bs**, at the southern end of the
beach look on Croyde Rd, which runs into
Hobbs Hill – the centre of the village. Close
to both the beach and the path you will find
Breakers (☎ 01271-890101, 🖳 croyde
breaks.co.uk; 2D/1T/1Tr, all en suite; Ⓛ;
Easter to end Oct), which charges from
£50pp (sgl occ £60), but does not usually
take one-night bookings; and the small and
family-run *Shuna Guesthouse* (☎ 01271-

890537, 🖳 shunaguesthouse.co.uk; 5D, all
en suite) which charges £40-50pp (sgl occ
£85). A little closer to the village is *The
Whiteleaf* (☎ 01271-890266, 🖳 thewhite
leaf.co.uk; 3D/1T/1Qd, all en suite; 🛆; Ⓛ);
the tariff here is £45-47pp (sgl occ from
£70).

More central still is *The Thatch* pub
(☎ 01271-890349, 🖳 thethatchcroyde.com;
fb; 10D/5T/2Tr, bunk-bed room, most en
suite but three rooms share facilities; 🛆; Ⓛ
; 🐾), whose rooms are in four different
buildings, including some at *Billy Budd's*
(see Where to eat), *Crosscombe Cottage*
and *The Priory*. B&B costs from £55pp
(sgl occ rates available on request). Two-
night minimum stay.

The most charming place to stay is
right in the village centre. The pretty,
thatched *Bridge Farm* (☎ 01271-890422;
2D en suite/1Tr private facilities; 🛆; 🐾;
Easter to end Oct/Nov), at 8 Jones Hill, is,
according to the owner, at least 400 years
old. The place is quirky and full of character – as you'd expect from a house this old
– and the owners are pleasant too. It also
provides a lovely contrast to the sometimes
brash and noisy street outside. The tariff is
from £35pp (sgl occ full room rate).

Where to eat and drink

Croyde Ice Cream Parlour (**fb**; summer
10am-10pm, spring & autumn to 5.30pm),
in the centre on Hobb's Hill, is famed in the
village because of its use of clotted cream
as one of its toppings!

New Coast Kitchen (formerly The
Stores Croyde; ☎ 01271-316026; 🖳 new
coastkitchen.co.uk; **fb**; Tue-Sat 9am-2pm
& 6-11pm, Sun 9am-3pm, closed Monday)
opened during the pandemic offering a regularly changing menu of brunch and dinner
dishes (mains from £14).

For a pub meal try *Billy Budd's* (☎
01271-890606, 🖳 billybudds.co.uk; **fb**;
daily noon-10pm; WI-FI) which has Sky TV
and does pizzas (£11-13.50), burgers
(£11.95-14.95), nachos (£7.95-12.95) and
the like.

Pretty much next door, *The Thatch*
(see Where to stay; daily 8am-10pm) is

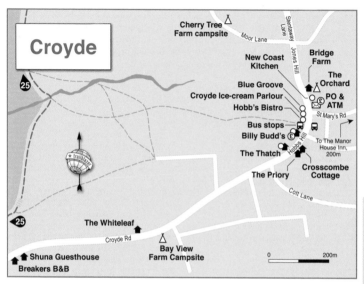

known for its beef nachos (£11-13), but does pub classics too (£13-14.50). It's a large pub with surfboards hanging off the walls and daily surf reports adorning them as well as real ales such as Proper Job and Tribute.

At *The Manor House Inn* (☎ 01271-890241, ☐ themanorcroyde.co.uk; **fb**; food daily noon-10pm), a few hundred metres from the village centre, at 39 St Mary's Rd, the menu is extensive and includes mains such as Thai red curry (£13.95) and steak and ale pie (£14.95). They also serve real ales.

Hobb's Bistro (☎ 01271-890256, ☐

hobbsbistrocroyde.co.uk; **fb**; daily 6-9pm, school hols Tue-Sat 9am-2pm) is the smartest place in town and does steak, burgers and pizza as well as more refined mains such as lamb tagine (£15.85) and Keralan cauliflower and red pepper curry (£13.95). Just a few yards down the hill, *Blue Groove* (☎ 01271-890111, ☐ blue-groove.co.uk; **fb**; mid Mar-Oct daily 9am-10pm, Nov & Dec Fri & Sat 10am-late, Sun & Mon 10am-4pm, closed Jan-mid Mar) serves breakfasts (from £5.95), lunches and evening meals, though it's best known for its mussels (small/large £9.75-16.50), especially *moules frites*.

Having navigated **Croyde Sands** a small headland, called **Downend**, from where you can sometimes see dolphins swimming off the coast, separates you from Saunton. Round this and the path drops down to the busy B3231 before running around the side, and then the front, of Saunton Sands Hotel (see p140).

From the car park below the hotel the path heads up the slope on the tarmac, turning off right halfway up (unmarked) to walk around the back of houses before rejoining the B3231 for an unpleasant, though short stretch of pavement-less road walking. Thankfully, there is an alternative.

The alternative route begins after you reach Saunton Sands Hotel, though the price you pay is to climb instead the biggest gradient between Woolacombe and Westward Ho!. This route then passes through a couple of fields before dropping down via elegant Saunton Court to a crossroads, where you rejoin the main trail. Turn left at the crossroads if going to Lobbs Field Caravan and Camping Park (see below).

SAUNTON [MAP 26]

Despite Saunton's far larger beach there are fewer amenities than in Croyde, with scant options for food and accommodation.

The beach is renowned for its wildlife, with the possibility of spying oystercatchers, cormorants, and numerous other birds. From the shore you might see porpoise, seals and possibly dolphins in summer. Fishermen have reported foxes and even otters sneaking up behind them in attempts to steal their catch!

If wishing to get a **bus** (see pp48-50), the No 21C service stops by Saunton Sands Hotel.

The nearest **campsite** is 1¼ miles along the road (B3231) although there is an alternative way, leading via a series of footpaths, to the top of the campsite; this is worth doing as the road is very busy. From the road by Saunton Court, turn left up unmade Hannaburrow Lane to Long Lane (first turning on the right). Follow this to the road junction, then take a right down Lobthorn Lane, following it down the hill until you can see Lobb Fields campsite. ***Lobb Fields Caravan and Camping Park*** (☎ 01271-812090, 🖳 lobbfields.com; **fb**; 🐕; walkers £6-8pp; mid Mar-late Oct) has its own snack bar and a laundry room.

The only other option, if you can afford it, is ***Saunton Sands Hotel*** (Map 25; ☎ 01271-890212, 🖳 sauntonsands.co.uk; **fb**; 11S/79D or T, all en suite; ▼; Ⓛ), which is something of a landmark. Owned by the local Brend chain, this whitewashed colossus can be seen along the coast from as far away as Westward Ho!. Rates start at around £80pp (sgl occ from £80), out of season, but they also have special offers so it is worth contacting them to check. The rooms are comfortable without being remarkable – but, given the magnificent views along the three-mile beach from most of them, who cares! – and some can have additional beds. Note that in the summer school holidays it's week-long stays only, and at Easter guests are required to stay for a minimum of three nights. **Food** is served daily from 7.30am till about 9.30pm.

There are two other options for **food** by the sand. ***Saunton Break Café*** (☎ 01271-890077; **fb**; summer Mon-Fri 9am-5pm, Sat & Sun to 6pm, weekends only in winter) is a takeaway which sells pasties and sandwiches. Note that their opening hours are variable depending on the season and the weather on the day. ***Beachside Grill*** (☎ 01271-891288, 🖳 beachsidegrill.co.uk; **fb**; food daily 11am-9.30pm) is owned by the hotel and has a sizeable balcony with magnificent views. The menu's impressive too, including open grilled sandwiches (£9-14), Exmoor steaks (£22-24) and mussels in Devon cider (£12).

The path then heads off along the edge of a **golf course** and through a **military training area** to **Braunton Burrows** (see box on p142). Note, it's very exposed here, with almost no shade along the path, so make sure you're carrying plenty of water.

Leaving the Burrows you take a sharp left-turn before **Crow Point**, a spit of land popular with fishermen, before taking a path atop an embankment that was built in 1857 to keep marsh, estuary and river apart. During WWII the marshes were turned into a dummy airfield in the hope of distracting the

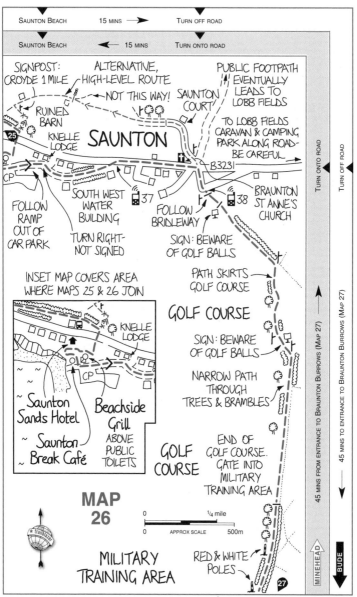

SAUNTON BEACH ◄ 15 MINS ──► TURN OFF ROAD

SAUNTON BEACH ◄── 15 MINS TURN ONTO ROAD

SIGNPOST: CROYDE 1 MILE

ALTERNATIVE, HIGH-LEVEL ROUTE

NOT THIS WAY!

SAUNTON COURT

PUBLIC FOOTPATH EVENTUALLY LEADS TO LOBB FIELDS

RUINED BARN

KNELLE LODGE

SAUNTON

TO LOBB FIELDS CARAVAN & CAMPING PARK ALONG ROAD - BE CAREFUL

25

B3231

FOLLOW RAMP OUT OF CAR PARK

SOUTH WEST WATER BUILDING

📱 37

FOLLOW BRIDLEWAY

📱 38

BRAUNTON ST ANNE'S CHURCH

TURN ONTO ROAD

TURN OFF ROAD

TURN RIGHT - NOT SIGNED

SIGN: BEWARE OF GOLF BALLS

INSET MAP COVERS AREA WHERE MAPS 25 & 26 JOIN

PATH SKIRTS GOLF COURSE

GOLF COURSE

KNELLE LODGE

SIGN: BEWARE OF GOLF BALLS

CP

NARROW PATH THROUGH TREES & BRAMBLES

~ Saunton Sands Hotel

~ Saunton Break Café

Beachside Grill ABOVE PUBLIC TOILETS

GOLF COURSE

END OF GOLF COURSE. GATE INTO MILITARY TRAINING AREA

45 MINS FROM ENTRANCE TO BRAUNTON BURROWS (MAP 27)

45 MINS TO ENTRANCE TO BRAUNTON BURROWS (MAP 27)

ROUTE GUIDE AND MAPS

MAP 26

0 ¼ mile
0 APPROX SCALE 500m

MILITARY TRAINING AREA

RED & WHITE POLES

27

MINEHEAD

BUDE

❏ **BRAUNTON BURROWS AND THE NORTH DEVON UNESCO**
BIOSPHERE RESERVE
Braunton Burrows is the centre of The North Devon UNESCO Biosphere Reserve (🖳 northdevonbiosphere.org.uk), an area of 3300 sq km that, according to the United Nations, encompasses a 'world-class environment' rich in wildlife and containing a mix of extraordinary landscapes. As well as the Burrows, the Biosphere Reserve includes **Braunton Marsh and Great Field**, the **Taw and Torridge Estuary**, **Fremington Quay** and **Northam Burrows Country Park**. No wonder, therefore, that there are over 60 SSSIs (see p61) within the area's boundaries.

The Burrows themselves are home to a wide variety of flora and fauna, as well as the largest sand dune system in England. There are nearly 500 recorded species of **flowering plants** on the site, including such rarities as the sand toadflax, which is unique to the Burrows, the water germander and the round-headed club-rush. There are also 33 species of **butterfly**, over half of Great Britain's regularly recorded species. For enthusiasts, resident is the small blue butterfly (*Cupido minimus*), although you are far more likely to spot a dark green fritillary (*Argynnis aglaja*) or marbled white (*Melanargia galathea*). **Guided tours** of the Burrows run regularly throughout the summer. Details can be found on the website of the Braunton Countryside Centre (🖳 brauntoncountrysidecentre.org).

enemy's attention away from the nearby Chivenor Airbase. Note, the path that goes around Horsey Island (Map 28) is no longer the official SWCP route as erosion has made it dangerous in places.

On the other side of the estuary you can see the villages of Appledore and Instow, possibly still a day's walk away. Wrecked boats and small fishing craft are dotted about in the sand as you stroll on along the riverside. Between Braunton and the Burrows lie the 350 acres of **Braunton Great Field** – a famous archaeological site and one of only two medieval field systems to survive in England. Some of the 'strip' system which parcelled up this land is still visible.

Eventually you arrive at **Velator Bridge** and, a few hundred metres further on, a roundabout where, on a hot day, you'll find it hard to resist stopping for a coffee or an ice cream at *Quay Café* (Map 29: ☎ 01271 268180, 🖳 thequay cafe.com; **fb**; daily 9am-6pm), a bright modern café that also does toasties, breakfast baps, sandwiches and pizza.

From here, you have a choice: turn right and continue along the Coast Path, which here, together with the Tarka Trail (see box p34), makes its merry way along a disused rail-track. Or you can turn left, cross the roundabout to South St and head along the disused railway line in the other direction on the marked footpath to Braunton. **Braunton** has several services and is a pleasant-enough village but if you feel up to walking a further 5½ miles there is more to distract you in Barnstaple. If you need a loo-stop or just wish to pick up supplies there is a **Tesco Superstore** (Mon-Sat 6am-midnight, Sun 10am-4pm) approximately 200 metres from the roundabout (see Map 29).

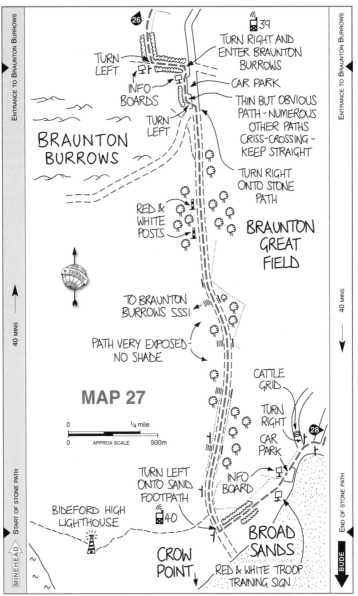

26

📱39
TURN RIGHT AND
ENTER BRAUNTON
BURROWS

TURN
LEFT

CAR PARK

INFO
BOARDS

THIN BUT OBVIOUS
PATH - NUMEROUS
OTHER PATHS
CRISS-CROSSING -
KEEP STRAIGHT

TURN
LEFT

BRAUNTON
BURROWS

TURN RIGHT
ONTO STONE
PATH

RED &
WHITE
POSTS

BRAUNTON
GREAT
FIELD

TO BRAUNTON
BURROWS SSSI

PATH VERY EXPOSED -
NO SHADE

CATTLE
GRID

TURN
RIGHT

28

CAR
PARK

MAP 27

0   ¼ mile
0   APPROX SCALE   500m

TURN LEFT
ONTO SAND
FOOTPATH
📱40

INFO
BOARD

BIDEFORD HIGH
LIGHTHOUSE

BROAD
SANDS

CROW
POINT

RED & WHITE TROOP
TRAINING SIGN

40 MINS

40 MINS

ROUTE GUIDE AND MAPS

MINEHEAD   START OF STONE PATH

BUDE   END OF STONE PATH

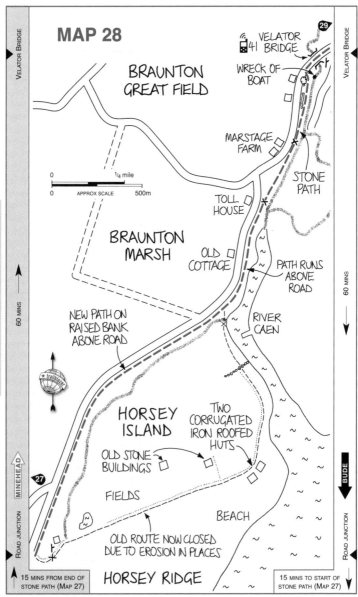

MAP 28

BRAUNTON
GREAT FIELD

VELATOR BRIDGE

29

📱41 VELATOR
BRIDGE

WRECK OF
BOAT

MARSTAGE
FARM

STONE
PATH

TOLL
HOUSE

0   1/4 mile
0   APPROX SCALE   500m

BRAUNTON
MARSH

OLD
COTTAGE

PATH RUNS
ABOVE
ROAD

RIVER
CAEN

NEW PATH ON
RAISED BANK
ABOVE ROAD

60 MINS

trailblazer

HORSEY
ISLAND

TWO
CORRUGATED
IRON ROOFED
HUTS

OLD STONE
BUILDINGS

MINEHEAD

27

FIELDS

BEACH

BUDE

OLD ROUTE NOW CLOSED
DUE TO EROSION IN PLACES

HORSEY RIDGE

15 MINS FROM END OF
STONE PATH (MAP 27)

15 MINS TO START OF
STONE PATH (MAP 27)

VELATOR BRIDGE

60 MINS

ROAD JUNCTION

ROAD JUNCTION

ROUTE GUIDE AND MAPS

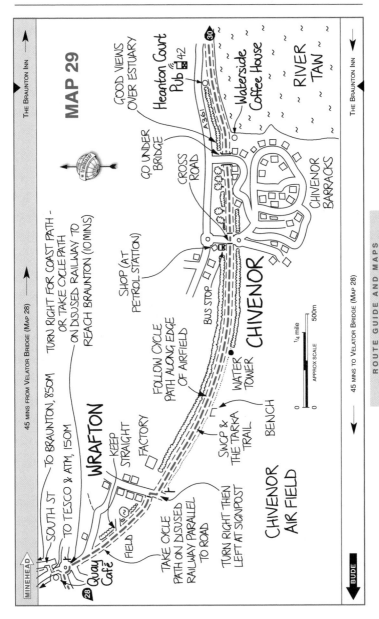

MAP 29

BRAUNTON

Recorded as Brantona in the Domesday Book, some claim Braunton to be the largest village in England and, as a result, it's more like a small town. Settlement is reputed to have begun in earnest around **St Brannock's Church**, originally founded by the eponymous saint in c550AD as part of his campaign to convert the Celts. His remains are said to be buried there. Braunton's debt to the saint is celebrated with a three-day festival of music, dance and literature around 26 June, St Brannock's Day.

Braunton and District Museum (☎ 01271-816688, 🖳 devonmuseums.net/braunton; Feb-Dec Mon-Fri 10am-3pm, Sat to 1pm; free but donations appreciated) has several interesting displays on the local area spread over two floors. **Braunton Countryside Centre** (☎ 01271-817171, 🖳 brauntoncountrysidecentre.org; May-Oct Wed & Sat 10am-4pm; donations also appreciated) has displays about the local nature and also offers 'Braunton Explorers' – personal GPS systems (£5 per day) that guide you via a set of headphones around different areas of interest in the area including the Burrows. Also available are tours of Braunton's industrial past and another entitled 'D-day and the dunes.'

The quirky **Museum of British Surfing** (☎ 01271-815155, 🖳 museumofbritishsurfing.org.uk; **fb**; Easter-Dec Tue-Sat 10am-3pm; £2) is next door.

Services

Braunton Information Centre (🖳 visitbraunton.co.uk) shares both its walls, phone number and opening hours with the town's museum and is staffed by exceedingly helpful local volunteers. They have information about accommodation but can't book it.

For an **ATM**, you'll have to go to the big Tesco supermarket, south of town, back near the coast path (off Map 29). For **food** there is a Co-op (daily 7am-10pm) on Exeter Rd, and a well-stocked local grocer's, Cawthornes Foodmarket (daily 8.30am-8pm) on Caen St. For a **chemist** there's a Lloyds Pharmacy (Mon-Fri 8.30am-6.30pm, Sat to 1pm) near the museums.

Braunton **launderette** (daily 6am-9pm) is on South St.

Transport

[See also pp48-50] For **buses**, the No 21 & 21C and the No 303 services pass through regularly whilst travelling to and from the surrounding towns and villages.

For a **taxi** try Shoreline Taxi (☎ 07812-104034, 🖳 shorelinetaxi.co.uk).

Where to stay

Centrally, *The George Inn* ☎ 01271-814903, 🖳 thegeorgeinnbraunton.com; **fb**; 5D, all en suite; 🐾 £10; (L) is a large establishment in the heart of Braunton; as well as its five rooms (from £50pp, sgl occ full room rate) it has a thriving bar and an à la carte restaurant (see Where to eat).

There are a few **B&Bs** on quiet South St: *The Brookfield* (☎ 01271-812382, 🖳 thebrookfield.co.uk; 4D or T/1Tr, all en suite; 🛏; (L); Apr-Dec) is a large, luxurious Georgian property which charges from £42pp (sgl occ £60-65); whilst comfortable *Stockwell Lodge* (☎ 01271-817128, 🖳 stockwell-lodge.co.uk; 2S shared bathroom/2D or T/1Tr, all en suite; 🛏; (L)), offers one-night stops, diary allowing, but this is unlikely in the summer months; from £42.50pp (sgl £45).

Closer to the village centre is the cute, thatched *Little Thatch Annexe* (☎ 01271-815328, 🖳 thatchbandbbraunton.co.uk; 1D, en suite). B&B here costs £40pp (sgl occ £50). The room is a self-contained annexe that was originally an 18th-century barn.

On North St you will find sweet little *North Cottage* (☎ 01271-812703, 🖳 northcottagebraunton.co.uk; 2S share bathroom, 1Tr/1D, both en suite; 🛏; 🐾) where B&B costs £40pp (sgl £40).

Where to eat and drink

Several pubs here serve good food. *The Agricultural Inn* (☎ 01271-817980, **fb** search 'The Aggi'; food summer daily 10.30am-9pm, winter Mon-Fri noon-

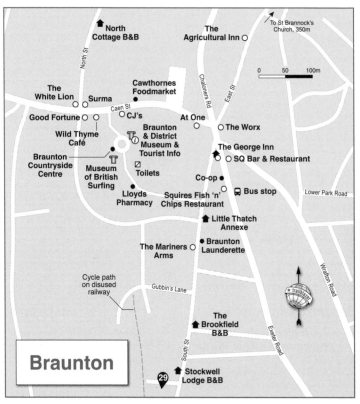

North Cottage B&B

The Agricultural Inn ○

To St Brannock's
Church, 350m

North St

Chaloners Rd

East St

0   50   100m

The White Lion ○ ○ Surma

Cawthornes Foodmarket

Caen St

Good Fortune ○ ○   ○ CJ's

At One   ○

○ The Worx

Wild Thyme Café

Braunton & District Museum & Tourist Info

The George Inn

○ SQ Bar & Restaurant

Braunton Countryside Centre

Museum of British Surfing

Toilets

Co-op ●

Lloyds Pharmacy

Squires Fish 'n' Chips Restaurant

○ ☐ Bus stop

Lower Park Road

Little Thatch Annexe

The Mariners ○ Arms

● Braunton Launderette

Cycle path on disused railway

Gubbin's Lane

Wrafton Road

The Brookfield B&B

South St

Exeter Road

Braunton

29 Stockwell Lodge B&B

2.30pm & 5-9pm, Sat 10.30am-9pm, Sun noon-8.30pm; 🐾), or '**The Aggi**' as it is known locally, is a family-friendly place with a beer garden and decent pub grub (most mains around £10).

If you fancy watching some sport or spending more time outside, *The Mariners Arms* (☎ 01271-813160, **fb**; food end May-Sep daily noon-2pm & 6.30-9.30pm, Oct-May Thur & Fri 6.30-9pm, Sat/Sun noon-2pm & 6-8pm; 🐾) has a big enclosed beer garden & Sky TV. All the food is home-cooked and you'll get a friendly welcome.

Opening earlier, cooked breakfasts (from £5.95) can be salivated over at *The George Inn* (see Where to stay; food daily

8am-2pm & 6-9.30pm) where main courses (mostly burgers and pizzas) cost from around £9 to £13.

On Caen St numerous dishes from pub classics to nachos (and many for less than £10) can be found at *The White Lion* (☎ 01271-813085, 🖥 thewhitelion.uk; **fb**; food Mon-Sat noon-9pm, Sun to 8pm). There are real ales, too, and a cosy wood burner in winter.

Also on Caen St there is *Good Fortune* (☎ 01271-817889; Mon & Wed-Sat 5-10.30pm, Sun 6-10.30pm), a fairly standard Chinese **takeaway**. and *Surma* (☎ 01271-817111, 🖥 surmatandoori.com; **fb**; Wed-Mon 5-10pm; mains from £7.95), an

Indian restaurant and takeaway.

A few metres further on *Wild Thyme Café* (☎ 01271-815191, 🖳 wildthyme cafe.co.uk; **fb**; Mon-Sat 9am-3pm) is a popular and award-winning café serving hand-roasted coffee, freshly-made smooth-ies (£3.95), cooked breakfasts (£7.95; including vegan and vegetarian versions), homemade pizza and a range of sandwich-es (£5-7). Nearby, *CJ's* (☎ 01271-812007, **fb**; Feb-Dec Mon-Sat 8.30am-3pm) is an excellent takeaway sandwich bar (sand-wiches £2.70-3.50).

If you just fancy a quick croissant and coffee, *The Worx* (🖳 theworxbraunton .co.uk; **fb**; Mon-Fri 8.45am-5pm, Sat 10am-5pm) is a dinky little coffee bar with a small back courtyard. Also serves Cornish lagers and pasties.

For an à la carte menu there is *At One* (☎ 01271-814444, 🖳 atonedining.co.uk; **fb**; Tue-Sat 10am-3pm & Wed-Sat 5.30-9.30pm) where there are also breakfasts (£5.90-8.95) and lunchtime toasties and ciabattas (£7.95-10.95). Main dishes include wild mushroom and parmesan risotto (£14.95) and slow-cooked pork belly (£14.95).

The best-known eatery in town is the renowned *Squires Fish 'n' Chips Restaurant* (☎ 01271-815533, 🖳 squires fishrestaurant.co.uk; **fb**; Mon-Sat noon-9pm, Sun noon-7.30pm, hours may change in winter) where they raise the frying of our humble national dish to an art form; **take-away** is also available. Their award-win-ning cod & chips costs £10.70, but there's also poached salmon, fish curry and numer-ous veggie and vegan options.

The Squires family's latest venture is *SQ Bar & Restaurant* (☎ 01271-815900, 🖳 sqdining.uk; **fb**; food daily 9am-9.30pm), a sleek, modern establishment that's proved an instant hit. You'll find West Country breakfasts (£6.50-8.25) and lunchtime sandwiches and wraps (£8.50-11.95) alongside mains such as North Devon sausage and mash (£9.50), River Exe mussels marinière (£14.50) and vegan butternut and sweet potato coconut curry (£9.95).

BRAUNTON TO INSTOW   [MAPS 29-34]

After the delights of the previous stages, this **12½-mile (20km; 5hrs inc 10 mins Braunton to Velator Bridge)** leg is distinctly low key. The path contin-ues with the Tarka Trail out of Braunton, hugging the banks of the Taw as it takes a riparian ramble into Barnstaple – the biggest town on this trail. It then continues along the tarmac until approximately two miles (45 mins) before Instow, where it suddenly deviates to follow a dyke around the marshes of East Yelland and Instow Barton. (You could, however, stay on the tarmac Tarka Trail which remains straight, providing an alternative to the SWCP.)

Scenically, this day is few people's favourite; but, while the terrain will not supply you with much to talk about, the day's walk does pass through some interesting areas. Bird-spotters will find much to enjoy with the views across the estuary where egret, curlew and oystercatchers stalk, as well as on Home Farm Marsh, a habitat for all sorts of wildlife.

Railway historians might also find something to titillate their senses during the long plod from Chivenor to Fremington, the path being decorated with var-ious bits of ironmongery from its days as part of the long-defunct London and South Western Railway. Gourmands will tuck in to the heavenly cream teas at Fremington Quay; while historians will enjoy the architecture of Barnstaple, which also offers numerous options for refreshment.

Even if none of the above particularly appeals there is always the consolation that both this walk and the next to Westward Ho! are, on the whole, pancake flat. As such, it's possible to count off the miles rapidly and indeed it's not unusual for walkers to notch up a mightily impressive 24 miles and combine the two stages in one long day. So, if disused railways, military airfields and mudflats aren't your thing, prepare to get your marching boots on, clock up the miles and look forward to the more spectacular sights on the path ahead.

The route

The day begins by following the edge of **Chivenor Airfield** (Map 29). Currently a base for the Royal Marines, the airfield also has two RAF search-and-rescue helicopters stationed there. Just after the barracks, and perfectly perched above the Taw Estuary, is *Waterside Coffee House* (☎ 01271-814086, 🖥 waterside-coffee-house.co.uk, **fb**; Wed-Sat 10am-6pm, Sun 10am-4pm; 🐾). You'll find a wide range of breakfasts as well as lunches including paninis, salads, burgers and homemade pizzas. They are fully licensed too.

Shortly after joining the estuary you come to *Heanton Court* (Map 29; ☎ 01271-816547, 🖥 vintageinn.co.uk, **fb**; food daily noon-10pm), a huge crenelated place that was once a manor house, but is now a **pub** serving decent food, craft beer and numerous varieties of gin. Most main dishes, such as chicken and mushroom pie or beef and red wine lasagne, cost from £12 to £16, lunches cost £7-12, and there are nice views over the estuary from its large garden.

The route continues along the River Taw to Barnstaple. If you don't wish to visit the town there is an alternative route over the busy new **Taw Bridge**. But if you've got the time, **Barnstaple** is worth a look.

BARNSTAPLE   [see map p153]

Barnstaple acts as a centre of sorts for North Devon. Historically one of the first four boroughs in England, by the advent of the Norman period the town was already busy and prosperous. Having originally been granted the right to mint coins during the reign of King Athelstan, it had long been a centre of commerce. Indeed, Athelstan also granted the town a charter to hold a market and a fair – both of which remain major cultural and financial contributors to the town today.

Barnstaple Fair is held each September and **Pannier Market** (☎ 01271-379084; Mon-Sat 9am-3pm) operates for most of the year. (*Pannier*, incidentally, are the wicker baskets that were once used by traders to bring their goods to the market.) Stalls differ daily but are usually a real smörgåsbord, varying from antiques and jewellery to pet supplies and home-made preserves. The market building was con-

structed in 1855 but plans for the area's development had already begun following the completion of the **Guildhall** in 1827. A remarkably impressive building, the Guildhall includes portraits of – amongst previous councillors – the poet John Gay, who was born in the town. A contemporary of both Samuel Johnson and Alexander Pope, Gay is best known for his satire *The Beggar's Opera*.

On the other side of Butcher's Row from the market and Guildhall are the **parish church** (St Peter's), in existence since 1107, and the Grade-I listed **St Anne's Chapel**. Dating from the early 14th century, the chapel has some splendid features including what some consider to have been a 'charnel house' – a place for storing bones. There are also some wonderfully gruesome gargoyles dotted around the place.

(cont'd on p152)

ROUTE GUIDE AND MAPS

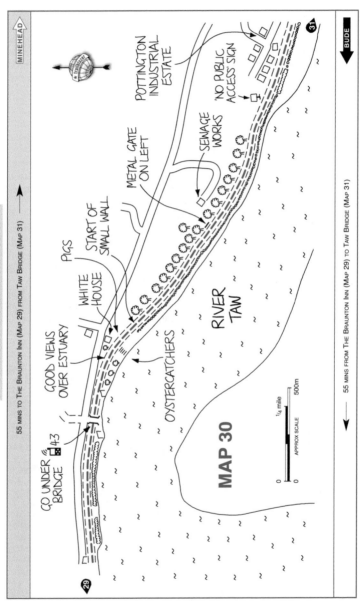

MINEHEAD

trailblazer

BUDE

POTTINGTON INDUSTRIAL ESTATE

'NO PUBLIC ACCESS SIGN'

METAL GATE ON LEFT

SEWAGE WORKS

START OF SMALL WALL

PIGS

WHITE HOUSE

GOOD VIEWS OVER ESTUARY

GO UNDER BRIDGE 43

RIVER TAW

OYSTERCATCHERS

MAP 30

APPROX SCALE
0 ¼ mile
0 500m

29

31

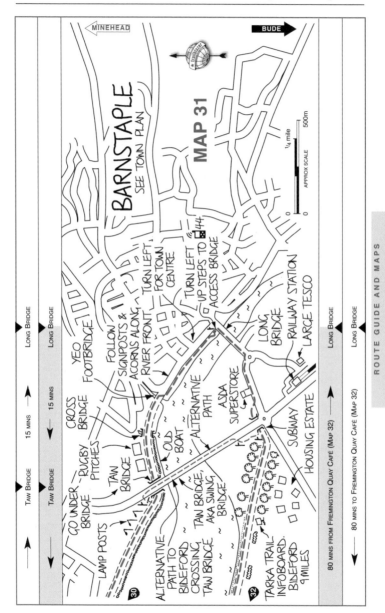

MINEHEAD

BUDE

BARNSTAPLE
SEE TOWN PLAN

MAP 31

¼ mile
500m
APPROX SCALE
0
0

LONG BRIDGE

LONG BRIDGE

15 MINS

15 MINS

TAW BRIDGE

TAW BRIDGE

CROSS
BRIDGE

YEO
FOOTBRIDGE

FOLLOW
SIGNPOSTS &
ACORNS ALONG
RIVER FRONT

TURN LEFT
FOR TOWN
CENTRE

TURN LEFT
UP STEPS TO
ACCESS BRIDGE

GO UNDER
BRIDGE

RUGBY
PITCHES

TAW
BRIDGE

OLD
BOAT

ALTERNATIVE
PATH

ASDA
SUPERSTORE

LONG
BRIDGE

RAILWAY STATION

LARGE TESCO

LAMP POSTS

ALTERNATIVE
PATH TO
BIDEFORD
CROSSING
TAW BRIDGE

TAW BRIDGE,
AKA SWING
BRIDGE

SUBWAY

HOUSING ESTATE

TARKA
TRAIL
INFOBOARD.
BIDEFORD
9 MILES

30

32

LONG BRIDGE

LONG BRIDGE

80 MINS FROM FREMINGTON QUAY CAFÉ (MAP 32)

80 MINS TO FREMINGTON QUAY CAFÉ (MAP 32)

(cont'd from p149) Other historical sites which may be of interest include the **Castle Mound**, across the bridge over the Yeo, which was originally the base of a wooden Norman castle; and, if you have the time to be inspecting the doors of almshouses, you'll find bullet holes from the Civil War in one of the doors at **Penrose Almshouses** in Litchdon St, which date from 1627.

The **Museum of Barnstaple & North Devon** (☎ 01271-346747, 💻 barnstaple museum.org.uk; **fb**; late Mar/Easter to Oct Tue-Sat 1030am-4.30pm, Oct to Easter to 4pm; free) has permanent exhibitions including The Tarka Gallery, which deals with the local wildlife, and North Devon at War. See p16 for details of festivals and events in Barnstaple.

Services

Barnstaple is not short of services and anything you need should be easy to source. In the same building as the museum, the **tourist information centre** (☎ 01271-346747; Mon-Sat 10am-4pm) is staffed by volunteers and has information on accommodation but can't make bookings. The **post office** (Mon-Sat 8.30am-5.30pm, Sun 10am-4pm) is inside WH Smith's on the High St.

The large number of computers in the town's **library** (☎ 01271-318780; daily 10am-5pm) on Tuly St, means getting **internet access** shouldn't be a problem. They also offer free wi-fi. There is also a local studies section (Wed-Fri 10am-5pm) that is well worth a perusal.

If you're in need of **walking gear** there's a Mountain Warehouse (☎ 01271-372253; Mon-Fri 9am-5.30pm, Sat to 6pm, Sun 10am-5pm) and a Millets (Mon-Sat 9am-5.30pm, Sun 10am-4pm) on the High St, while for **cameras and repairs** J & A Cameras (☎ 01271-375037; Mon-Sat 9am-5.30pm) is on Gammon Walk.

Back on the High St there's a Boots **chemist** (Mon-Sat 8.30am-6.30pm, Sun 10.30am-4.30pm) and a Superdrug (Mon-Sat 9am-5.30pm, Sun 10am-4pm), a Waterstone's **bookshop** (Mon-Sat 9am-5.30pm, Sun 10.30am-4.30pm), and a

Tesco Express **supermarket** (daily 7am-10pm). Out near the railway station, across the river, there is also a large Tesco and an Asda superstore.

There are several **ATMs** in the centre including at both HSBC and NatWest.

Transport

[See also pp48-50] Barnstaple is the only place on the path to be connected with the national **rail** network. Great Western Railway runs regular services to Exeter, from where you can connect with other services.

Barnstaple is also very well served by **buses**, with regular services (Filers' Nos 301, 303, 309 & 310; Stagecoach's Nos 5B, 21, 21A, 21C, 85, 155, & 319) to and from surrounding towns and villages. Bude can be accessed by connecting with Stagecoach's 219 service from Hartland. The bus station is on Belle Meadow Rd.

Where to stay

For a town this size there is scant accommodation. No campsite, no hostel and few budget choices. At the cheaper end of the scale is ***Rolle Quay Inn*** (☎ 01271-345182, 💻 therollequayinn.co.uk; **fb**; 2D/1T/1Tr), a friendly pub on Rolle St with room-only rates starting at £22.50pp (sgl occ full room rate). They serve food from lunchtime onwards, but don't do breakfast.

For a more traditional B&B, on the other side of town is ***The Old Vicarage*** (☎ 01271-328504, 💻 oldvicaragebarnstaple .co.uk; 1S/1D/1D or T/1Tr/1Qd, all en suite; ●), once home to the vicar for the nearby Holy Trinity Church but now finding a purpose by providing accommodation for tired walkers. The owners have walked the path so they have maps and are happy to help people plan itineraries; their website also includes a very useful guide describing how you could stay here for as long as you need to complete the stretch of SWCP between Lynmouth and Hartland using public transport. They charge from £47.50pp (sgl from £57.50, sgl occ from £80).

For **hotels**, the local Brend chain has three fine representatives in Barnstaple. Right in the centre, there is the elegant

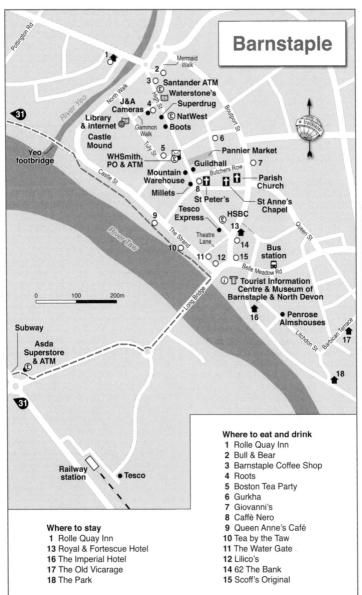

Barnstaple

Mermaid Walk

1 Rolle Quay Inn

2

3 Santander ATM

Waterstone's

J&A Cameras

North Walk

High St

Superdrug

4 € NatWest

Library & internet

Gammon Walk

Boots

Castle Mound

Tuly St

5 ⊠

6

Pannier Market

WHSmith, PO & ATM

Guildhall

7

Castle St

Mountain Warehouse

Butchers Row

Parish Church

Millets

8

St Peter's

St Anne's Chapel

River Yeo

Potlington Rd

31

River Taw

Yeo footbridge

Tesco Express €

HSBC

13

9

Theatre Lane

14

Bus station

10

The Strand

11 12 15

Belle Meadow Rd

Boulport St

Queen St

0   100   200m

Long Bridge

ℹ️ 🎭 Tourist Information Centre & Museum of Barnstaple & North Devon

16

Penrose Almshouses

Subway

17

Asda Superstore & ATM €

Litchdon St

Barbican Terrace

31

18

ROUTE GUIDE AND MAPS

Railway station ● Tesco

Where to eat and drink
1 Rolle Quay Inn
2 Bull & Bear
3 Barnstaple Coffee Shop
4 Roots
5 Boston Tea Party
6 Gurkha
7 Giovanni's
8 Caffè Nero
9 Queen Anne's Café
10 Tea by the Taw
11 The Water Gate
12 Lilico's
14 62 The Bank
15 Scoff's Original

Where to stay
1 Rolle Quay Inn
13 Royal & Fortescue Hotel
16 The Imperial Hotel
17 The Old Vicarage
18 The Park

Georgian *Royal & Fortescue* (☎ 01271-342289, 🖥 royalfortescue.co.uk; **fb**; 4S/44D or T, all en suite; ☛; 🐾). Room only costs from £47.50pp (sgl £85, sgl occ full room rate); breakfast is an extra £10pp.

The second, *The Park* (☎ 01271-372166, 🖥 parkhotel.co.uk; **fb**; 2S/17D/15D or T/4T, all en suite; ☛), is only a 5-minute walk away on quieter Taw Vale. A modern, less inspiring building, it is, nonetheless, very comfortable and overlooks Rock Park and the Taw beyond. Room only from £53pp (sgl £96, sgl occ full room rate); breakfast is an extra £12.50pp.

Surpassing both in terms of style, however, *The Imperial* (☎ 01271-345861, 🖥 brend-imperial.co.uk; **fb**; 10S/63D or T/2Tr, all en suite; ☛; 🐾 annexe only) has rooms with extra sumptuousness and luxury. Room only costs from £67.50pp (sgl £100, sgl occ from £127.50); bed-and-breakfast rates here are often just a couple of pounds higher than room-only rates.

Where to eat and drink

There are quite a few options for food in Barnstaple; some right on the coast path. There are two lovely **cafés** on The Strand, for instance. *Queen Anne's Café* (☎ 01271-325232, 🖥 cafeonthestrand.co.uk; **fb**; Mon-Sat 9am-5pm; 🐾 outside) is housed inside a building known as Queens Anne's Walk, which consists of a Grade I-listed colonnade built in 1708 and a Grade II-listed building which was added later. It serves a range of breakfasts (£4-8) and sandwiches (£5-8) plus soups, jacket potatoes, quiche and daily seafood specials and has outdoor riverside seating too. Slightly further along, *Tea by the Taw* (☎ 01271-370032, 🖥 teabythetaw.co.uk; **fb**; summer Mon-Fri 10am-4pm, Sat to 5.30pm, winter hours variable; 🐾 outside) is a vintage-style tearoom, and is also housed in a heritage building. They sell sandwiches, paninis, jacket potatoes, cakes and cream teas (£6) and also have outdoor seating. Both cafés are fully licensed.

For a café in the town centre, the best option is *Boston Tea Party* (☎ 01271-316777, 🖥 bostonteaparty.co.uk; Mon-Sat 8am-5pm, Sun 9am-5pm; 🐾), on Tuly St; a spacious and modern café that serves a

great and varied menu. The West Country breakfast (£9.15) is just one of 19 all-day breakfast options, whilst a burger will set you back £10.50. There is also a fine selection of homemade cakes and pastries.

Other places for a coffee include *Barnstaple Coffee Shop* (☎ 01271 323636; **fb**; Mon-Sat 9am-4pm, Sun 10.15am-3.30pm), which does a variety of breakfasts and light lunches, and the unusual *Roots* (☎ 07539-353550, 🖥 roots-devon.business .site; **fb**; Mon-Sat 10.30am-3.30pm), which specialises in Middle Eastern and Asian street-food snacks (£1.50-4.50) such as falafels and bhajis.

For something more mainstream, there's a *Caffè Nero* (☎ 01271-379247; **fb**; Mon-Sat 7.30am-5.30pm, Sun 9.30am-5pm) on the High St.

There are a few **pubs** that serve food. *Rolle Quay Inn* (see Where to Stay; food Tue-Wed noon-2pm & 6-8pm, Thur noon-2pm, Fri noon-2pm & 6-9pm, Sat noon-4pm & 6-9pm, Sun noon-3pm) does good-value pub grub every day except Mondays. Mains (£8-14) include penang curry, chilli con carne and veggie burger. They also serve real ales, and have darts, pool and skittles.

Nearby, on Mermaid Walk, *Bull & Bear* (☎ 01271-323238, 🖥 ilovebulland bear.com; **fb**; food Mon-Sat 11am-9pm, Sun 11am-5pm) is an America-style sports bar serving buffalo wings (£5.50-13.95) and 'totally freaking awesome burgers' (£9.95-18.95), all ready to be washed down with a glass of Bourbon or a tin-can cocktail (juice, soda and spirits).

Wetherspoons also has a representative – *The Water Gate* (☎ 01271-335410, 🖥 www.jdwetherspoon.com; food daily 8am-11pm) – which faces towards the river on The Strand and serves the standard Wetherspoons' menu.

Barnstaple isn't short on **restaurants** either. With a great decorative ceiling, finer dining can be found at *62 The Bank* (☎ 01271-324446, 🖥 62thebank.co.uk; **fb**; daily 11.30am-2.30pm & 6-9.30pm), adjoining Royal & Fortescue Hotel, which started life as a merchant's house some 300 years ago. The menu is imaginative and varied and includes items such tiger prawn, garlic and chilli linguine (£13.95) and Japanese katsu curry (£13.95-15.95).

Nearby, opposite Long Bridge, *Lilico's Tapas Bar & Lounge* (☎ 01271-372933, 🖳 lilicos-barnstaple.foodndrink.uk; **fb**; Tue-Sat 11am-11pm, Sun noon-5pm) serves delights such as deep-fried calamari with sweet chilli and honey, as well as a range of rums.

At 35 Boutport St, *Giovanni's* (☎ 01271-321274, 🖳 giovannisdevon.co.uk; Mon-Sat noon-2.30pm & 5.30-10.30pm) is, as you may have already guessed, an Italian restaurant with pasta and pizza mains from

£9 to £11. Takeaway is also available.

Tucked away between Boutport St and the Pannier Market, Nepalese cuisine can be found at *Gurkha* (☎ 01271-377665, 🖳 gurkhabarnstaple.co.uk; Tue-Sat 5-11pm, Sun 5-10pm). The interesting menu includes such dishes as lamb sherpa (£10.95) and *tori macha* (Nepalese-style fish curry; £13.95).

For **takeaway**, at 1 The Square, *Scoff's Original* (☎ 01271-346671; **fb**; Mon-Sat 11am-8pm, closed Bank Hol Mons) won't disappoint. A portion of fish 'n' their signature lightly battered chips costs £6.10, and you can eat in, too.

From Barnstaple, you cross over historic Long Bridge (built in 1796), and pass the huge Asda **supermarket** (Mon-Fri 7am-11pm, Sat 7am-10pm, Sun 10am-4pm) before following the long straight path – decorated with benches and shelters – along the disused Barnstaple to Torrington railway line with mud and sand to one side and mainly fields on the other, eventually turning in just before **Penhill Point** and arriving at **Fremington Quay**.

FREMINGTON QUAY [MAP 32, p156]

A tranquil spot and a lovely place for a rest, Fremington Quay used to be the busiest port between Bristol and Land's End. The import of coal and the export of, amongst other things, local clay and pottery led to the area thriving throughout the first half of the 20th century. The railway finally closed in 1982; a replica railway station (the old one is on the other side of the trail) houses **Fremington Quay Heritage Centre**.

The centre shares a building and space

with *Fremington Quay Café* (☎ 01271-268720; **fb**; daily 10am-5pm; 🐾 outside), a popular place with walkers, cyclists and locals. Serving breakfast until 11am, plus lunches, drinks and snacks, their cream teas are, to put it simply, divine. Doggy biscuits for four-legged friends are baked on the premises.

Stagecoach's No 5B, 21 & 21A **bus** services call at the New Inn in Fremington; see pp48-50 for details.

Leaving the quay behind, the path crosses the small **bridge** to some disused **lime kilns** on your right. Fields continue to accompany the path on the one side, marshes on the other. **Home Farm Marsh** used to be the site of a dairy farm but since 2002 has been owned by the Gaia Trust, a charity that aims to protect the countryside by promoting sustainable farming and wildlife conservation. Due to the trust's work in returning much of the marsh to its original state as a wetland, wild flowers and birds are once again flourishing – look out for little egret, skylark and bittern. There is a 2km walking route that you can follow around the marsh with information boards helping you to ascertain what wildlife to look out for. Stray off the path towards the water and you may come across a **granite cross**, erected in memory of Lady Hilda McNeill who drowned there whilst trying to rescue a child in 1904. Be warned that **the waters of the estuary are very fast-running – do not go in**! Note also, that **dogs** are not allowed within the marsh.

ROUTE GUIDE AND MAPS

FREMINGTON QUAY CAFÉ

← 80 MINS TO LONG BRIDGE (MAP 31) →

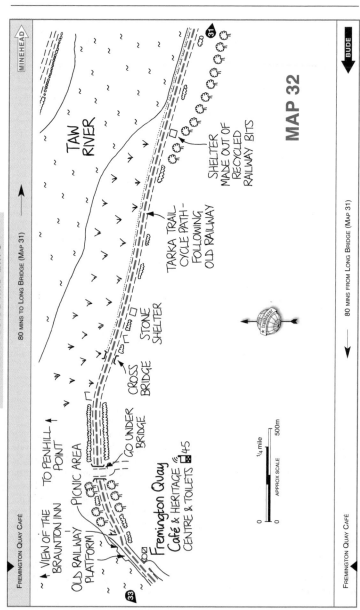

MINEHEAD ⊳

TAW RIVER

MAP 32

SHELTER MADE OUT OF RECYCLED RAILWAY BITS

TARKA TRAIL CYCLE PATH – FOLLOWING OLD RAILWAY

STONE SHELTER

CROSS BRIDGE

GO UNDER BRIDGE

VIEW OF THE BRAUNTON INN

TO PENHILL POINT ←

OLD RAILWAY PLATFORM

PICNIC AREA

Fremington Quay Café & Heritage Centre & Toilets 🚻 45

Trailblazer

¼ mile
500m
APPROX SCALE
0 . . . 0

31

33

BUDE ◄

FREMINGTON QUAY CAFÉ

←— 80 MINS FROM LONG BRIDGE (MAP 31) —→

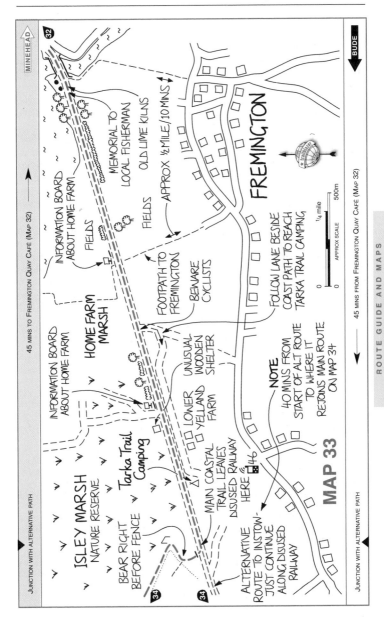

MINEHEAD

BUDE

JUNCTION WITH ALTERNATIVE PATH

45 MINS TO FREMINGTON QUAY CAFÉ (MAP 32)

JUNCTION WITH ALTERNATIVE PATH

32

ISLEY MARSH
NATURE RESERVE

INFORMATION BOARD
ABOUT HOME FARM

Tarka Trail
Camping

BEAR RIGHT
BEFORE FENCE

HOME FARM
MARSH

INFORMATION BOARD
ABOUT HOME FARM

FIELDS

MEMORIAL TO
LOCAL FISHERMAN

OLD LIME KILNS

APPROX ½ MILE/10 MINS

FIELDS

FOOTPATH TO
FREMINGTON

BEWARE
CYCLISTS

FREMINGTON

LOWER
YELLAND FARM

UNUSUAL
WOODEN SHELTER

MAIN COASTAL
TRAIL LEAVES
HERE

NOTE
40 MINS FROM
START OF ALT ROUTE
TO WHERE IT
REJOINS MAIN ROUTE
ON MAP 34

FOLLOW LANE BESIDE
COAST PATH TO REACH
TARKA TRAIL CAMPING

0   ¼ mile
0   APPROX SCALE   500m

MAP 33

ALTERNATIVE
ROUTE TO INSTOW-
JUST CONTINUE
ALONG DISUSED
RAILWAY

DISUSED
RAILWAY

34

34

45 MINS FROM FREMINGTON QUAY CAFÉ (MAP 32)

ROUTE GUIDE AND MAPS

On the south side of the trail, at Lower Yelland Farm, is ***Tarka Trail Camping*** (Map 33; ☎ 01271-861011 or 07944-247417, ☐ tarkatrailcamp ing.co.uk; **fb**; Easter-Sep; 🐾), the only campsite for miles, and perfectly located right on the coast path. It's aimed at walkers and cyclists (no campervans allowed) and is pretty basic (no showers; just portaloo toilets and a washing-up sink), but friendly and welcoming, and there's a microbrewery next door! Expect to pay £10 for a pitch, £3 for a pint. Note, unless you fancy jumping a fence with a big rucksack on, you'll have to come off the coast path before Lower Yelland Farm and follow the lane alongside the coast path to reach the campsite.

The path then runs between **Isley Marsh Nature Reserve** and **East Yelland Marsh** (Map 34), both of which form part of the estuary's SSSI. Isley Marsh, whilst owned by the RSPB, is mostly consumed by the sea at high-tide so has no breeding birds nesting on it. It is, however, an important habitat for resting birds and between there and the other marshes there is a chance of seeing anything from barn owls to kingfishers. East Yelland Marsh is also known to be home to greater horseshoe bats, which are perhaps less spectacular than kingfishers but every bit as fascinating. The path ambles around Instow Barton Marsh before following the sands of the estuary into **Instow**.

Note: if walking around windswept marshes doesn't appeal, you can continue along the disused railway track all the way into Instow. This will also give you the opportunity to stop at the friendly little ***Sandbanks Café*** (Map 34; ☎ 01271-320650; **fb**; daily 9am-4pm, winter hours variable; 🐾) which does good breakfasts as well as paninis, sandwiches, ice creams and coffee. There's indoor and outdoor seating and dogs are welcome.

INSTOW   [map p160]

Instow is a pretty little village, the main highlight of which is its beach and the views it commands across the confluence of the Taw and Torridge rivers. It is a pleasant place to relax in at the end of a day's walk and contrasts splendidly with the hustle and bustle of Barnstaple.

For railway enthusiasts, where the North Devon Yacht Club (Map 35) now stands used to be Instow Railway Station and for those with a nose for trivia, Instow **signal box** (Bank Hols and some Suns Easter-Oct 2-5pm, Nov-Easter 2-4pm; free, donation appreciated) was the UK's first Grade-II listed signal box.

On the other side of the estuary, through the sails and seagulls, Appledore glistens on a summer's day and if you are willing to bypass Bideford there is a **ferry** (☐ appledoreinstowferry.com; **fb**;) that will take you directly there. Weather permitting, it runs (Apr-Oct daily; adults £2

one way; 🐾 free, but at the skipper's discretion) for two hours either side of high tide; the service operates between Instow ferry slip, opposite Johns of Instow, and Appledore Quay. You should always check notices in the villages themselves for the actual operating times.

Services and transport
There's an air of serenity about the village, though there are a few amenities here. For **general supplies** there is *Johns* (see also Where to eat; ☎ 01271-860310, ☐ johns ofinstow.co.uk; **fb**; daily 8.15am-5.30pm, hours variable in winter), a long-running deli-cum-bakery-cum-grocery, which also includes a café (see Where to eat). **Cashback** is available.

Instow is well served by public transport. In addition to the **ferry** service (see above) Stagecoach's Nos 5B, 21 & 21A **buses** call here (see pp48-50).

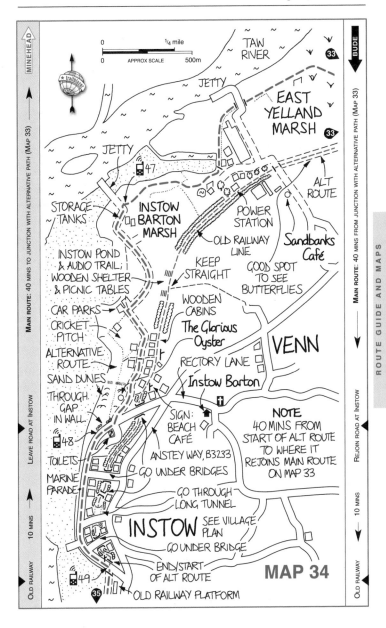

MINEHEAD

BUDE

MAIN ROUTE: 40 MINS TO JUNCTION WITH ALTERNATIVE PATH (MAP 33)

MAIN ROUTE: 40 MINS FROM JUNCTION WITH ALTERNATIVE PATH (MAP 33)

ROUTE GUIDE AND MAPS

0 ¼ mile

0 APPROX SCALE 500m

TAW RIVER

JETTY

33

EAST YELLAND MARSH

33

JETTY

47

ALT ROUTE

STORAGE TANKS

INSTOW BARTON MARSH

POWER STATION

Sandbanks Café

OLD RAILWAY LINE

GOOD SPOT TO SEE BUTTERFLIES

INSTOW POND & AUDIO TRAIL; WOODEN SHELTER & PICNIC TABLES

KEEP STRAIGHT

WOODEN CABINS

CAR PARKS

The Glorious Oyster

VENN

CRICKET PITCH

RECTORY LANE

ALTERNATIVE ROUTE

Instow Barton

SAND DUNES

THROUGH GAP IN WALL

48

SIGN: BEACH CAFÉ

NOTE 40 MINS FROM START OF ALT ROUTE TO WHERE IT REJOINS MAIN ROUTE ON MAP 33

TOILETS

ANSTEY WAY, B3233

GO UNDER BRIDGES

MARINE PARADE

GO THROUGH LONG TUNNEL

INSTOW SEE VILLAGE PLAN

GO UNDER BRIDGE

49

END/START OF ALT ROUTE

35 OLD RAILWAY PLATFORM

MAP 34

LEAVE ROAD AT INSTOW

10 MINS

OLD RAILWAY

REJOIN ROAD AT INSTOW

10 MINS

OLD RAILWAY

Where to stay

For accommodation close to the path try *The Wayfarer Inn* (☎ 01271-860342, ☐ thewayfarerinn.co.uk; 4D/1T/2Qd, all en suite; ➤; ⓛ; 🐾). It is the first place you come to as you head into Instow along the beach and is also signed from the Tarka Trail. The rooms (from £45pp, sgl occ £70) are simple but smart and the whole place is very welcoming. One of the doubles has an extra attached room so can sleep up to six. Note, the multi-person rooms include bunk beds.

Other possibilities in Instow include the rather austere-looking *Springfield House* (☎ 01271-860895, ☐ springfield-instow.co.uk; 2D both private bathroom; ➤; ⓛ; 🐾), up the hill on New Rd, which charges £47.50-60pp (sgl occ £85-110). There are drying facilities for walkers, a wood-burner, and afternoon tea is served on arrival. They rarely take single-night bookings, particularly in summer, but, subject to prior arrangement, for a two-night stay they can pick you up and drop you off and can also do your laundry. Up to two children can be accommodated on a sofa bed in one of the rooms for an extra £10 per child.

More established, *The Commodore Hotel* (☎ 01271-860347, ☐ commodore-instow.co.uk; fb; 24D or T, all en suite; ➤; ⓛ;) is the largest place on the front and is a grand and sophisticated whitewashed affair. B&B costs from £57.50pp (sgl/sgl occ from £100). Dinner, bed and breakfast packages are also available.

A five-minute amble away from the SWCP is *Instow Barton* (Map 34; ☎ 01271-860845, ☐ instowbarton.co.uk; fb; 4D or T/1Tr, all en suite; ➤; ⓛ; well-behaved 🐾), where B&B is available in a farmhouse near to the church. The tariff (from £47.50pp, sgl occ £95) not only includes breakfast but also afternoon tea.

Where to eat

For food and refreshments there are several good options. As you approach Instow, you'll pass *The Glorious Oyster* (Map 34; fb; daily 11am-5pm), a wooden-shack café on the dunes, specialising in perfectly-shucked oysters (£2.75, or 6 for £15) and

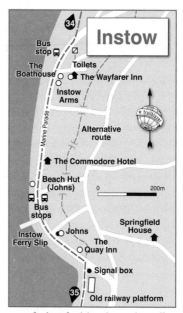

super-fresh seafood, but also serving coffee, cake and ice cream. Outdoor seating only.

Johns Café (also see services, p160) incorporates an award-winning café and deli (daily 8.15am-5pm, hot food until 4.30pm, sometimes closes later in summer) and also runs a **beach hut** (11am-4.30pm, depending on weather, summer only) selling drinks and ice creams, which you pass as you follow the path through Instow. The menu in the café is splendid, featuring cooked breakfasts, bagels, cream teas and cakes, as well as ploughman's platters, Devon pasties, Mediterranean mezze and homemade quiche.

Overlooking the harbour and estuary, *The Quay Inn* (☎ 01271-860624, ☐ the quayinninstow.co.uk; fb; food Tue-Sat 10am-3pm & 6-9pm, Sun 10am-4pm; 🐾) serves real ales and pub-classic mains (£10-14) like fish and chips, sausage and mash and steak and ale pie.

Make sure you look up and check out the wonderful painting on the ceiling by a local artist if you choose to eat in *Instow*

Arms (☎ 01271-860608, 🖥 instowarms .com; **fb**; food daily noon-9.30pm; 🐾 in the bar). There is a strong focus on locally sourced seafood; the *moules marinière* uses River Exe mussels and costs £16.

The Boathouse (☎ 01271-861292, 🖥 theboathouseinstow.co.uk; **fb**; food daily noon-4pm & 5-10pm; 🐾) is also decorated splendidly, with surfboards hanging off the ceiling and mopeds displayed on the walls.

Much of its seafood is served straight off the beach and it has an extensive fish-themed menu (most mains £12-18) including Devon crab linguine, ale-battered cod, and homity pie with leek, potato and smoked cheddar. If you're after a beer garden *The Wayfarer Inn* (see Where to Stay; daily noon-2/3pm & 6-8.30/9.30pm) has a well-priced pub-grub menu (most mains £10).

INSTOW TO WESTWARD HO! [MAPS 34-39]

This **11-mile (17.6km; 4hrs 50 mins)** stage is where the coastal path and the Tarka Trail shake hands, embrace and bid a final, fond farewell to each other. Nevertheless, though you finally leave the otter and its old railway line behind at Bideford by crossing the Torridge River, the path still remains flat and easy all the way to Westward Ho!.

From Bideford the route follows a slightly incoherent path that twists and turns its way between estuary-edge, road and woodland all the way to Appledore. Leaving this pretty village behind, the route meanders through Northam Burrows Country Park before finally arriving in Westward Ho!, which is not as bad as some will have you believe (though the exclamation mark at the end of the name does tend to raise expectations that the town

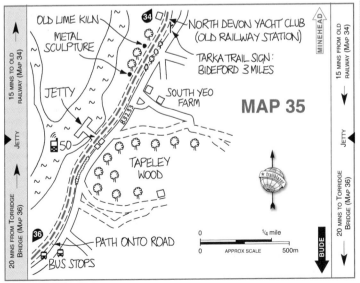

ROUTE GUIDE AND MAPS

struggles to satisfy). There are plenty of options for refreshment on this straightforward stage and you would be well advised to enjoy them as tomorrow the easy walking ends. So, get a good night's sleep in Westward Ho! and prepare yourself to re-embrace the sharp ups and nigh-on-vertical downs of the jagged North Devon coast!

The route

From Instow continue along the tracks to **East-the-Water** where you cross the Torridge via the historic Long Bridge to **Bideford**. Looking across the river you can see the route you will follow when leaving the town, as well as the one you've just finished.

EAST-THE-WATER   [MAP 36]

Blink and you could miss East-the-Water as you march on towards Long Bridge and Bideford.

There's little here to distract you but English history buffs may wish to visit **Chudleigh Fort**. Located above the path, the fort was erected between 1642 and 1643, during the Civil War, to defend Bideford. It was rebuilt in the 19th century and it is now an ornamental garden.

The Nos 15A & 15C **bus** services call here; see pp48-50.

For **accommodation**, just before you cross Long Bridge is *The Royal Hotel* (☎ 01237-472005, ☐ royalbideford.co.uk; **fb**; 4S/12D/4T/7D or T/2Tr, all en suite; ✒; ℂ; 🐾). The prices (B&B from £50pp, sgl from £75, sgl occ from £85) are fair and The Kingsley Bedroom is gorgeous, with an ornate, plastered ceiling and original panelling.

Recommended by coastal path walkers, approximately two miles from Bideford Quay (and once you've left the road, 1½ miles down a single track lane), is *Old Keepers Cottage* (off Map 36; ☎ 01237-479113, ☐ oldkeeperscottage.net; **fb**; 1D/1D or T/1Qd all en suite, 1D/1T private bathroom; ✒; ℂ; Feb-Oct; laundry facilities); so named as the main building is

an old gamekeeper's cottage built in 1835. Set in 35 acres of field, garden and woodland, subject to prior arrangement free pick up/drop offs from the path are available. There's a Tesco one mile away for any urgent purchases. B&B costs £30pp (sgl occ £45) for the non en suite rooms and from £60pp (sgl occ £105) for the en suites in peak season, when there is also a two-night minimum stay.

For **food**, *East of the Water* (☎ 01237-425329; **fb**; Tue-Thur & Sun 5-9.30pm, Fri-Sat 5-10pm) is a notch above most Chinese restaurants, with an imaginative menu including Indonesian chicken satay starter, and mains such as Peking-style lamb (strips of lamb stir-fried in wine, chilli, beans, hoi sin & soy sauce) served with vegetables and rice. Ordering both – or two similar dishes – will cost approximately £15.

Up on the old railway-station platform is *Tea on the Train*, a quirky café where you can sit down at small tables inside a train carriage, or at picnic tables on the platform. It was closed pending a change of ownership at the time of research, but hopefully will be trading again by the time you are passing by.

❏ WHERE TO STAY: THE DETAILS

In the descriptions of accommodation in this book: ✒ means at least one room has a bath; ℂ means a packed lunch can be prepared if arranged in advance; 🐾 signifies that dogs are welcome in at least one room but also subject to prior arrangement, an additional charge may also be payable; **fb** indicates a Facebook page. See also p74.

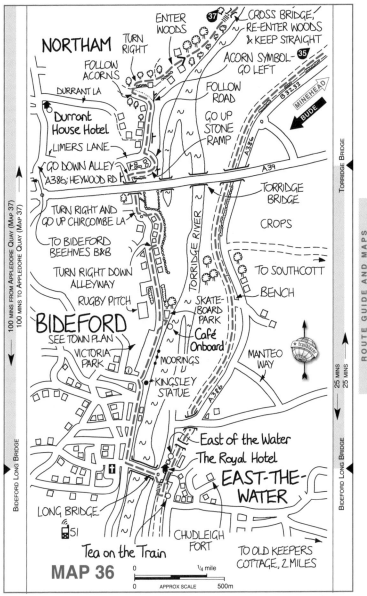

ENTER WOODS

TURN RIGHT

CROSS BRIDGE, RE-ENTER WOODS & KEEP STRAIGHT

37

NORTHAM

FOLLOW ACORNS

ACORN SYMBOL- GO LEFT

35

DURRANT LA

FOLLOW ROAD

B3233

MINEHEAD

Durrant House Hotel

GO UP STONE RAMP

BUDE

A386

LIMERS LANE

A39

GO DOWN ALLEY

A386; HEYWOOD RD

TORRIDGE BRIDGE

TORRIDGE BRIDGE

TURN RIGHT AND GO UP CHIRCOMBE LA

CROPS

TORRIDGE RIVER

TO BIDEFORD BEEHIVES B&B

TURN RIGHT DOWN ALLEYWAY

TO SOUTHCOTT

BENCH

RUGBY PITCH

SKATE-BOARD PARK

BIDEFORD

SEE TOWN PLAN

Café Onboard

VICTORIA PARK

MANTEO WAY

MOORINGS

KINGSLEY STATUE

East of the Water

The Royal Hotel

EAST-THE-WATER

BIDEFORD LONG BRIDGE

BIDEFORD LONG BRIDGE

LONG BRIDGE

51

CHUDLEIGH FORT

Tea on the Train

TO OLD KEEPERS COTTAGE, 2 MILES

MAP 36

0   1/4 mile

0   500m

APPROX SCALE

100 MINS FROM APPLEDORE QUAY (MAP 37)
100 MINS TO APPLEDORE QUAY (MAP 37)

25 MINS
25 MINS

BIDEFORD

'All who have travelled through the delicious scenery of North Devon must needs know the little white town of Bideford, which slopes upwards from its broad tide-river paved with yellow sands, towards the pleasant upland in the west.'

Charles Kingsley, *Westward Ho!*

The 'little white town' of Bideford has a long and rich history spanning from Roman times. Pivotal to the town's existence is its position on the Torridge and since the 16th century onwards its primary function has been as a port and place of trade. One of the town's most famous residents, Sir Richard Grenville, set sail from Bideford on several expeditions to the New World. He is also, famously, the subject of Tennyson's poem, *Revenge*, following his death fighting the Spanish during the Battle of Flores in 1591.

There is evidence of **The Quay** having been here in some form since 1619 and it was refurbished in 2006, a project that included the construction of the **Quay Fountain**, which at high tide shoots 24 jets of water up into the air and out over the river. The 24 jets are supposed to mirror the 24 arches that hold up **Long Bridge**. First constructed from oak in 1280 as a packhorse bridge, it replaced what was a dangerous ford – the name Bideford is derived from 'By the ford'. Originally the bridge had a chapel at either end. The Quay is also a departure point for ferries to Lundy Island (see box p122).

The current church, **St Mary's**, is actually the third to have been built on the site, having been constructed in 1865 around the original Norman tower. Inside, the font is thought to be from 1080 and is thus the oldest relic in town.

Other sites in Bideford include the **Pannier Market** – held in Bideford since 1272, when the town was granted charter to hold a market by Henry III, and located on the same site since 1675, though the current building dates 'only' from 1884. Today, as ever, there is as rich a variety of stalls, with trading taking place on Tuesdays and Saturdays year-round. The area is now slightly rundown in parts, though it is also

the most interesting of quarters to browse around. Should you have the time, **Bideford Heritage Trail** takes you on a tour around the town's most historically significant areas. Information about the tour can be found at the tourist office.

If more walking isn't your idea of fun, **Burton Art Gallery & Museum** (☎ 01237-471455, 🖳 burtonartgallery.co.uk; Mon-Sat 10am-4pm, Aug to 5pm, Sun 11am-4pm; free) boasts a number of interesting artefacts and houses a scale replica of Long Bridge, displaying its various forms down the ages. There is also information on many of the town's most famous residents including Edward Capern (1819-94), aka the Postman Poet, a man who could obviously multitask; and the story of the trial of the Bideford witches – who in 1682 became the last women in England to be hanged for witchcraft.

Services

Bideford has a good selection of services. The **tourist information centre** (☎ 01237-477676; opening hours same as for Gallery) is in Burton Art Gallery; the staff can do accommodation booking (see box p42) over the counter but not over the phone.

The **post office** (Mon-Fri 9am-5.30pm, Sat 9am-12.30pm) is nearby on The Quay.

For **internet access**, or wi-fi, try Bideford **Library** (☎ 01237-476075; Mon, Tue, Thur & Fri 9.30am-6pm, Sat 9.30am-1.30pm) near Long Bridge. There are several **ATM**s dotted along The Quay.

For **food** there is a Co-op (Mon-Sat 7am-10pm, Sun 10am-4pm), on Mill St in the centre, and should you need a **chemist** there's a Boots (Mon-Sat 8.30am-5.30pm) on High St.

Transport

[See also pp48-50] The 5B, 15A, 15C, 21, 21A, 85 & 319 **bus** services connect Bideford with most surrounding towns and villages. Buses stop on The Quay.

For a **taxi** try A1-Taxis (☎ 01237-666060, 🖳 a1taxisbideford.co.uk).

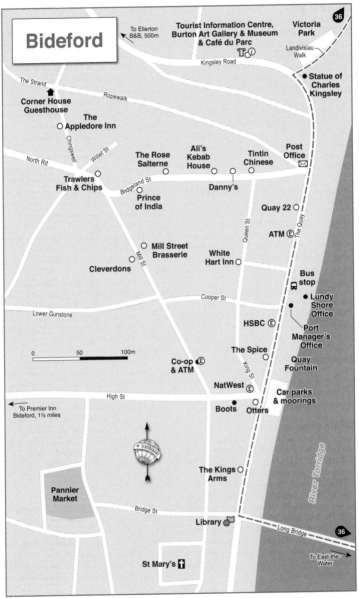

Bideford

To Ellerton B&B, 500m

Tourist Information Centre, Burton Art Gallery & Museum & Café du Parc

Victoria Park

36

Kingsley Road

Landivisiau Walk

Statue of Charles Kingsley

The Strand

Ropewalk

Corner House Guesthouse

The Appledore Inn

Chingswell

Willet St

North Rd

The Rose Salterne

Ali's Kebab House

Tintin Chinese

Post Office

Bridgeland St

Danny's

Trawlers Fish & Chips

Prince of India

Quay 22

ATM £

The Quay

Queen St

Mill St

Mill Street Brasserie

White Hart Inn

Cleverdons

Cooper St

Bus stop

Lundy Shore Office

Lower Gunstone

Port Manager's Office

HSBC £

0   50   100m

The Spice

Quay Fountain

Co-op & ATM

King St

NatWest £

Car parks & moorings

High St

Boots

Otters

To Premier Inn Bideford, 1½ miles

trailblazer

River Torridge

Pannier Market

The Kings Arms

Bridge St

Library

Long Bridge

36

St Mary's

To East-the-Water

Where to stay

Campers looking to pitch their tents in the area should continue walking to Northam. Indeed, there is a distinct lack of accommodation in Bideford, which may make the extra 3½ miles to Appledore – or stopping at one of the B&B options en route (see Northam p167; Map 36) – seem appealing.

B&B accommodation can be found on The Strand at *Corner House Guesthouse* (☎ 01237-473722, 🖳 cornerhouseguesthouse.co.uk/bideford.html; 2D/2T/1Tr all en suite; 👄; 🐾), where you can sleep and devour breakfast in a pretty 18th-century merchant seaman's house. They charge from £44pp (sgl occ from £44, though full room rate at peak times).

Less than half a mile from the town centre on Glenburnie Rd (off Southwood Dr, which is off Chanters Rd) is *Ellerton B&B* (☎ 01237-470393, 🖳 ellertonbandb .com; 2D both en suite, 1S/1D both with private bathroom; 👄). Rates are from £37.50pp (sgl/sgl occ £50).

Hotel-wise, there is an option in East-the-Water (see p162), and also *Premier Inn Bideford* (☎ 0871-527 9564, 🖳 premierinn .com; 70D or T, all en suite; 👄), which is on Clovelly Rd, opposite Atlantic Village, a couple of miles from the centre of town. Room rates start from as little as £32 but expect to pay more than double that in peak periods. Breakfast costs £8.99pp. The hotel is also near Abbotsham and approximately 3½ miles from Westward Ho!.

Where to eat and drink

There are lots of **cafés** in Bideford, including two right on The Quay. *Otters* (☎ 01237 237190; **fb**; Mon-Sat 8.30am-5pm, Sun 10am-4pm) is a friendly place with tables spilling out onto the pavement and a menu that includes breakfasts, sandwiches and jacket potatoes as well as beer, wine and gin! Further along, and also fully licensed, *Quay 22* (☎ 01237 423057; **fb**; Mon-Sat 10am-4pm) is classier, serving excellent coffee, delicious cakes and the likes of poached eggs on avocado toast. It also has pavement seating.

Up on Mill St you'll find *Cleverdons* (☎ 01237-472179; **fb**; Mon & Tue 9am-4pm, Wed-Sat 9am-7pm, Sun 11am-4pm; 🐾 at other customers' discretion) which provides cream teas and lunches, while not far away, at No 49 is *Mill Street Brasserie* (☎ 01237-700245, **fb**; lunch: Tue-Sat noon-3pm, dinner: Thu-Sat 6.30-11pm). Locally-sourced Mediterranean-style menu (*moules*, cassoulet, crab) along with burgers and delicious homemade cakes.

On your way out of Bideford, and attached to the museum and tourist information, is *Café du Parc* (☎ 01237-429317; **fb**; daily 10am-4pm, Aug to 5pm), selling authentic French *galette* and *crêpes* as well as soups, sandwiches and excellent coffee. A little further along the coast path, you pass the floating *Café Onboard* (Map 36; ☎ 07403 194194; **fb**; Easter-Nov Wed-Sun 10am-5pm, rest of year to 4pm, open Mondays if it's school or public holidays; 🐾), which offers a brew and a butty on a boat!

As for **pubs**, the *White Hart Inn* (☎ 01237-473203; 🐾), secreted away on Queen St, serves local real ales, and has a lovely beer garden, but doesn't serve food at the moment. Likewise, the *Kings Arms* (☎ 0121 272 5499), on The Quay, is drinks only now.

For **pub food**, there's good Thai cuisine, to eat in or takeaway, at *The Appledore Inn* (☎ 01237-476956, 🖳 appledoreinn bideford.co.uk; food Tue-Sat 4-9pm; 🐾 bar area only), on Chingswell St. Mains start from £7.50. Complementing the spicy food are local real ales including Grenvilles from Jolly Boats and Doom Bar from Cornwall. *The Rose Salterne* (☎ 01237-426110, 🖳 www.jdwetherspoon.com; food daily 8am-11pm), on Bridgeland St, is Bideford's Wetherspoons' offering, serving their standard, reliably cheap fare.

Bideford has plenty of **takeaways**. For Chinese food there is *Tintin Chinese* (☎ 01237-429633; **fb**; Sun, Mon, Wed & Thur 5-10pm, Fri & Sat to 10.30pm), and for Indian, *Prince of India* (☎ 01237-424295; **fb**; daily 5-11pm); both are on Bridgeland St. You can also eat in at Prince of India.

Indian food can also be found at *The Spice* (☎ 01237-471133, 🖥 thespice1.co.uk; **fb**; daily 5pm-midnight), on The Quay, where you can also eat in.

For pizzas, kebabs and burgers try *Danny's* (☎ 01237-474555, 🖥 dannysbideford.co.uk; Mon-Thur 4pm-midnight, Fri 4pm-1am, Sat 4pm-3.30am, Sun 4-10.30pm) or *Ali's Kebab House* (☎ 01237-

474621; Mon-Fri 4pm-midnight, Sat 4pm-3am, Sun 4-11pm); both are on Bridgeland St. Further up the same road, there's *Trawlers Fish & Chips* (☎ 01237 476546; **fb**; Mon-Wed noon-8pm, Thur to 8.30pm, Fri & Sat to 9pm, Sun 4-8pm), at No 38, which has a restaurant as well as a take-away.

From Bideford the path takes a slightly convoluted route to Appledore. It initially follows the river. Where the road turns away from the water as you leave town you'll find a **statue of Charles Kingsley** (Kingsley is said to have written much of *Westward Ho!* in Bideford, which is also where the beginning of the novel is set).

Beyond this, for about 275 metres, the tarmac path is known as **Landivisiau Walk** – named after the town's French twin. The park to your left is **Victoria Park**. Hidden amongst the flowerbeds and playing children are a couple of old cannons, thought to have been captured from the Spanish Armada in 1588. There is also a tree in the park planted in 1944 by American Lt Col F Holmes to commemorate the good relations the US army had with the people of Bideford whilst stationed there between 1940 and 1944.

As the ugly but necessary new **Torridge Bridge** looms ever closer, the path seems to lose its sense of direction somewhat. The bridge was built in 1987 due to the long-existing problems with the sheer weight of traffic crossing Bideford Long Bridge; indeed, in 1968 some of the bridge had even collapsed.

The path meanders between river and farmland and passes by the turning for **Northam**, emerging, after a short road-walk, at **Appledore**.

NORTHAM [MAP 36, p163]
The village of Northam provides a couple of B&B options as well as a campsite.

Follow Limers Lane up to the A386 Heywood Rd for *Bideford Beehives B&B* (☎ 01237-421139, 🖥 bidefordbeehivesbb.co.uk; 1D en suite, 1Qd private facilities; 🐾) charges £45pp (sgl occ £80). The family room is made up of one double room and one twin room, with a shared bathroom between them.

The tariff for a standard room at the plush *Durrant House Hotel* (☎ 01237-472361, 🖥 durranthousehotel.com; 5S/50D/50T/8Tr, all en suite; ☛; WI-FI most

rooms; 🐾) is £40-55pp (sgl occ £60-75); a jacuzzi room will set you back £85-90pp.

Marshford Camping and Caravan Site (Map 37; ☎ 01237-477160, 🖥 marshfordcamping.co.uk; **fb**; hiker & tent £8; WI-FI variable; 🐾; Apr-end Oct) is approximately a kilometre to the south of Appledore. They also run an organic food **shop** (🖥 marshford.co.uk; Tue-Sat 11am-5pm) at the same site. There is a short-cut to the site from the SWCP before you reach Appledore (see Map 37).

Stagecoach's No 21A **bus** service calls here (see pp48-50).

APPLEDORE

Quaint and quirky, Appledore is a lovely little village, and although its location
between Bideford and Westward Ho! probably means you won't stay here for the
night, it really deserves as much of your
time as you can give it.

At heart it's a typical old West Country
fishing village, but one onto which a vivid
coat of creativity and craftsmanship has
been painted, its centre a jumble of tiny cottages connected by narrow cobbled alley-
ways in which you'll find galleries and
workshops, studios and showrooms.

There's an interesting museum at the
top of the village. In a house once owned
by the father of Jerome K Jerome, author
of *Three Men in a Boat*, **North Devon
Maritime Museum** (☎ 01237-422064, 💻
northdevonmaritimemuseum.co.uk; Apr-
Oct daily 10.30am-5pm; £4) contains exhibitions on Appledore's seafaring history,
including displays on shipbuilding, fishing
and shipwrecks.

See p16 for details of festivals and
events in Appledore.

Services

There are some **tourist information**
leaflets in the **library** (☎ 01237-477442;
Tue 10am-1pm, Wed 2-5pm, Thur & Sat
10am-noon) on the front, but possibly a
better source of information is 💻 apple
dore.org. The library also has **internet
access** (£1/30 mins, free wi-fi).

Close by is the **post office** (Mon-Fri
9am-5.30pm, Sat 9am-12.30pm), located
inside the **general store** called Johns, which
is twin to the branch of Johns in Instow (see
p160) and which, similarly, is made up of a
grocery (daily 8.15am-5.30pm), a deli
(8.30am-5pm) and a café (see *Where to eat*).
Cashback is available here.

In the summer months, for those who
want to return to Instow (or are heading in
the other direction and are happy to miss
Bideford) a **ferry** (see p158) runs daily,
weather and tide permitting, from The
Quay.

Transport

[See also pp48-50] The only **bus** service is
the No 21C to Barnstaple, although it does
connect there with the 21/21A to
Ifracombe. Buses stop on The Quay.

Where to stay

For **camping** see Northam (p167). For
B&B accommodation there are three
options: *One End House* (☎ 01237-473846,
💻 appledoreoneendhouse.wixsite.com/b
andb; 1D en suite, 1S/1T share facilities if
both rooms booked; ➥; 🦮) is on the lane
of the same name and is one of the charming little 18th-century terraced cottages that
make up the centre of the village. Rates here
are from £45pp (sgl occ from £65).

Up the hill at 19 Bude St, *Torridge
House* (☎ 01237-477127, 💻 devon-bed-
and-breakfast.com; 2D/1T, all en suite; ➥;
🕐; 🦮) is a lovely Georgian place, tasteful-
ly furnished and with chickens in a pretty
back garden; rates from £49pp (sgl occ
£85). They are happy to pick up and drop
off guests who stay two nights.

Completing the trio is *The Seagate* (☎
01237-472589, 💻 theseagate.co.uk; fb;
1S/15D/1T, all en suite; ➥; 🦮), a pub

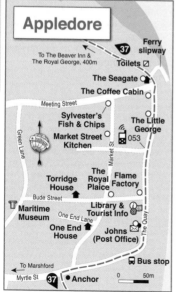

Appledore

Ferry
slipway
To The Beaver Inn &
The Royal George, 400m
Toilets ☑
The Seagate
The Coffee Cabin
Meeting Street
Sylvester's
Fish & Chips
Market Street
Kitchen
The Little
George
053
The
Torridge Royal Flame
House Plaice Factory
Bude Street
Maritime Library &
Museum One End Lane Tourist Info
One End Johns
House (Post Office)
Green Lane
Market St
The Quay
To Marshford
Bus stop
Myrtle St 37 Anchor
0   50m

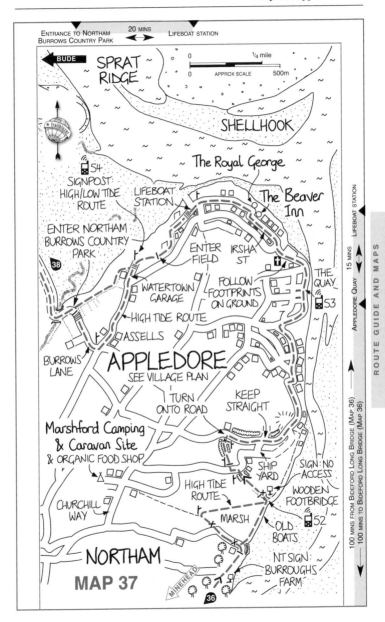

ENTRANCE TO NORTHAM
BURROWS COUNTRY PARK

20 MINS

LIFEBOAT STATION

BUDE

SPRAT RIDGE

SHELLHOOK

0   ¼ mile
0   500m
APPROX SCALE

trailblazer

54
SIGNPOST
HIGH/LOW TIDE
ROUTE

The Royal George

The Beaver Inn

LIFEBOAT STATION

ENTER NORTHAM
BURROWS COUNTRY
PARK

38

ENTER
FIELD

IRSHA
ST

WATERTOWN
GARAGE

FOLLOW
FOOTPRINTS
ON GROUND

THE
QUAY

53

HIGH TIDE ROUTE

ASSELLS

APPLEDORE
SEE VILLAGE PLAN

BURROWS
LANE

TURN
ONTO ROAD

KEEP
STRAIGHT

Marshford Camping
& Caravan Site
& ORGANIC FOOD SHOP

SHIP
YARD

SIGN: NO
ACCESS

WOODEN
FOOTBRIDGE

52

CHURCHILL
WAY

HIGH TIDE
ROUTE

MARSH

OLD
BOATS

NT SIGN
BURROUGHS
FARM

NORTHAM

MAP 37

MINEHEAD

36

LIFEBOAT STATION

15 MINS

APPLEDORE QUAY

ROUTE GUIDE AND MAPS

100 MINS FROM BIDEFORD LONG BRIDGE (MAP 36) →
← 100 MINS TO BIDEFORD LONG BRIDGE (MAP 36)

housed in a 17th-century building at the end of The Quay, with 10 rooms in the main building and a further seven larger 'boutique' rooms in a nearby building. The tariff is from £55pp (sgl £60, sgl occ from £100).

Where to eat and drink

Food-wise, during the day there are several options. Along The Quay – so right on the SWCP – is *Johns* (☎ 01237-425870, ⌨ johnsofinstow.co.uk; **fb**; café daily 8am-4pm), part of the local group of delicatessens, where there are breakfast, brunch, lunch, and 'deli platters' as well as sandwiches and bagels; whilst further along The Quay is *The Coffee Cabin* (☎ 01237-475843; **fb**; daily 9am-5pm): the staff are friendly, the sandwiches magnificent. Between the two, *The Little George* (summer 9am-5pm, winter noon-5pm) is a take-out shop connected to the Royal George pub (see below) and sells ice creams, coffee and crèpes.

Hiding away on narrow Market St, at No 25, *Market Street Kitchen* (☎ 01237-474168, ⌨ marketstkitchen.com; **fb**; Tue-Sun 10am-4pm) sells homemade cakes, cream teas, sandwiches (from £4.95) and main meals (£10).

For restaurant meals, *The Royal Plaice* (☎ 01237-478673, ⌨ theroyalplaiceappledore.co.uk; **fb**; Mon-Sat 10am-2pm & 5-9pm) is an unpretentious fish restaurant and takeaway, with a rival takeaway, *Sylvester's Fish & Chips* (☎ 01237-423548; **fb**; Mon-Sat noon-2pm & 5-8pm),

at the other end of Market St. Both are excellent.

Nearby, *Flame Factory* (☎ 01237-475261, ⌨ flamefactory.org.uk; **fb**; summer noon-9pm, winter 6-9pm) serves wood-fired pizza (£10-14) and flame-grilled burgers (£12-14) as well as mouth-watering Clovelly longhorn steaks (£19-22).

There's some smashing food at *The Seagate* (see Where to stay; food Mon-Fri 8am-9pm, Sat & Sun 9am-9pm) including fisherman's pie (£15.25) and dressed Devon crab (£18). They also do breakfasts (£3.50-9.50).

At the northern end of town (see Map 37), with sea views and outdoor seating, two pubs sit almost side-by-side on Irsha St. Both are popular. *The Beaver Inn* (Map 37; ☎ 01237-474822, ⌨ beaverinn.co.uk; **fb**; food daily 10am-9pm; 🐾 bar area), is a locals' favourite, serving real ales, sandwiches (from £6.95), pub-grub classics (£10-14) and locally caught fish specials such as Appledore mussels (£14.95). More upmarket is *The Royal George* (Map 37; ☎ 01237-424138, ⌨ trgpub.co.uk; **fb**; food Mon-Sat 9-11am, noon-2.30pm & 5-9pm, Sun 9-11am, noon-2.30pm & 3-9pm), serving the likes of roast Exmoor pork loin (£14.50), cauliflower *shawarma* (Middle-Eastern kebab; £12.95) and roast cod with beer-butter mussels (£17.95). The George tries to keep things as local as possible, and even lists the food miles of every dish on its menu.

Leaving Appledore you have a choice between two routes – although as one of them is only accessible at low tide, nature may well make your decision for you. The two paths soon reunite at the entrance to **Northam Burrows Country Park**. Consisting of 253 hectares of coastal plain and sand dunes the Burrows are an SSSI, due partly to the pebble ridge that separates the Burrows from the sea. The golf course you skirt is The Royal North Devon – the oldest links course in England. Be warned: it's not unknown for half-blind amateur golfers to send a wayward shot too close! The main route passes by a public **toilet** (open Easter-Sept only) then takes a long, straight, wide path along the back of the pebble ridge. If you find walking with golfers not to your taste, at low tide you can cross the ridge and stroll along the beach all the way to **Westward Ho!**. Note that dogs must be on a lead here.

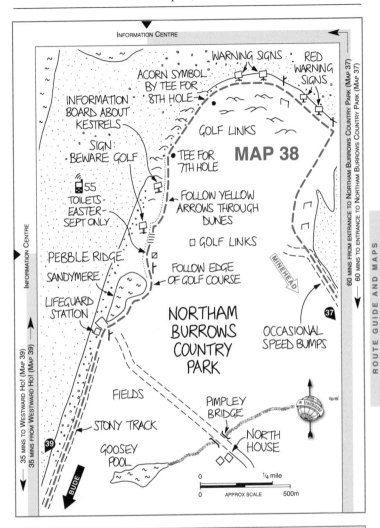

INFORMATION CENTRE

WARNING SIGNS

RED WARNING SIGNS

ACORN SYMBOL BY TEE FOR 8TH HOLE

INFORMATION BOARD ABOUT KESTRELS

SIGN: BEWARE GOLF

GOLF LINKS

MAP 38

TEE FOR 7TH HOLE

55

TOILETS - EASTER - SEPT ONLY

FOLLOW YELLOW ARROWS THROUGH DUNES

GOLF LINKS

PEBBLE RIDGE

SANDYMERE

FOLLOW EDGE OF GOLF COURSE

LIFEGUARD STATION

MINEHEAD

37

NORTHAM BURROWS COUNTRY PARK

OCCASIONAL SPEED BUMPS

FIELDS

PIMPLEY BRIDGE

STONY TRACK

NORTH HOUSE

39

GOOSEY POOL

BUDE

trailblazer

0   ¼ mile
0   500m
APPROX SCALE

60 MINS FROM ENTRANCE TO NORTHAM BURROWS COUNTRY PARK (MAP 37)
60 MINS TO ENTRANCE TO NORTHAM BURROWS COUNTRY PARK (MAP 37)

INFORMATION CENTRE

35 MINS TO WESTWARD HO! (MAP 39)
35 MINS FROM WESTWARD HO! (MAP 39)

ROUTE GUIDE AND MAPS

❑ **IMPORTANT NOTE – WALKING TIMES**
Unless otherwise specified, **all times in this book refer only to the time spent walking**. You will need to add 20-30% to allow for rests, photography, checking the map, drinking water etc, not to mention time simply to stop and stare. When planning the day's hike count on 5-7 hours' actual walking.

WESTWARD HO!

The town of Westward Ho! may come as something of a disappointment to those for whom the name (the only one in England with an exclamation mark and, as far as we know, the only one named after a novel as opposed to the other way round) conjures up images of seafarers, buccaneers and adventure on the high seas.

It's true that this once ramshackle but now much rejuvenated conglomeration of residential care homes and static caravan sites may not challenge Clovelly or Appledore for beauty awards. It also lacks the history of other towns around here, having been built as a holiday resort (the first hotel, The Westward Ho!, was built in 1864, when it was decided that there was money to be made in a tourist development overlooking the Pebbleridge described in the book).

But having said that, those who bother to spend some time in the town often find that they grow to like it. The warmth and openness of the locals is undoubtedly one of the reasons why this is so – and the fact that they all seem so proud of the place is quite infectious after a while. So, while you may not take too many photos as you pass through (though the view over the town's massive beach from the top of town is quite magnificent), don't dismiss Westward Ho! out of hand, despite what other walkers may tell you. The SWCP is all about variety, and whatever else you may think of it, there's nowhere else quite like Westward Ho! on the entire path.

Services

The Co-op **supermarket** (daily 7am-10pm) boasts the usual lengthy opening hours; its rival round the corner, Londis (Mon-Sat 8am-8pm, Sun 8am-5pm) also houses the **post office** (Mon-Fri 9am-5pm, Sat to 12.30pm).

There's a free-to-use **ATM** on the corner of Golf Links Rd and Nelson Rd next to the **pharmacy** (Mon-Fri 9am-5.30pm, Sat 9am-1pm). Note, this is the last ATM on the path before Bude, though the hotel at Hartland Quay does cashback.

Transport

[See also pp48-50] Westward Ho! is fairly well served by **buses**. Stagecoach's No 21 regularly operates to Ilfracombe, Braunton and Barnstaple as well as other towns and villages in the area.

Prior to the pandemic, some National Express coaches called here so check 🖥 nationalexpress.com to see if this service has resumed.

For a **taxi** call A1 Taxis (☎ 01237-666060, 🖥 a1taxisbideford.co.uk).

Where to stay

Campers need to either return to Northam (see p167), 1½ miles inland, or walk 3½ miles further to Abbotsham (see p174 and Map 40).

There are three **B&B** options in Westward Ho!. The views from the premier rooms at the Victorian *Culloden House* (☎ 01237-479421, 🖥 culloden-house.co.uk; 5D/1T/2S, all en suite; WI-FI reception area; Mar-Oct; no children), Fosketh Hill, are hard to surpass, looking out directly along the main swathe of sand. With its huge rooms the inside of this guest house is a joy too. The tariff is from £42.50pp (sgl £59, sgl occ full room rate). Single-night stays may not be available on summer weekends.

The pub, *The Village Inn* (☎ 01237-477331; 2D/1Tr/1Qd, all en suite; 🛏; Ⓛ; 🐾) provides B&B from £45pp (£80 sgl occ) in quite old fashioned but spacious rooms.

Your third option is on Golf Links Rd. *The Waterfront Inn* (☎ 01237-474737, 🖥 waterfrontinn.co.uk; **fb**; 11 rooms, all en suite, incl twins, doubles and family rooms; 🛏; Ⓛ; 🐾) is fairly characterless but is comfy enough. B&B costs from £52 (sgl occ rates on request). If requested they can provide a packed lunch instead of breakfast.

Where to eat and drink

There are a couple of decent cafés on Golf Links Rd: *The Rock Pool Café* (☎ 01237-477763, 🖥 rockpooltakeaway.com; **fb**; daily 9am-4pm; 🐾 outside) does breakfasts (including bacon baps; £4.25) as well as

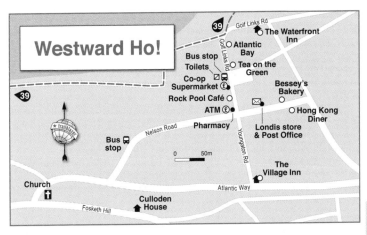

baguettes (£5.95-6.95) and jacket potatoes (£5.50-7.50); it's a friendly and bustling establishment and has outside seating. For cream teas and lunches (£5-10), *Tea on the Green* (☎ 01237-429406, 🖥 teaonthe-green.net; **fb**; Wed-Sun 11am-5pm; 🐾 outside) is hard to beat. There are six different cream teas – three savoury, three sweet – and the homemade cake cabinet (with gluten-free options) is always kept full.

Pub food can be found in a few places. Near the coast path, at the bottom of Golf Links Rd, *The Waterfront Inn* (see Where to stay; food daily noon-9pm) has an extensive menu including many breakfast options (£4-9), and a good choice of sandwiches (£7), burgers (£10-14) and pub-grub mains (£10-12). They also do a Sunday carvery (£9.95) and a smaller carvery (£6.95) on Thursdays, Fridays and Saturdays. At the top of the hill on Youngaton Rd, *The Village Inn* (see Where to stay; food served daily 10-11am, noon-2pm & 6-9pm), which feels a bit neglected these days, is more of a locals' pub, serving real ales and standard pub food.

For **fish & chips**, try *Atlantic Bay* (☎ 01237 470815, 🖥 atlanticbayfishandchips .com; **fb**; daily 11.45am-8.30pm), on Golf Links Rd. It's a takeaway and an eat-in restaurant with sea-view terrace seating out front. Cod and chips costs £7.50.

There's a Chinese restaurant with a **takeaway** section: *Hong Kong Diner* (☎ 01237-477661; **fb**; summer daily 5-10.30pm, winter Tue-Sun hours variable), on Nelson Rd, opposite which is the friendly *Bessey's Bakery* (☎ 01237-478570, Mon-Sat 8am-4.30pm) where you can buy good-value sandwiches (£2.50-3.50) and pasties (£1.80-3.40).

As you leave Westward Ho! on the coast path, there are a couple of **restaurants** with wonderful seaside locations: *M'Rock N'Bowl* (Map 39; ☎ 07745-085147, **fb**; Mon, Tue, Thur & Fri 10am-3pm & 6-8.30pm, Sat 10.45am-8.30pm, Sun 10.45am-6.30pm, closed Wed) is a bit of a gem – a tiny Moroccan restaurant with an unrivalled seaside perch; sit either inside at one of the cute, mosaic-topped circular tables or out on the rooftop terrace to enjoy your Bissara soup (£5) and chicken tagine (£12) followed by a Moroccan crepe (£3) and a pot of authentic mint tea (£2.50).

A bit further along is *The Pier House* (Map 39; 01237-477777, 🖥 thepier-house .co.uk; **fb**; Sun-Thur 10am-11pm, Fri & Sat 10am-midnight), a huge family-friendly restaurant with mains (most costing from £13 to £15) that include burgers, steaks, salads and seafood. It also has rooftop seating.

WESTWARD HO! TO CLOVELLY   [MAPS 39-43]

This **11-mile (17.7km; 4hrs 35 mins)** section is very much a tale of two terrains. Leaving Westward Ho!, the path assumes a southerly direction along exposed and open cliffs, lacerated, once again, by several deep and fairly testing combes. On reaching Peppercombe, however, the path not only takes a more westerly direction but also changes in nature from clifftop clamber to woodland walk.

Aside from a visit to the small huddle of houses that is Buck's Mills, as well as the occasional field, you remain under the forest canopy for pretty much the rest of the stage as the trail leads you towards and then onto Hobby Drive – a wide and gentle tree-shaded track coaxing you to lovely Clovelly.

Note that (except for possibly in Buck's Mills, see p178) there is nowhere to get any refreshments on the way nor is there anywhere to stay on the path (though there are several places a short walk inland), so do remember to bring supplies and plan your day properly.

The route
Though the first half of this walk is undoubtedly more testing than the second, it begins in a fairly gentle manner as you escape from Westward Ho! along the path of a disused railway that used to run inland to Bideford.

After passing Westward Ho!'s wonderful **sea pool** (Map 39), and two restaurants (M'Rock N'Bowl and The Pier House; see p173), the trail leaves the tarmac to head towards **Abbotsham Cliff** (Map 40) and then **Green Cliff**, both owned by the National Trust. Pause at the top of either and you should, weather permitting, make out Saunton Sands and even Baggy Point, which you probably walked around about four days ago! Look south, on the other hand, and the keen-eyed may just be able to make out Clovelly in the cliffs ahead.

Just after crossing a wooden bridge beside an old kiln, campers can detour inland towards **Abbotsham.**

ABBOTSHAM   [MAP 40, p176]
Approximately 15-20 mins (¾ mile) inland is **Westacott Farm** (☎ 01237-472351, 🖥 westacottfarm.co.uk; 🐾; hiker £5pp; open year-round), a very welcoming **campsite** with good toilet and shower facilities, a small kitchen (kettle and microwave), a laundry and a kids play area. You can sit outside the farmhouse and connect to the owner's wi-fi if needed. Note that although they do have occasional pizza or fish-and-chips evenings, there's nowhere to buy provisions here so come prepared.

The nearest option to the campsite for **food** is a 25-minute stroll away, although the food at *The Thatched Inn* (off Map 40; ☎ 01237-471321, 🖥 thethatchedinn.com; **fb**; food daily 11am-2.30pm & 5-9pm; WI-FI temperamental; 🐾 in the bar area) is certainly worth the trek! There's a large and varied menu which includes vegetable Penang curry (£11.95), fish pie (£13.95) and beer-battered cod and chips (£12.95). There's also a range of burgers, loaded sandwiches and jacket potatoes. It's the kind of place where you could easily forget that you're camping and not notice it getting dark … and then end up leaving far too late!

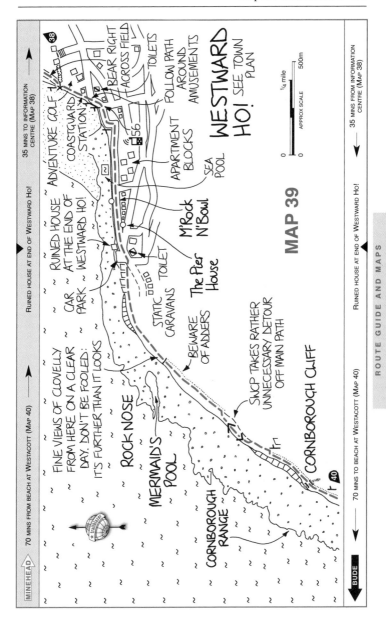

35 MINS TO INFORMATION CENTRE (MAP 38)

BEAR RIGHT

TOILETS

FOLLOW PATH AROUND AMUSEMENTS

WESTWARD HO! SEE TOWN PLAN

ACROSS FIELD

ADVENTURE GOLF

COASTGUARD STATION

56

APARTMENT BLOCKS

SEA POOL

M'ROCK N'BOWL

The Pier House

RUINED HOUSE AT THE END OF WESTWARD HO!

CAR PARK

STATIC CARAVANS

TOILET

BEWARE OF ADDERS

MAP 39

0   ¼ mile
0   500m
APPROX SCALE

FINE VIEWS OF CLOVELLY FROM HERE ON A CLEAR DAY. DON'T BE FOOLED: IT'S FURTHER THAN IT LOOKS

MERMAID'S POOL

ROCK NOSE

CORNBOROUGH RANGE

SWCP TAKES RATHER UNNECESSARY DETOUR OFF MAIN PATH

CORNBOROUGH CLIFF

40

BUDE

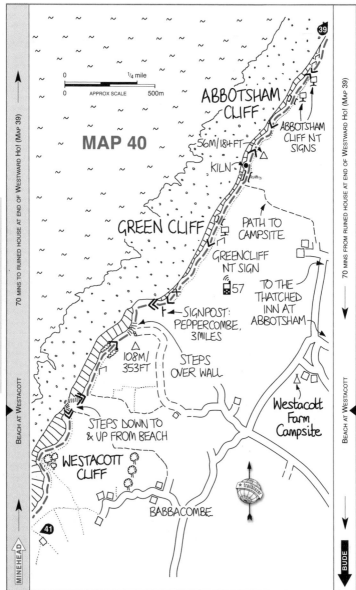

ROUTE GUIDE AND MAPS

0   ¼ mile
0   APPROX SCALE   500m

MAP 40

70 MINS TO RUINED HOUSE AT END OF WESTWARD HO! (MAP 39)

ABBOTSHAM CLIFF

56M/184FT

ABBOTSHAM CLIFF NT SIGNS

KILN

70 MINS FROM RUINED HOUSE AT END OF WESTWARD HO! (MAP 39)

GREEN CLIFF

PATH TO CAMPSITE

GREENCLIFF NT SIGN

57

TO THE THATCHED INN AT ABBOTSHAM

SIGNPOST: PEPPERCOMBE, 3 MILES

108M/ 353FT

STEPS OVER WALL

BEACH AT WESTACOTT

Westacott Farm Campsite

STEPS DOWN TO & UP FROM BEACH

WESTACOTT CLIFF

BABBACOMBE

trailblazer

MINEHEAD

41

BEACH AT WESTACOTT

BUDE

39

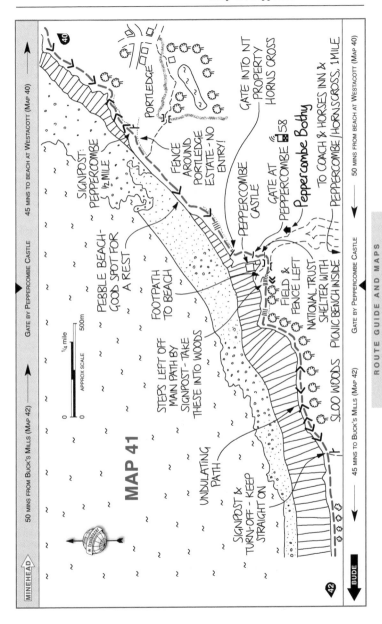

50 MINS FROM BUCK'S MILLS (MAP 42)

GATE BY PEPPERCOMBE CASTLE

45 MINS TO BEACH AT WESTACOTT (MAP 40)

MAP 41

APPROX SCALE

0   500m
0   ¼ mile

SIGNPOST:
PEPPERCOMBE
½ MILE

PEBBLE BEACH-
GOOD SPOT FOR
A REST

FOOTPATH
TO BEACH

STEPS LEFT OFF
MAIN PATH BY
SIGNPOST - TAKE
THESE INTO WOODS

UNDULATING
PATH

SIGNPOST &
TURN-OFF - KEEP
STRAIGHT ON

SLOO WOODS

FENCE
AROUND
PORTLEDGE
ESTATE - NO
ENTRY!

PORTLEDGE

GATE INTO NT
PROPERTY
HORNS CROSS

PEPPERCOMBE
CASTLE

GATE AT
PEPPERCOMBE

Peppercombe Bothy

NATIONAL TRUST
SHELTER WITH
PICNIC BENCH INSIDE

FIELD &
FENCE LEFT

TO COACH & HORSES INN &
PEPPERCOMBE/HORNSCROSS, 1 MILE

58

50 MINS FROM BEACH AT WESTACOTT (MAP 40)

GATE BY PEPPERCOMBE CASTLE

45 MINS TO BUCK'S MILLS (MAP 42)

BUDE

40

42

For those not camping there's plenty of walking still to be done. The gradients increase as you drop to the beach, briefly, at **Westacott**, and again by the private **Portledge Estate**, before you reach Peppercombe, another National Trust property. **Peppercombe Castle**, labelled on OS maps, is actually an Iron-Age fort though little remains today. Nearby, and right on the path, is a National Trust **shelter** with a picnic table inside it, while around 200m south of the path is *Peppercombe Bothy* (Map 41; ☎ 0344-3351296, 🖥 nationaltrust.org.uk; 2D; £22 per night for the whole bothy; 🐾), another National Trust-run property. It's basic (no heating, electricity or cooking facilities), but you get two double sleeping platforms, a cold-water sink (which is safe to drink from) and an attached toilet hut. Officially there's a minimum three-night stay policy, but it's worth enquiring about single-night stays, especially outside peak season.

Further inland along the same path, about three-quarters of a mile from the coast path, is *Coach & Horses Inn* (off Map 41; ☎ 01237-451214, fb; 1D/1T/1Tr, all en suite; Ⓛ). They have **B&B** rooms from £42.50pp (sgl occ from £77) and serve **food** daily (noon-9pm, winter hours may differ).

The path now meanders along the slopes through **Sloo** and **Worthygate woods** (the border between the two being unmarked) before dropping down to the hamlet of **Buck's Mills** (Map 42). Unless you require a refreshment from *Buck's Ice Cream* (Map 42; fb; Mar-Oct daily noon-6pm though not reliably open so don't depend on it), which sells hot drinks, snacks and, er… ice-cream, there's little to detain you here. There are, though, two old **limekilns** down at the bottom of the road by the beach, and on the way is **Look-out Cottage**, a tiny studio used from the 1920s to the 1970s by artists Mary Stella Edwards and Judith Ackland, who renamed it The Cabin and whose work now hangs in Burton Art Gallery (see p164) at Bideford. It has barely been touched in the 40 years since the artists left it. If you're desperate for supplies, you can walk one mile inland to **Buck's Cross Post Office** (Map 42; Mon-Sat 8am-6pm, Sun 9am-1pm) which is a well-stocked store. There is also a **shop** at the huge Bideford Bay Holiday Park, further along, but closer to the path, though you can't camp here.

The woods on the other side of Buck's Mills are, if anything, even more beautiful than those you've just left, with some huge beech trees and gigantic rhododendron bushes shading the way. Emerging briefly into meadows above the trees, the path plunges into the shade again to reach **Hobby Drive**, a 19th-century 'bridleway' that provides an easy and picturesque stroll into Clovelly, leisurely snaking its way along the cliffside, with benches placed here and there to the right of the trail to encourage wayfarers to tarry a while and appreciate the views down onto the rooftops of **Clovelly**. Hard to believe in such a tranquil place that, according to legend, in a giant cave below the trail lived a certain John Gregg and his family, who made their living robbing, murdering and eating passers-by around 250 years ago. These days, the most dangerous creature you're likely to encounter is the occasional grouse strutting along the path or scampering through the undergrowth. Just over an hour after joining the Drive you reach its end and arrive at one of the more unique and individual settlements on the entire South-West Coast Path.

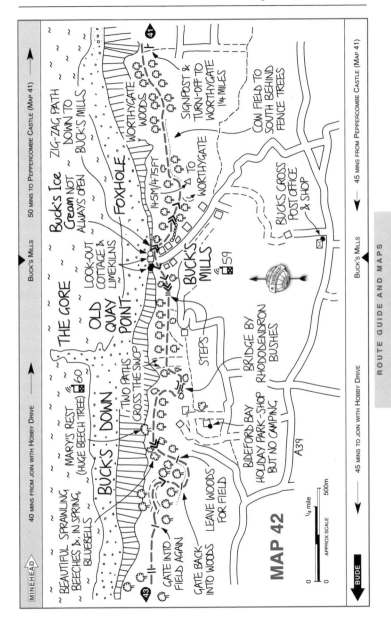

MINEHEAD ▷

← 40 MINS FROM JOIN WITH HOBBY DRIVE

50 MINS TO PEPPERCOMBE CASTLE (MAP 41) →

◀ BUCK'S MILLS ▶

45 MINS FROM PEPPERCOMBE CASTLE (MAP 41) →

BUCK'S MILLS

← 45 MINS TO JOIN WITH HOBBY DRIVE

▣ BUDE

BEAUTIFUL SPRAWLING
BEECHES & IN SPRING
BLUEBELLS

MARY'S REST
(HUGE BEECH TREE) 📷 60

THE GORE

LOOK-OUT
COTTAGE &
LIMEKILNS

Buck's Ice
Cream NOT
ALWAYS OPEN

ZIG-ZAG PATH
DOWN TO
BUCK'S MILLS

FOXHOLE

WORTHYGATE
WOODS

43

BUCK'S DOWN

7 TWO PATHS
CROSS THE SWCP

OLD QUAY
POINT

II-SM/475FT

↙ TO
WORTHYGATE

SIGNPOST &
TURN-OFF TO
WORTHYGATE
¼ MILES

COW FIELD TO
SOUTH BEHIND
FENCE TREES

BUCK'S
MILLS

BUCKS CROSS
POST OFFICE
& SHOP

📷 59

LEAVE WOODS
FOR FIELD

STEPS

BRIDGE BY
RHODODENDRON
BUSHES

GATE BACK
INTO WOODS

GATE INTO
FIELD AGAIN

43

BIDEFORD BAY
HOLIDAY PARK-SHOP
BUT NO CAMPING

A39

MAP 42

0   ¼ mile
0   APPROX SCALE   500m

CLOVELLY & HIGHER CLOVELLY
[map p183]

Clovelly is one of the loveliest villages on the entire SWCP. Four-hundred feet of cobbled street rolling down a narrow cleft in the coastline of North Devon, lined on either side by wonderfully preserved cottages which, viewed from the sea, appear to have been stacked on each other's shoulders. It really is the most photogenic of places.

The gradient of the main street – which bears the names Up-a-Long and Down-a-Long – is enough to prevent traffic from driving down it (though there is a road linking the harbour with the top of the village which is used by Land Rovers to shuttle paying passengers to and from the harbour). Instead, goods are brought in by sled from the top of the village, while rubbish is taken to the bottom where it is removed by boat. In between are some gorgeous little cottages, each full of character and entirely individual.

Much of the credit for this wonderful state of preservation is down to the fact that Clovelly is actually privately owned, the Hamlyn family acquiring the fishing village as part of their purchase of the entire Clovelly Estate in 1738. One of the family, Christine Hamlyn, spent years restoring many of the cottages on the main street; her initials and a date can be seen carved into many of the structures. It is now in the hands of her great-grandnephew, the Hon. John Rous.

For such a small village (the estimated population for the entire ward of Clovelly Bay is about 1600), Clovelly has a surprising number of claims to fame: the village was a boyhood home of Charles Kingsley,

who returned here years later to write some of his best work, including *The Water Babies*; Charles Dickens also wrote about it (though he calls it, appropriately enough, 'Steepways'); Rex Whistler painted it, as did JMW Turner; and Wedgewood used cameos of the village on their china service. It is also mentioned in the Domesday Book.

The opening of the huge **visitor centre** above the village – and the subsequent charging of an **entrance fee** (£7.95) to visit the village – are controversies over which coast-path walkers can remain in blissful ignorance, for the entrance into Clovelly along The Hobby bypasses the entrance gates altogether, thus allowing walkers to enter the village without paying. There are two small museums (daily approx 9am-5pm; entry charge inc in village fee): **Kingsley Museum** celebrates the life and work of the author, but perhaps more interesting is the **Fisherman's Cottage**, across the courtyard, where the cob-and-stone dwelling has been preserved in a 1930s' style with a sail loft and even a covered well. At the foot of the village, beyond the 19th-century **Lifeboat Station**, is a **waterfall**, behind which you'll find a cave where the Arthurian wizard Merlin was supposedly born.

On the coast path at the top of the village are the **Donkey Stables** which have been here for more than 100 years, and are currently home to more than a dozen donkeys and mules, and two **Craft Workshops**, one focussing on pottery, the other on silk. Both are open from around 10am to 5pm throughout the summer and are free to look around.

❏ **'STEEPWAYS'**

The village was built sheer up the face of a steep and lofty cliff. There was no road in it, there was no wheeled vehicle in it, there was not a level yard in it. From the sea-beach to the cliff-top two irregular rows of white houses, placed opposite to one another, and twisting here and there, and there and here, rose, like the sides of a long succession of stages of crooked ladders, and you climbed up the village or you climbed down the village by the staves between, some six feet wide or so, and made of sharp irregular stones.   **Charles Dickens**, *Message from The Sea*

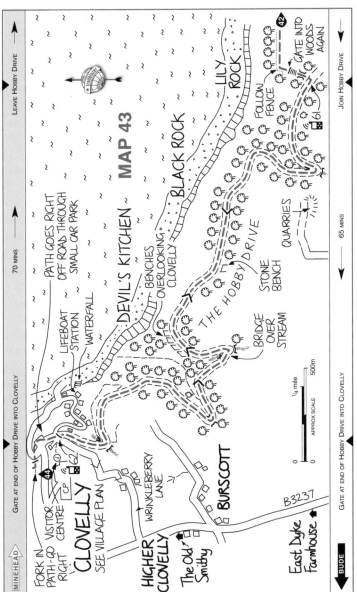

MINEHEAD ↑

LEAVE HOBBY DRIVE →

← 70 MINS →

GATE AT END OF HOBBY DRIVE INTO CLOVELLY

MAP 43

PATH GOES RIGHT OFF ROAD THROUGH SMALL CAR PARK

DEVIL'S KITCHEN

WATERFALL

LIFEBOAT STATION

BENCHES OVERLOOKING CLOVELLY

BLACK ROCK

LILY ROCK

FOLLOW FENCE

42

GATE INTO WOODS AGAIN

61

JOIN HOBBY DRIVE ↓

QUARRIES

THE HOBBY DRIVE

STONE BENCH

BRIDGE OVER STREAM

← 65 MINS →

GATE AT END OF HOBBY DRIVE INTO CLOVELLY

FORK IN PATH-GO RIGHT

VISITOR CENTRE

CP

44

62

CLOVELLY
SEE VILLAGE PLAN

HIGHER CLOVELLY

The Old Smithy

WRINKLEBERRY LANE

BURSCOTT

East Dyke Farmhouse

B3237

BUDE ↓

¼ mile

500m

0

0

APPROX SCALE

Services
The **Visitor Centre** (☎ 01237-431781, 💻 clovelly.co.uk; daily Easter-Oct 9.30am-5.30pm, longer in school summer holidays, Nov-Easter 10am-4pm) is very much concerned with Clovelly and information about other parts of Devon is slight. It does, though, have a large **souvenir shop** and an equally large **café**, meaning you can grab some food if you're just passing through without having to climb down to (and all the way back up from) the village. In the village itself you'll find a small **shop** (daily 9.30am-5pm) selling pasties, ice cream and fudge, but little else.

Transport
[See also pp48-50] Stagecoach's No 319 **bus** leaves from the visitor centre and connects Clovelly with Barnstaple and Hartland.

The **Land Rover service** shuttles paying passengers between the quay and the donkey stables (£1.50) or the Visitor Centre car park (£2.50).

Where to stay
The iconic **Red Lion Hotel** (☎ 01237-431237, 💻 redlion-clovelly.co.uk; **fb**; 16D/2D or T, all en suite; ➛; ⓛ; 🐾) is run by the Clovelly Estate, which is also in charge of the visitor centre. It's a lovely old place, and a bit of a landmark in the village, situated right by the harbour. However, B&B starts at a whopping £90pp (sgl occ full room rate). Some rooms can also sleep up to two children.

Bookending Clovelly at the top end of the village, is **New Inn Hotel** (☎ 01237-431303, 💻 thenewinnclovelly.co.uk, **fb**; 1S/6D/1Tr, all en suite; ➛; ⓛ;🐾). It is arguably the most elegant place to stay in Clovelly; the smart rooms have a sea view or, in one case, a balcony overlooking part of the street. B&B starts at £70pp, sgl/sgl occ from (£140).

Alternatively, and specialising in short stays for coast-path walkers, **Hamlyn's Hostel** (☎ 01237 431303; 5T/6D/1Qd, 2 en suite, rest shared facilities; ➛; ⓛ; 🐾) is across the cobbles from the New Inn and run by the same people. Despite the name,

it's not really a hostel, though some rooms do share bathrooms, so prices are cheaper. Rates are for room only, and start at £34pp with en suite, or £20pp with shared bathrooms (sgl occ from £49). Breakfast, taken in the New Inn, costs £8pp.

In the centre of the village is **Harbour View B&B** (☎ 01237 432215, 💻 clovelly cottage.co.uk; 3D/1T shared facilities; ➛; ⓛ; 🐾), a delightful old cottage situated beside the village tearooms. The four comfortable rooms (one on the ground floor, three upstairs) share two first-floor bathrooms. The breakfast is excellent, the owners are very welcoming and the front garden is filled with flowers. B&B rates are £32.50-35pp (sgl occ usually full room rate).

Where to eat and drink
There are only a few choices for food in the village. The fabulous **Cottage Tearooms** are open during the day (☎ 01237-431494; **fb**; Easter-Oct daily 10.30am-5pm) and boast a lovely outside eating area with sea views. Cream teas cost £6.50. They also do excellent baguettes (from £6.50), and a generous Ploughman's (£8.25).

The two hotels also serve food: **Red Lion Hotel** (see Where to stay; daily 10am-noon & 6-9pm to eat in, takeaway also available noon-4pm & 5-8.30pm) unsurprisingly boasts some fine fresh seafood dishes in its **restaurant**. Pan-seared fillet of sea trout will set you back £16.25, while the Clovelly-landed lobster costs £45. Other dishes include tomato gazpacho (£11) and free-range duck breast with roasted chicory and cherries (£16.95). More traditional pub grub, including pizza, is available in the **bar** (mains £10-14). There's also pub grub at the **New Inn Hotel** (see above; daily noon-2.30pm & 6.30-8.30pm, winter hours variable), which serves the likes of beef lasagne, ham, egg and chips or cod and chips for under a tenner, alongside a selection of local real ales.

A simple pasty or ice-cream can be found by the harbour at **Quay Shop** (Easter-Oct daily 10am-5pm, weather dependent), housed inside one of the Red Lion's old arched cellars.

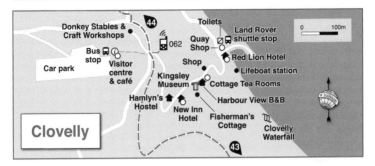

Higher Clovelly

There are two more B&B options further up the hill, about 2km from the top of the main village. *The Old Smithy* (Map 43; ☎ 01237-431202, 🖳 oldsmithybandbclovelly .co.uk; **fb**; 1D/1Tr both en suite; ➖; ⒧) has two rooms, one of which has its own attached lounge. B&B costs £39.50pp (sgl occ £70). *East Dyke Farmhouse* (Map 43; ☎ 01237-431216, 🖳 bedbreakfastclovelly .co.uk; **fb**; 1D/1Tr both en suite; ➖; ⒧; 🐾) is a lovely friendly place, a grand 19th-century building with exposed beams and flagstone floors. B&B costs £45pp (£85 sgl occ). You are free to explore Clovelly Dykes, a 200-year-old Iron Age hill fort, lying just beyond their back garden. They even have bedding and bowls for dogs! To get here from the end of Hobby Drive, take the path signposted towards Wrinkleberry. Keep walking through the tiny hamlet, then turn left at the end of the road and The Old Smithy (200m) and East Dyke Farmhouse (850m) will both be on your right.

CLOVELLY TO HARTLAND QUAY   [MAPS 43-48]

The final two stages of this walk are renowned for being amongst the wildest, most remote and most spectacular on the entire SWCP. The paucity of amenities and accommodation on the trail also mean that walkers really need to plan carefully for their walk on this stretch. True, when it comes to **accommodation** there are several B&Bs, a (YHA) hostel and a campsite, but these are sometimes a fair hike away and should definitely be booked in advance. Similarly, for **food** you need to plan well: the first stage has only a seasonal snack kiosk on the trail, though it does have a fabulous hotel with food and ale at the end, while the second stage has nothing actually on the path until Sandymouth Café which is only two miles before Bude. It does, though, offer the option of an excellent tearoom and a pub at Morwenstow, if you're willing to divert about a third of a mile (500 metres) off the trail (it's a flat path, thankfully).

One way round this, of course, is to ask your accommodation to make a packed lunch for you, or else stock up on pasties from the shop in Clovelly or takeouts from the Cottage Tearooms or the Visitor Centre café.

However, assuming you *have* planned properly, there is much to look forward to on both these stages. The reputation of the second stage for being the toughest and amongst the most awe-inspiring on the entire path is well known but there's plenty to appreciate on this first stage to Hartland Quay too.

The first part of this **10½-mile (16.9km; 5hrs 5mins)** walk is gentle enough, beginning with a stroll through the woods of Gallantry Bower and Snaxland before you indulge in a meadowside meander along the clifftops of Brownsham and Beckland. So far, so familiar. But when you round Hartland Point, the path takes an abrupt turn to the south... and things get a little more dramatic. Wild seas crash against rocks carved by time and tide into alcoves and archways, canyons and caves, tunnels and towers, where grey seals slumber and seagulls soar. It's a land of rock and reef, storm and shipwreck, lonely, baleful shorelines and looming, brooding skies; while, above it all, a 19th-century lighthouse and the enigmatic ruins of a much older tower sit in stoical silence – untouched and untroubled by the chaos below.

The route

Your first task on this stage is to avoid the scary-looking (but presumably benign) steers of the Clovelly Court estate as you skip through fields and forest, passing on your way two curious man-made structures tucked away among the trees. The first, just 10 minutes from Clovelly itself, is **The Wilderness Summerhouse Cabin** (Map 44; 🖳 clovelly.co.uk/map/wilderness-summerhouse-cabin), built in the 19th century by Sir James Hamlyn Williams (a former owner of Clovelly Estate) and now used, bizarrely, as a venue for weddings. It is open-sided with a bench inside, but provides some shelter from the elements. The second, reached via a tunnel of rhododendrons, is an ornate wooden pagoda-style structure known as **Angel's Wings**, which was carved by a former butler of the estate. Again, it is a shelter of sorts (though open on all sides), with a bench to rest on while you make a start on your sandwiches.

More woodland wandering ensues as you make your way to **Mouthmill Beach**, once the haunt of smugglers but now the home to a ruined limekiln and, more famously, **Blackchurch Rock** with its two sea-sculpted 'windows'.

Climbing out of the valley you now follow an endless series of fields towards Hartland Point, the only features of note being **Windbury Castle** (Map 45), an Iron Age fort that has largely disappeared due to erosion, though the keen-eyed expert can still make out parts of the southern ramparts amongst the undergrowth; and, just a short walk further on, a **memorial to a Wellington bomber** that crashed at the foot of Beckland Cliff in 1942. Eventually, around four hours after setting off, you pass the turn-off to *West Titchberry Farm* (Map 46; ☎ 01237-441287, 🖳 westtitchberryfarm.weebly.com; 1Qd en suite, 1D/1T share facilities; 🐾; (Ⓛ), a typical Devon longhouse and B&B that charges £32.50pp (sgl occ £55), and offers evening meals (by prior arrangement, from £13) as well as a pick-up/drop-off service (subject to a small charge) for walkers. (Its neighbour, by the way, **East Titchberry Farm**, is a 17th-century National Trust property with its own malthouse that's unfortunately closed to the public.)

Shortly afterwards – though it's been visible a long way beforehand – is the giant white golf-ball-on-a-tee that is the **radar station**. At its foot is a car park where you will find *Hartland Point Refreshment Kiosk* (Map 46; Easter-Oct 10.30am-5pm), which sells hot drinks, snacks and ice creams.

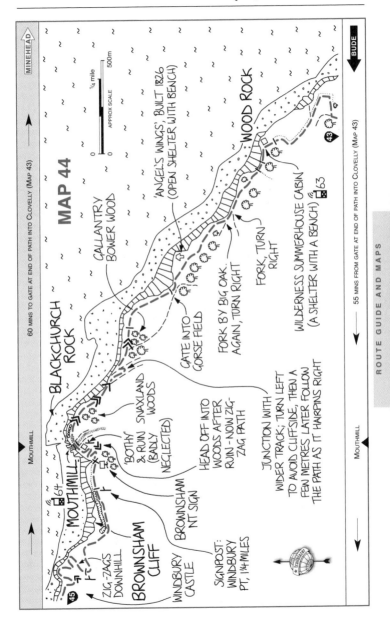

MINEHEAD

BUDE

60 MINS TO GATE AT END OF PATH INTO CLOVELLY (MAP 43)

55 MINS FROM GATE AT END OF PATH INTO CLOVELLY (MAP 43)

Minehead

Mouthmill

Mouthmill

MAP 44

BLACKCHURCH ROCK

GALLANTRY BOWER WOOD

WOOD ROCK

'ANGEL'S WINGS', BUILT 1826 (OPEN SHELTER WITH BENCH)

GATE INTO GORSE FIELD

FORK BY BIG OAK. AGAIN, TURN RIGHT

FORK, TURN RIGHT

WILDERNESS SUMMERHOUSE CABIN (A SHELTER WITH A BENCH)

MOUTHMILL

SNAXLAND WOODS

'BOTHY' & RUIN (BADLY NEGLECTED)

HEAD OFF INTO WOODS AFTER RUIN – NOW ZIG-ZAG PATH

JUNCTION WITH WIDER TRACK; TURN LEFT TO AVOID CLIFFSIDE, THEN A FEW METRES LATER FOLLOW THE PATH AS IT HAIRPINS RIGHT

BROWNSHAM NT SIGN

SIGNPOST: WINDBURY PT, 1¼ MILES

WINDBURY CASTLE

BROWNSHAM CLIFF

ZIG-ZAGS DOWNHILL

¼ mile

500m

APPROX SCALE

0

0

ROUTE GUIDE AND MAPS

45

43

63

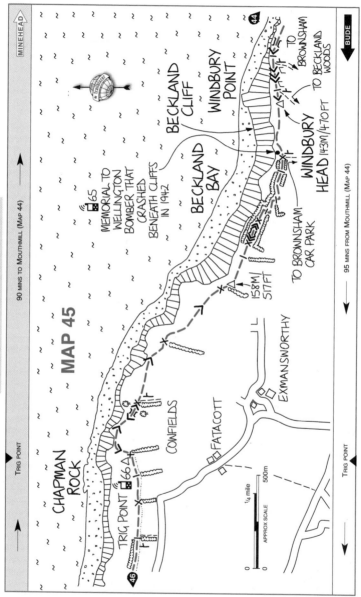

MINEHEAD

MAP 45

CHAPMAN ROCK

TRIG POINT

90 MINS TO MOUTHMILL (MAP 44)

MEMORIAL TO WELLINGTON BOMBER THAT CRASHED BENEATH CLIFFS IN 1942

BECKLAND CLIFF

WINDBURY POINT

BECKLAND BAY

TO BROWNSHAM

TO BECKLAND WOODS

WINDBURY HEAD 143M/470FT

158M/ 517FT

TO BROWNSHAM CAR PARK

COWFIELDS

FATACOTT

EXMANSWORTHY

TRIG POINT

¼ mile

APPROX SCALE

0   500m

TRIG POINT

95 MINS FROM MOUTHMILL (MAP 44)

BUDE

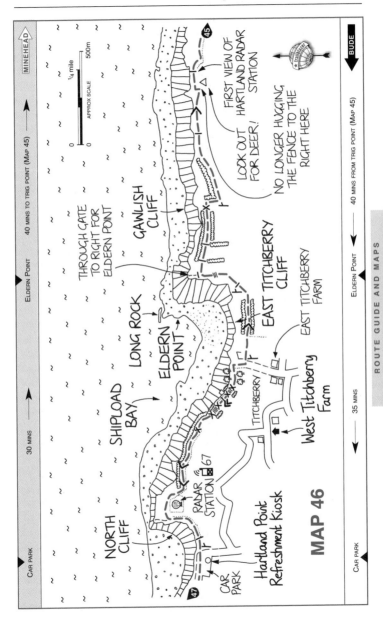

MINEHEAD

CAR PARK | 30 MINS | ELDERN POINT | 40 MINS TO TRIG POINT (MAP 45)

¼ mile
500m
APPROX SCALE
0

45

FIRST VIEW OF HARTLAND RADAR STATION

LOOK OUT FOR DEER!

NO LONGER HUGGING THE FENCE TO THE RIGHT HERE

THROUGH GATE TO RIGHT FOR ELDERN POINT

GAWLISH CLIFF

LONG ROCK

ELDERN POINT

SHIPLOAD BAY

EAST TITCHBERRY CLIFF

EAST TITCHBERRY FARM

NORTH CLIFF

TITCHBERRY

West Titchberry Farm

RADAR STATION 67

Hartland Point Refreshment Kiosk

CAR PARK

MAP 46

47

From here, it's but a short skip to **Hartland Point** (Map 47), where the Bristol Channel meets the Atlantic and the SWCP begins to head in a more southerly direction after so long heading west. The point is marked by the **lighthouse**, built in 1874 and said to be visible up to 25 miles away.

Though you're on the homeward stretch, there's still plenty to be done on this leg before you can finally call it a day. Passing a **memorial** to *Glenart Castle* (a hospital ship that was torpedoed by a German U-boat in 1918 with the loss of 153 men and women out of a total of 186 on board), the path takes you on several steep descents, the second leading towards **Gull Rock**, the third towards the isolated valley of **Blackpool Mill**. Heading up and out of here, the path finally flattens as it crosses **The Warren**, decorated by the ruins of a **tower** – once a folly, so it is believed, but which now makes a nice frame for your photo of the village church in the distance. From here, the way is straightforward to **Hartland Quay**, turning right down the hill by Rocket House.

❑ HARTLAND ABBEY   [OFF MAP 47]

Just a short walk from the village of Stoke, and a little over a mile from the coast path, **Hartland Abbey** (☎ 01237-441496, 🖥 hartlandabbey.com; grounds 11am-5pm, house 2-5pm, last entry 4pm) is a palatial country house that served as a monastery from the 12th century until 1539 when it became the last monastery in the country to be dissolved by Henry VIII. Today it is home to Sir Hugh and Lady Stucley and their family, but is also open to the public. There's a museum, photographic exhibitions, a tea room and extensive public gardens that include a woodland garden with more than 100 different camellias, an 18th century walled garden and winding paths and terraces that lead to a bog garden and Victorian fernery. Tickets for the house, gardens, grounds and exhibitions cost £13.50 (child £5.50) or £10 (child £5) for the gardens, grounds and exhibitions only. Note that there is no access to the tea room without a valid entry ticket.

HARTLAND QUAY   [MAP 48, p191]

There's little to Hartland Quay other than the hotel, but it's a hotel which, converted from what were once stables and customs houses, hints at the importance of this spot as a major port in Tudor times. A storm in 1887 destroyed the quay, and these days there's only a small modern slipway. Nevertheless, the past can still be glimpsed in the hotel's very own museum, with photos and mementoes of various shipwrecks that have occurred on this stretch of shoreline over four centuries. They've plenty of source material to choose from, for it's said that this coastline has approximately ten shipwrecks per mile!

As for the accommodation, *Hartland Quay Hotel* (☎ 01237-441218, 🖥 hartland quayhotel.co.uk; **fb**; 1S/1T/5D/3Tr/2Qd/

annexe sleeps up to 6; all en suite; 🛏; 🐾 stay in annexe only) offers rooms (from £55pp, sgl/sgl occ £70/80) that are the perfect place to nurse sore feet while gazing out over the crashing surf.

The hotel's bar, *The Wreckers' Retreat* (food daily noon-2.30pm & 6-9pm plus 3-5.30pm at weekends and in summer) is also decorated with photos and souvenirs of local shipwrecks. The bar serves local ales (including many from St Austell brewery) and does a nice line in healthy portions of resuscitating food. There are sandwiches, pasties and jacket potatoes at lunchtime (£5-8), while evening mains (£8.50-19) range from simple chicken kiev and chips to 8oz steaks.

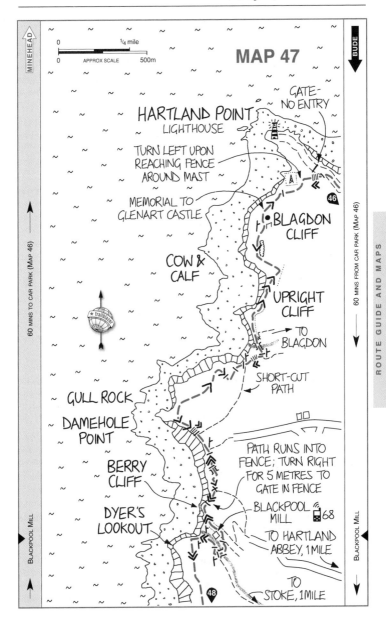

MINEHEAD

BUDE

MAP 47

0 ¼ mile
0 APPROX SCALE 500m

GATE - NO ENTRY

HARTLAND POINT LIGHTHOUSE

TURN LEFT UPON REACHING FENCE AROUND MAST

MEMORIAL TO GLENART CASTLE

A

46

BLAGDON CLIFF

COW & CALF

UPRIGHT CLIFF

TO BLAGDON

SHORT-CUT PATH

GULL ROCK

DAMEHOLE POINT

BERRY CLIFF

DYER'S LOOKOUT

PATH RUNS INTO FENCE; TURN RIGHT FOR 5 METRES TO GATE IN FENCE

BLACKPOOL MILL 68

TO HARTLAND ABBEY, 1 MILE

TO STOKE, 1 MILE

48

60 MINS TO CAR PARK (MAP 46)

60 MINS FROM CAR PARK (MAP 46)

BLACKPOOL MILL

BLACKPOOL MILL

ROUTE GUIDE AND MAPS

STOKE [OFF MAP 48]

If you can't get a room at Hartland Quay Hotel, you'll have to head half a mile inland to this tiny settlement, centred around the 14th-century **Church of St Nectan**, known and famed for its soaring tower, said to be the highest in Devon and for centuries a vital landmark to sailors at sea.

Nearby is an excellent **campsite**. *Stoke Barton Farm* (☎ 01237-441238 or 07766-766176, 🖳 westcountry-camping .co.uk; **fb**; adult/child £9/3.50; WI-FI shop only; 🐾; end Mar to end Oct) is a great place with hot showers and owners who are helpful. They have a small camp **shop** (8.30-10.30am) with the main essentials, a spacious laundry room and a good-sized dining hut with a picnic table, microwave and kettle. Booking is recommended,

though they will always accommodate walkers if at all possible. They even have their own short-cut from the path (see Map 48). They also have two '**pixie huts**' (1D, £32.50pp with bedding, sgl occ £50, £5 less without bedding) – essentially a cute log cabin with a proper double bed in it, and a kettle but no cooking facilities.

The only other option is halfway between Stoke and Hartland, on the lane linking the two. The lovely *Hartland Mill B&B* (☎ 01237-440181, 🖳 hartlandmill.co .uk; **fb**; 3D all en suite; 🍽) has three beautifully decorated rooms (from £49.50pp, sgl occ full room rate) and pleasant forest views. Two-person sharing-platter evening meals (£10pp) are also available.

HARTLAND [map p192]

Though around 2½ miles (3.75km) from the path, and 1½ miles beyond Stoke, Hartland is still visited by coastal walkers as it's the nearest village to this section of the path with shops and facilities, as well as a few places providing B&B.

As the name suggests, Hartland Store & Post Office, on Fore St, contains the local **post office** (Mon-Fri 9am-5.30pm & Sat 9am-12.30pm) and a well-stocked **general store** (Mon-Sat 8am-9pm, Sun 8am-1pm & 4.30-7.30pm). You can withdraw cash from the post office if it is open and you have a suitable account; if not there is an **ATM** that charges for withdrawals. About 100m away, also on Fore St, *The Pop-in* (☎ 01237-441488; **fb**; daily 8am-7.30pm) is equally well stocked, selling hot drinks, hot pasties and sandwiches to take away as well as general food supplies.

Hartland is the only place on the peninsula connected by a **bus service**. Stagecoach's 319 runs via Bideford and Clovelly to Barnstaple, connecting with their 219 service between Hartland & Bude; see pp48-50.

Next to The Hart Inn (see p192), **B&B** is available at *Two Harton Manor* (☎ 01237-441670, 🖳 twohartonmanor.co.uk; 1S/1T shared facilities/1D en suite; 🍽;

🍽), which is actually the west wing of a 400-year-old manor house. B&B costs £45-50pp, and the double room has a four-poster bed.

Alternatively try *Home from Home B&B* (☎ 01237-441652, 🖳 john.sheppard12 @gmail.com; 2D, both en suite; 🍽; Ⓛ; 🐾), which charges £45pp (call for sgl occ rates). The breakfast is splendid and there's a garden to relax in.

The Acorns (☎ 01237-441543; 1D/1Tr, both en suite; 🍽) is a 5-minute walk from the centre of Hartland at 19 Pengilly Way. They charge from £40pp (sgl occ £40).

For accommodation above a pub, *The Anchor Inn* (☎ 01237-441414; 🖳 anchor hartland.co.uk; **fb**; 7D or T/1Qd, all en suite; 🍽; Ⓛ; 🐾 bar only), on Fore St, sits in the centre of the village and is one of three decent pubs here. It is a traditional boozer with real ale (they are in the CAMRA guide), pool and darts and the occasional live music or karaoke evening. The newly refurbished rooms start from £32.50pp. The Anchor also does decent **food** (daily 6-9pm; Sun lunch noon-2pm), with authentic goan curry (£12) and goats cheese and vegetable pancake (£8) sharing a menu with more traditional pub-grub

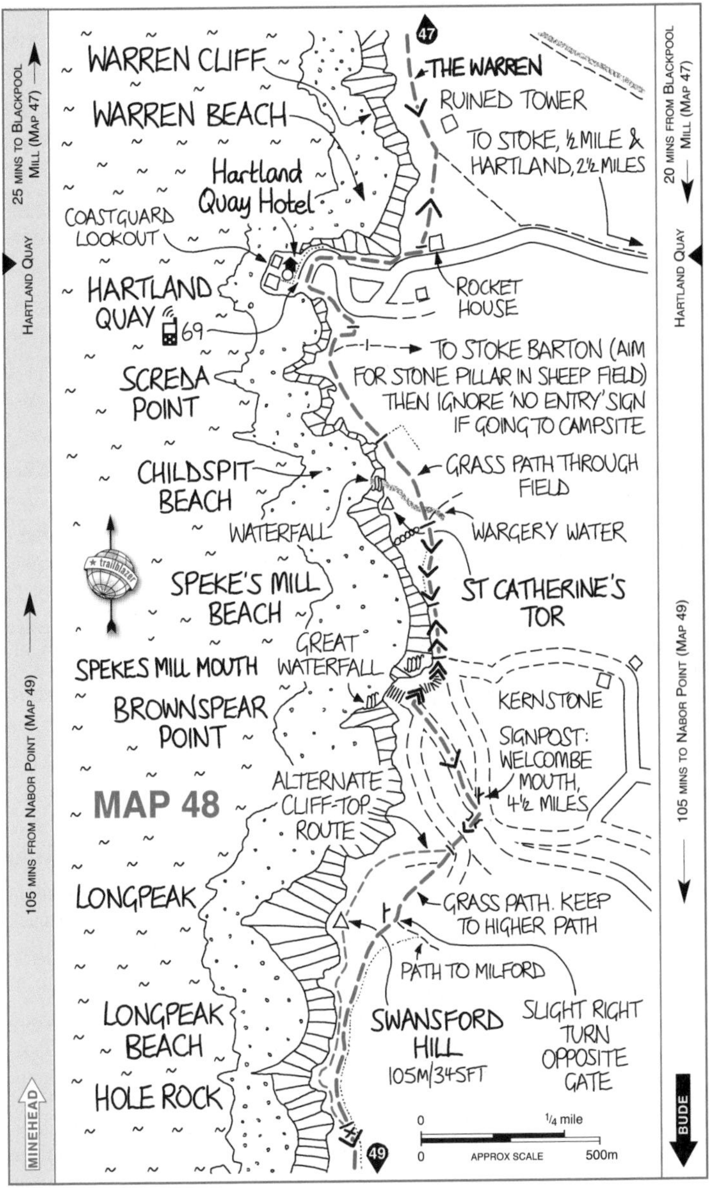

WARREN CLIFF

WARREN BEACH

Hartland Quay Hotel

COASTGUARD LOOKOUT

HARTLAND QUAY 📱 69

SCREDA POINT

CHILDSPIT BEACH

WATERFALL

SPEKE'S MILL BEACH

SPEKES MILL MOUTH

BROWNSPEAR POINT

GREAT WATERFALL

MAP 48

ALTERNATE CLIFF-TOP ROUTE

LONGPEAK

LONGPEAK BEACH

HOLE ROCK

THE WARREN

RUINED TOWER

TO STOKE, ½ MILE & HARTLAND, 2½ MILES

ROCKET HOUSE

TO STOKE BARTON (AIM FOR STONE PILLAR IN SHEEP FIELD) THEN IGNORE 'NO ENTRY' SIGN IF GOING TO CAMPSITE

GRASS PATH THROUGH FIELD

WARGERY WATER

ST CATHERINE'S TOR

KERNSTONE

SIGNPOST: WELCOMBE MOUTH, 4½ MILES

GRASS PATH. KEEP TO HIGHER PATH

PATH TO MILFORD

SWANSFORD HILL 105M/345FT

SLIGHT RIGHT TURN OPPOSITE GATE

0   ¼ mile
0   APPROX SCALE   500m

25 MINS TO BLACKPOOL MILL (MAP 47)

HARTLAND QUAY

105 MINS FROM NABOR POINT (MAP 49)

MINEHEAD

20 MINS FROM BLACKPOOL MILL (MAP 47)

HARTLAND QUAY

105 MINS TO NABOR POINT (MAP 49)

BUDE

ROUTE GUIDE AND MAPS

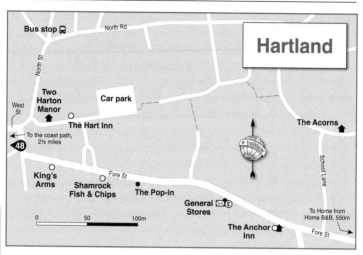

classics. There's also a Sunday carvery.

Stone-baked pizzas (£9.50-12.50) are on the menu at the *King's Arms* (☎ 01237-440151; **fb**; food daily 5-8.30pm), also on Fore St, as well as pub staples like cod and chips and lasagne. They also serve Tribute ales, and have a garden with a play area for kids.

Nearby, behind St John's Chapel, on a lane called The Square, *The Hart Inn* (☎ 01237-441474; **fb**; food Tue-Sat 6-9pm, Thur-Sun noon-3pm; 🐾) is an old place with roots going back to the 14th century.

The menu includes curry of the day (£13.95) and pan-fried seabass (£16.95) as well as burgers and steak; sandwiches are available at lunch time. Sunday roasts start from £10.95. Nice garden, too.

For **takeaway**, head to *Shamrock Fish and Chips* (☎ 01237-488123; **fb**; Mon & Tue 5-7.30pm, Fri noon-2pm & 5-8pm, Sat 5-8pm, closed Sun, Wed & Thur), also on Fore St, where cod and chips cost £7. They can deliver to Stoke Barton Farm campsite.

HARTLAND QUAY TO BUDE   [MAPS 48-55]

By the time you reach this stage you should be well on your way to becoming acclimatised to your new, itinerant way of life; your feet hardened, your back strong, and your legs like two solid tubes of reinforced steel emanating from the legs of your shorts.

You are now, in short, a walker.

Which is just as well, for this stage is said to be the most taxing in the entire book; indeed, by common consent it's actually the hardest on the entire South-West Coast Path! It's a **15½-mile (24.9km; 9hrs)** slog across soaring summit and plunging combe that includes, by our reckoning, ten *major* ascents and descents as you scramble across valley after valley, with no refreshments along the way until right near the end (though it's possible to divert off the path to

Morwenstow – see Map 51 – where there is both a wonderful tea room and a marvellous pub).

Thankfully, the rewards are manifold: the views along the way, especially the panorama at Higher Sharpnose Point, the vista south from Steeple Point and the aspect from Yeolmouth Cliff back to Devil's Hole, are little short of magnificent. If surveying the scenery is difficult due to inclement conditions you can find shelter in the huts of writers Robert Hawker, near Morwenstow, and Ronald Duncan, above the border with Cornwall. While if the weather is good, it seems churlish not to pay a visit to the endless stretch of sand before Bude, the perfect place to cool one's corns and paddle in the sea. All this, and we haven't even mentioned the waterfalls (with a particularly fine example at Speke's Mill Mouth), Iron Age forts, Roman sites, radio stations, and the sheer joy of being on one of the remotest and most beautiful stretches of coastline this country can offer. Plus of course, nothing can beat the feeling that, at the end of this day, you will have completed the walk described in this book – which is no small achievement. While for those who are walking the entire trail – and thus for whom this book was little more than an *hors d'oeuvre* – you too can celebrate the fact that you've finished your time in North Devon, and you won't be seeing this county again for another 300 miles!

The route

Despite the fearsome reputation of this stage, the beginning of the walk is rather gentle as you leave Hartland Quay to head towards the triangular promontory of **St Catherine's Tor**. The path ignores the scramble up the Tor (which is believed to have had a Roman villa on its summit), preferring instead to follow **Wargery Water** upstream, a waterway that ends its journey in impressive fashion by plummeting over the cliffs to the north of the Tor. Those who miss this waterfall (which, after all, is not actually on the path) needn't be too concerned, for the next valley, **Speke's Mill Mouth**, has, if anything, an even more spectacular version, and one that is easily visible just a few metres from the path.

Climbing out of the combe – the first of many calf-popping ascents – takes you up **Swansford Hill** and past the turn-off to **Elmscott**.

ELMSCOTT   [OFF MAP 49, p194]

Elmscott is an easy, short walk from the path (10-15 mins) and the accommodation is rather pleasant. Privately-owned, but YHA-affiliated, *YHA Elmscott* (☎ 01237-441367 or 01237-441276, 🖳 elmscott.org.uk, or yha.org.uk/hostel/elmscott-bunk house; 1T/3 x 4- & 3 x 6-bed dorms, shared facilities; Mar-Oct) was originally built as a school in Victorian times, but is now a cosy hostel (approx £22/25pp members/non-members) with a small **shop** (8-10am & 5-10pm), good kitchen facilities (which is just as well as meals aren't provided and there's

nowhere to eat around here) and a drying room. **Camping** is also available (£10pp), although they only have room for four tents; booking is therefore recommended.

Elmscott Farm, on which it is set, is also a **B&B** (☎ 01237-441276, 🖳 elms cott.org.uk; 2D en suite/1T private bathroom; ☛; (L)) under the same ownership as the hostel. They charge £40pp (sgl occ £40) for bed and breakfast. They don't do evening meals but will direct you to the local pub.

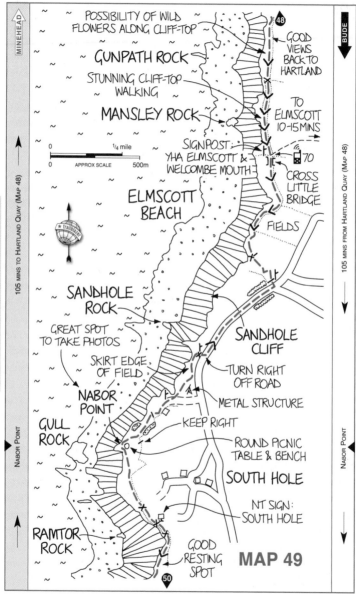

MINEHEAD

BUDE

ROUTE GUIDE AND MAPS

105 MINS TO HARTLAND QUAY (MAP 48)

105 MINS FROM HARTLAND QUAY (MAP 48)

NABOR POINT

NABOR POINT

POSSIBILITY OF WILD
FLOWERS ALONG CLIFF-TOP

GUNPATH ROCK

STUNNING CLIFF-TOP
WALKING

MANSLEY ROCK

48

GOOD
VIEWS
BACK TO
HARTLAND

TO
ELMSCOTT
10-15 MINS

SIGNPOST:
YHA ELMSCOTT &
WELCOMBE MOUTH

70

CROSS
LITTLE
BRIDGE

ELMSCOTT
BEACH

FIELDS

1/4 mile

APPROX SCALE   500m

SANDHOLE
ROCK

GREAT SPOT
TO TAKE PHOTOS

SKIRT EDGE
OF FIELD

NABOR
POINT

GULL
ROCK

SANDHOLE
CLIFF

TURN RIGHT
OFF ROAD

METAL STRUCTURE

KEEP RIGHT

ROUND PICNIC
TABLE & BENCH

SOUTH HOLE

NT SIGN:
SOUTH HOLE

RAMTOR
ROCK

GOOD
RESTING
SPOT

MAP 49

50

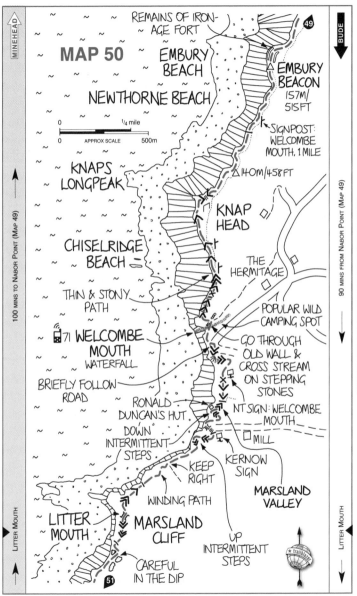

MINEHEAD

BUDE

MAP 50

REMAINS OF IRON-AGE FORT

EMBURY BEACH

49

EMBURY BEACON
157M/515FT

NEWTHORNE BEACH

SIGNPOST:
WELCOMBE
MOUTH, 1 MILE

0   ¼ mile
0   500m
APPROX SCALE

140M/458FT

KNAPS LONGPEAK

KNAP HEAD

CHISELRIDGE BEACH

THE HERMITAGE

POPULAR WILD CAMPING SPOT

THIN & STONY PATH

GO THROUGH OLD WALL & CROSS STREAM ON STEPPING STONES

71 WELCOMBE MOUTH
WATERFALL

BRIEFLY FOLLOW ROAD

NT SIGN: WELCOMBE MOUTH

RONALD DUNCAN'S HUT

MILL

DOWN INTERMITTENT STEPS

KERNOW SIGN

KEEP RIGHT

MARSLAND VALLEY

WINDING PATH

LITTER MOUTH

MARSLAND CLIFF

UP INTERMITTENT STEPS

CAREFUL IN THE DIP

51

trailblazer

100 MINS TO NABOR POINT (MAP 49)

90 MINS FROM NABOR POINT (MAP 49)

ROUTE GUIDE AND MAPS

LITTER MOUTH

LITTER MOUTH

The path is rather uneventful to **Nabor Point**, even joining a road at one point, and only gets exciting again at **Embury Beacon** (Map 50), where the path runs alongside the defensive earthwork of an Iron Age fort. Yet another vertiginous descent follows, this time at **Welcombe Mouth**, where the path crosses the stream on stepping stones. It's a beautiful spot – and popular with wild campers – but it's surpassed in its noteworthiness for walkers by the next laceration in the surface of the land: **Marsland Valley**. Another steep combe, it is here on its northern slopes that you'll find **Ronald Duncan's hut**. Author, poet, playwright and pacifist, Duncan is perhaps best known for writing the libretto of Benjamin's Britten's opera *The Rape of Lucretia*; but also for this lovely stone hut that he constructed so he could have views over the sea while writing. It's been well restored by members of his family in recent years, and inside is a writing table and chair, a bench, and a noticeboard with information about Duncan.

Struggle down the steps to the floor of the valley and you cross the **border into Cornwall**, the exact boundary marked by a bridge and a signpost welcoming you to 'Kernow' (as they call it round here). But while the county might have changed, the path remains as challenging as ever as you traverse yet more stamina-sapping undulations at **Litter Mouth** and **Yeol Mouth** (Map 51) and around **St Morwenna's Well** – so easy to write, so exhausting to complete.

Thankfully, soon after the latter, it's possible to get off the rollercoaster for a while by taking the short diversion to the hamlet of **Morwenstow**.

MORWENSTOW   [MAP 51]

There's little more to this ancient settlement than a church, a tearoom, and a pub. All three, however, are full of character. The church is dedicated to St Morwenna and St John the Baptist, and while the earliest part of the current church is Norman, there is believed to have been a church on this site since Anglo-Saxon times. The Rev Hawker, of Hawker's Hut fame (see box p198), was one of the vicars here.

Morwenstow is connected with Bude by the No 217 **bus** which runs three times a day; see pp48-50 for details.

Opposite the church sits the award-winning *Rectory Farm Tearoom* (☎ 01288-331251, 🖳 rectory-tearooms.co.uk; **fb**; late Mar/Easter-end Oct daily 11am-4.30pm, winter hours variable; 🐾 outside area), part of a charming 13th-century farm that's been serving cream-topped scones (from £6) to hungry walkers for 60 years. Gluten-,

wheat-, and dairy-free options are available and they also do sandwiches, pasties, cakes and tarts, as well as beer, cider, coffee, loose-leaf teas and clotted-cream vanilla ice cream. Dogs are welcome in the outside area.

To the south, the 13th-century *Bush Inn* (☎ 01288-331242, 🖳 thebushinnmor wenstow.com; **fb**; 2D/2T, all en suite; 🛏; Ⓛ; 🐾) provides B&B (£47.50pp, sgl occ £80) and serves **food** (daily noon-2.30pm & 5.30-8pm). The menu includes fish and chips, slow-roasted pork belly and three-bean chilli, and there are real ales on tap. Ask the owners to point out some of the ancient features of the inn, including the lepers' squint, through which the diseased of the parish were fed scraps, and a monastic cross carved into a flagstone in the floor. Note: there is sometimes a minimum two-night stay in high season.

Those who forego the delights of Morwenstow will continue along **Vicarage Cliff**, in time coming to the cliff-face path to **Hawker's Hut** (see box on p198), built by a local vicar from the timbers of shipwrecked craft.

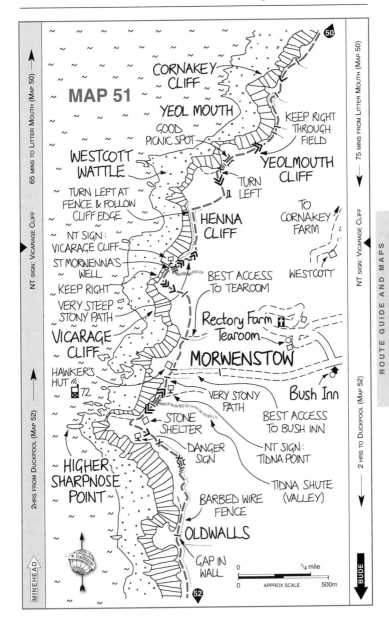

MAP 51

CORNAKEY CLIFF

YEOL MOUTH

GOOD PICNIC SPOT

KEEP RIGHT THROUGH FIELD

WESTCOTT WATTLE

YEOLMOUTH CLIFF

TURN LEFT

TURN LEFT AT FENCE & FOLLOW CLIFF EDGE

TO CORNAKEY FARM

HENNA CLIFF

NT SIGN: VICARAGE CLIFF

ST MORWENNA'S WELL

WESTCOTT

KEEP RIGHT

BEST ACCESS TO TEAROOM

VERY STEEP STONY PATH

Rectory Farm Tearoom

VICARAGE CLIFF

MORWENSTOW

HAWKER'S HUT 72

Bush Inn

VERY STONY PATH

BEST ACCESS TO BUSH INN

STONE SHELTER

DANGER SIGN

NT SIGN: TIDNA POINT

HIGHER SHARPNOSE POINT

TIDNA SHUTE (VALLEY)

BARBED WIRE FENCE

OLDWALLS

GAP IN WALL

0   1/4 mile
0   APPROX SCALE   500m

trailblazer

65 MINS TO LITTER MOUTH (MAP 50)

NT SIGN: VICARAGE CLIFF

2HRS FROM DUCKPOOL (MAP 52)

MINEHEAD

75 MINS FROM LITTER MOUTH (MAP 50)

NT SIGN: VICARAGE CLIFF

2 HRS TO DUCKPOOL (MAP 52)

BUDE

ROUTE GUIDE AND MAPS

Still the relentless gradients of the path continue as you clamber in and out of the valleys of **Tidna Shute** and **Stanbury Mouth** (Map 52), the latter, in this author's reckoning, the steepest of all today's climbs. Your reward at the top is the enormous **GCHQ Bude** site from where, at its southern end, the first views of Bude can be glimpsed. Another steep valley, **Duckpool**, follows, where in July at dusk you can see the rare spectacle of glow worms. Along this coast, over 150 ships have been wrecked between Morwenstow and Bude. No wonder Alfred, Lord Tennyson, described this stretch thus:

But after tempest, when the long wave broke
All down the thundering shores of Bude and Bos.
Alfred, Lord Tennyson, *The Birth of King Arthur*

Duckpool is also the last serious challenge on this stage. The gradients finally relent now and the path, though still long and undulating, is more merciful than it has been previously on this stage.

ROUTE GUIDE AND MAPS

❑ **HAWKER AND HIS HUT**   [MAP 51, p197]
Writer, maverick and saviour of shipwrecked sailors, Robert Stephen Hawker was born in 1803 and became vicar of St Morwenna and St John the Baptist Church at Morwenstow in 1834. Prior to his arrival the church had had no serving clergy for well over a century and, lacking any guiding moral influence, the coastline in this region had instead become a base for smugglers and wreckers (who used to lure passing ships onto the rocks, regardless of the safety of those onboard, so they could then loot the wreck of its cargo).

Hawker, horrified at the behaviour of many of his parishioners, went out of his way to both ameliorate their behaviour and educate them in the errors of their ways. The hut that he built out of driftwood into the cliff-face, and which still carries his name, was originally designed as a lookout, so Hawker could warn any ships of the dangers of navigation. He also used the hut as his study, from where he could compose such works as '*Footprints of Former Men in Far Cornwall*', which included an account of the wrecking of the *Caledonia* in 1842, and where he also received friends such as Charles Kingsley and Alfred, Lord Tennyson.

Contemporary sources describe Hawker as a bit of an eccentric, given to wearing colourful clothes, dressing up as a mermaid, and excommunicating his cat for mousing on a Sunday. But he was also extremely compassionate and introduced the practice of giving the bodies of shipwrecked sailors a Christian burial (where previously they had been allowed to bob in the ocean for days). The **figurehead of** *Caledonia* marks the spot in Morwenstow Church where the crew are buried. Nearby is a granite cross into which the words 'Unknown Yet Well Known' are carved, a tribute to the thirty or so bodies of seafarers that he buried nearby. He is most remembered, however, as the man who introduced the Harvest Festival into the Christian calendar, having invited his congregation to a service in October 1841 to give thanks to God for his bounty; and as the composer of '*The Song of the Western Men*', which has become something of a 'national' anthem for Cornwall.

Hawker died in 1875, the mourners at his funeral wearing purple rather than the traditional black. He was survived by his wife, who was forty years his junior – plus, of course, by his small driftwood hut, today the smallest building in the entire portfolio of the National Trust.

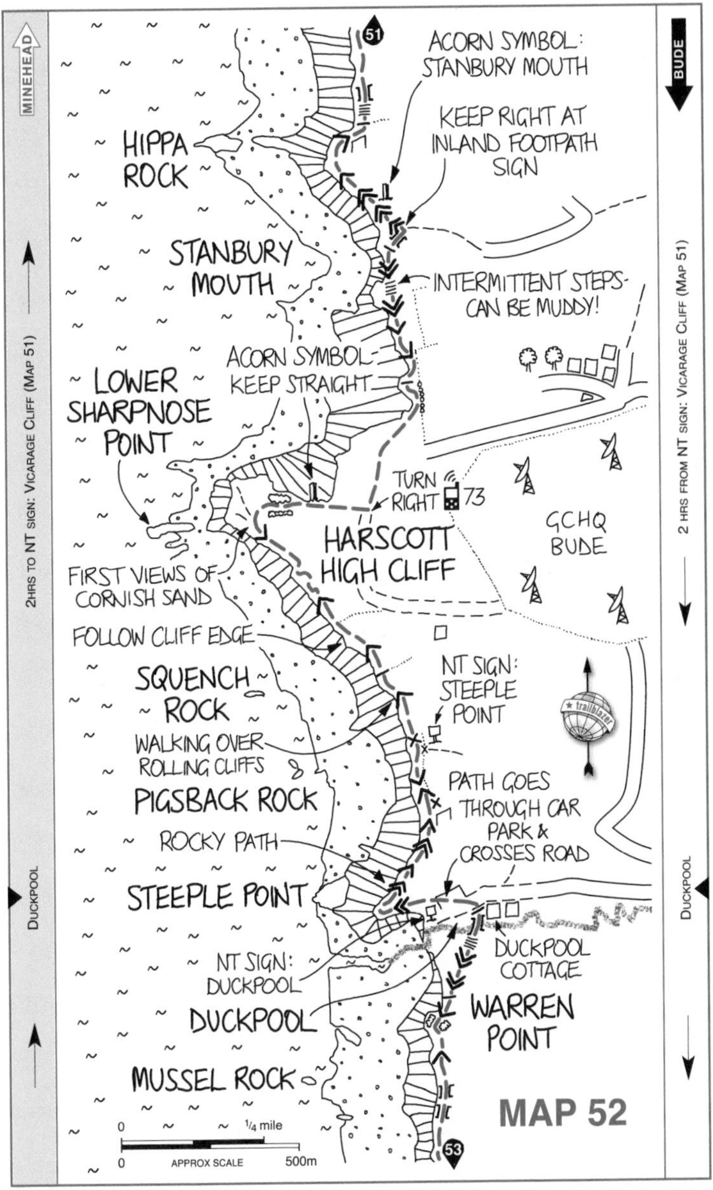
MINEHEAD
2HRS TO NT SIGN: VICARAGE CLIFF (MAP 51)
DUCKPOOL
BUDE
2 HRS FROM NT SIGN: VICARAGE CLIFF (MAP 51)
DUCKPOOL
51
ACORN SYMBOL: STANBURY MOUTH
KEEP RIGHT AT INLAND FOOTPATH SIGN
HIPPA ROCK
STANBURY MOUTH
INTERMITTENT STEPS- CAN BE MUDDY!
ACORN SYMBOL- KEEP STRAIGHT
LOWER SHARPNOSE POINT
TURN RIGHT
73
HARSCOTT HIGH CLIFF
GCHQ BUDE
FIRST VIEWS OF CORNISH SAND
FOLLOW CLIFF EDGE
SQUENCH ROCK
NT SIGN: STEEPLE POINT
trailblazer
WALKING OVER ROLLING CLIFFS
PIGSBACK ROCK
PATH GOES THROUGH CAR PARK & CROSSES ROAD
ROCKY PATH
STEEPLE POINT
NT SIGN: DUCKPOOL
DUCKPOOL COTTAGE
DUCKPOOL
WARREN POINT
MUSSEL ROCK
MAP 52
0
1/4 mile
0
APPROX SCALE
500m
53

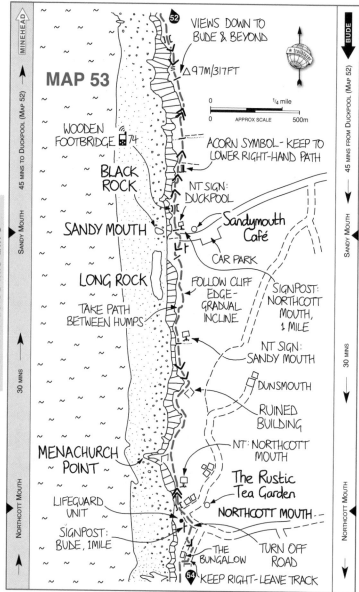

MINEHEAD

45 MINS TO DUCKPOOL (MAP 52)

SANDY MOUTH

30 MINS

NORTHCOTT MOUTH

BUDE

45 MINS FROM DUCKPOOL (MAP 52)

SANDY MOUTH

30 MINS

NORTHCOTT MOUTH

MAP 53

VIEWS DOWN TO
BUDE & BEYOND

△ 97M/317FT

0   1/4 mile
0   APPROX SCALE   500m

WOODEN
FOOTBRIDGE   74

ACORN SYMBOL – KEEP TO
LOWER RIGHT-HAND PATH

BLACK
ROCK

NT SIGN:
DUCKPOOL

Sandymouth
Café

SANDY MOUTH

CAR PARK

LONG ROCK

FOLLOW CLIFF
EDGE –
GRADUAL
INCLINE

SIGNPOST:
NORTHCOTT
MOUTH,
½ MILE

TAKE PATH
BETWEEN HUMPS

NT SIGN:
SANDY MOUTH

DUNSMOUTH

RUINED
BUILDING

MENACHURCH
POINT

NT: NORTHCOTT
MOUTH

The Rustic
Tea Garden

LIFEGUARD
UNIT

NORTHCOTT MOUTH

SIGNPOST:
BUDE, 1MILE

THE
BUNGALOW

TURN OFF
ROAD

KEEP RIGHT – LEAVE TRACK

Cafés start to appear on the route too, including popular ***Sandymouth Café*** (Map 53; ☎ 01288-354286, daily 10am-4pm, later in summer), with bacon baps for £3.95 and paninis, burgers and jacket potatoes for around £8.

Further on is the lovely eatery, ***The Rustic Tea Garden*** (Map 53; ☎ 07494-289546, **fb**; Easter-early Oct Tue-Sun 10am-6pm), by the stream at **Northcott Mouth**. It was run by the redoubtable Margaret Frost, known as the Queen of Bude, for 54 years until her death in 2020. It has since been taken on by a local family who serve, to quote from an article in *The Sunday Times*, 'a cracking cream tea for just £4'. But by now even this idyllic place may not be enough to halt your determined march to Bude, which you should reach, weary, exhausted and happy, about 2-2½ hours after leaving Duckpool.

Should you begin to wane just before Bude, however, there are more food and drinks options at **Crooklets Beach**, though it's a less pleasant place to rest up than the previous two cafés, so you may as well push on to Bude. ***Rosie's Kitchen*** (Map 54; ☎ 01288-354238, 🖥 rosieskitchen.co.uk; **fb**; summer Sun-Wed 10am-4pm, Thur-Sat 10am-8pm; winter hours variable) does breakfasts, burgers and wood-fired pizza, and serves booze, while ***Crooklets Beach Café*** (Map 54; ☎ 01288 350009; **fb**; daily 9am-6pm, winter to 5pm), also fully licensed, serves pasties, all-day breakfasts, including baps, and has plenty of vegan options.

BUDE [MAP 55 p205]

Bude is a small, compact seaside town with plenty of charm and character that sprawls out from its famous beach, Summerleaze. Summer and bank holidays are when this normally sleepy little town springs into life and it can become quite hectic. However, arrive at any other time and you shouldn't have any trouble booking accommodation and making your way around town.

Built in 1830, the town's small **castle** (☐ thecastlebude.org.uk; daily 10am-4/5pm winter/summer; free) is worth exploring. Its **heritage centre** contains exhibitions on shipwrecks and lifeboats as well as displays on the Bude Canal and the geology of the Cornish coast. Inside, too, is **Willoughby Gallery**, which holds local art exhibitions, a gift shop and the pleasant Limelight Café (see Where to eat).

Pretty **Bude Canal** (see box below) runs from the beach past the castle and can be followed for a mile or so along the towpath or in **boats** (£8-10 for 30 mins). Also nearby is **Bude Light**, a Millennium project built to commemorate the life of Sir Goldsworthy Gurney, a Cornish scientist and inventor for whom the castle was originally built.

The marvellous **Bude Sea Pool** (Map 54; ☐ budeseapool.org; **fb**; open year-round; free) is a man-made tidal swimming pool, built in 1930 to provide a safe place for people to go sea swimming.

Bude is also known for its **Jazz Festival** (see p16).

Services

The excellent **Bude Tourist Information and Canal Centre** (☎ 01288-354240, ☐ visitbude.info; **fb**; Easter-Oct Mon-Sat 10am-5pm, Sun 10am-4pm, Oct-Easter daily to 4pm) has a comprehensive listing of accommodation in the area (you can book accommodation in the centre and through its website too) and the enthusiastic staff are willing to help. Wi-fi is free if you log in through Facebook but if not you can buy a voucher for £1 which is valid for three hours. They are happy to store luggage for the day (£1.50). Hot drinks are available here too, and they also have a good selection of Cornwall books, including Trailblazer's guidebook to the Cornwall Coast Path.

There is **internet access** (free for 30 mins) at **Bude Library** (Mon, Wed & Fri

---

❑ BUDE CANAL

Bude Canal (☐ bude-canal.co.uk) was dug to transport mainly sand inland from the seashore so that it could be spread on the fields to improve the soil which was rather poor in parts of north Cornwall. The Canal was the brainchild of one John Endyvean, the intention being to link up with the River Tamar at Calstock, thus providing a waterway between the Bristol Channel and the English Channel, 90 miles of canal to span just 28 miles as the crow flies.

The full scheme was never realised although by 1823 some 35 miles of canal were in operation. Once the railways were built the use of the canal began to decline and by WWII it became ineffective as a waterway. Today only a short stretch remains between Bude and Helebridge.

A project to restore the canal with the aid of a £45m grant from the Heritage Lottery Fund was completed in 2009. Whilst the lock-gates giving access to the open sea suffered damage in the early part of 2008 during some huge storms, the canal itself is currently in good working order. At the Helebridge end, **Weir Nature Centre** at Whalesborough Farm opened in 2011. It is a 40-minute walk along a flat tarmac path by the side of the canal.

You can also hire rowing boats (£8 for 30 mins), pedalos and canoes (both £10 for 30 mins) to take out on the canal from **Bude Rowing Boats** (☎ 07968-688782 or 07432-199447, ☐ budeboathire.co.uk; **fb**; Good Fri to end Sep daily 11am-6pm).

9.30am-5pm, Sat 10am-1pm), which has a good Cornish reference section. All cafés, restaurants and pubs have free wi-fi.

Bude's main **post office** (Mon-Fri 9am-5pm, Sat 9am-12.30pm) is at the top of Belle Vue, the main shopping street. There's also a **sub-post office** which is part of a newsagent (daily 7am-5.30pm) almost directly opposite the tourist office.

For **food** shopping, there is a Sainsbury's (Mon-Sat 8am-8pm, Sun 10am-4pm), and a Co-op (daily 7am-10pm). There is a Boots **pharmacy** (Mon-Sat 9am-5.30pm, Sun 10am-4pm) while, for **walking and camping gear**, there is a Mountain Warehouse (Mon-Fri 9am-5.30pm, Sat 9am-6pm, Sun 10am-5pm) and a good camping section in Wroes (Mon-Sat 9.30am-5pm).

Spencer Thorn Bookshop (☎ 01288-352518; Mon-Sat 9am-5pm, summer school hols Sun 10am-4pm) has a good selection of books on Cornwall, including Trailblazer's Cornwall Coast Path.

There are several **banks** including a TSB (Mon-Fri 9am-5pm, Sat 9am-1pm) and a Barclays (Mon-Fri 9.30am-4.30pm, Sat 9.30am-noon); both of which have **ATMs**. You will also find ATMs outside the town's supermarkets.

There's a **launderette** (Mon-Thur 8.30am-5pm, Fri to 8pm, Sat 9am-5pm, Sun 10am-5pm) tucked away off Lansdown Rd.

Transport

[See also pp48-50] **Bus**-wise, for destinations north, some of Stagecoach's No 85 services go from here to Barnstaple, where you'll find the nearest railway station. Alternatively, their Nos 6 & 6A run to the main rail hub at Exeter. The No 217 operates to Morwenstow and the 218/219 service travels to Hartland from where you can connect with the 319 to Bideford and Barnstaple. Plymouth Citybus's No 12 service heads to Launceston, while the 95 runs to Wadebridge. Buses stop on The Strand.

For a **taxi**, try Trev's Taxi (☎ 07799-663217, 🖥 trevstaxi.co.uk).

Where to stay

Campsites For **campers**, the 10-minute stroll out of town to *Upper Lynstone Caravan & Camping Park* (☎ 01288-352017, 🖥 upperlynstone.co.uk; 🐾 on lead; Apr-Sep; walker & small tent £8-10, 2 people & tent £16-23) is well worth the effort. The quiet location is perfect for those continuing on the trail as it backs on to the cliffs and the coastal path to Upton and Widemouth Bay. There is a well-stocked **shop** and **laundry** facilities; the free showers are roomy and spotlessly clean. To get here, keep walking along Falcon Terrace, which becomes Vicarage Road, and the campsite will eventually be on your right.

The fabulous *Cerenety Eco Campsite* (☎ 07789-718446, 🖥 cerenetycampsite.co .uk; **fb**) was temporarily closed in 2021 but planning to reopen from 2022 so it's worth calling them to check. It's in **Upton**, just off the coast path towards Crackington Haven, so not really in Bude itself, although not much further away than Upper Lynstone. It's basic (solar-heated showers, compost toilets) but well organised and genuinely eco-conscious.

B&Bs, guesthouses and pubs B&B-style accommodation is mostly located at the northern end of town, near the golf course. On Burn View you will find: *Links Side Guest House* (☎ 01288-352410, 🖥 linkssidebude.co.uk; **fb**; 1S/4D/1T all en suite, 1D private facilities) where B&B costs from £32.50pp (sgl/sgl occ from £45); *Sea Jade Guest House* (☎ 01288-353404, 🖥 seajadeguesthouse.co.uk; **fb**; 2D/4Tr all en suite, 1D private bathroom) where the tariff is from £37.50pp (sgl occ £35-55); *Sunrise* (☎ 01288-353214, 🖥 sunrise-bude .co.uk; **fb**; 2S/1T/3D/1D or T, all en suite; 🛑; 🐾), which charges £35-45pp (sgl occ £40-60); and *Tee-Side Guest House* (☎ 01288-352351, 🖥 tee-side.co.uk; **fb**; 1S private facilities, 4D or T, all en suite), from where, as its name suggests, you can enjoy views overlooking the golf course while eating your breakfast. Rates here are from £40pp (sgl/sgl occ from £50/65).

Brendon Arms (☎ 01288-354542, 🖥

brendonarms.co.uk; **fb**; 1S/5D/3T, all en suite; ●) is a popular **pub** which also has rooms (from £42pp, sgl/sgl occ from £42).

Hotels Overlooking the beach from a great vantage point on the edge of Summerleaze Down, *The Beach* (☎ 01288-389800, 🖥 thebeachatbude.co.uk; 2T/14D, all en suite; ●) is Bude's most boutique-like hotel, with heated floors and very smart, modern rooms, half of which have sea views. The terraces from the bar and restaurant have sea views too. B&B in low season starts at around £65pp (sgl occ from £125), but you'll often have to pay more than £100pp; room only and dinner, bed & breakfast package rates are also available.

On the same road, *The Edgcumbe* (☎ 01288-353846, 🖥 edgcumbe-hotel.co.uk; **fb**; 6D/5D or T/1Tr, all en suite; ●; Feb-Dec) is a friendly place, with a young vibe to it. Rates are from £50pp (sgl occ from £40). There's a small bar-restaurant with excellent meals, and a drying room too; handy for wet tents and soggy walking boots.

Atlantic House (☎ 01288-352451, 🖥 atlantichousehotel.com; **fb**; 1S private bathroom, 12D/3D or T, all en suite; ●) has some nice sea-view rooms, although some of the rear rooms are a bit poky. Rates are £45-87.50pp (sgl from £45, sgl occ £70-150). Next door is *The Grosvenor* (☎ 01288-352062, 🖥 thegrosvenorbude.co.uk; 1S/3D/1D or T/1T/1Tr, all en suite; Mar-Nov), which has two rooms with sea views and one en suite room can connect with a bunk bed room for children aged 7-16 (£110-120 for a family). They charge £35-49pp (sgl occ from £50) but they have a two-night minimum stay at weekends (mid July to mid Sep).

On the other side of the canal, *Falcon Hotel* (☎ 01288-352005, 🖥 falconhotel .com; **fb**; 4S/7T/18D, all en suite; ●) is an impressive place, and a more traditional, classier alternative to its main top-end rival, The Beach. B&B starts at £55pp (sgl occ from £97.50).

At the lower end of the hotel scale, *The Globe Hotel* (☎ 01288 352085, 🖥 the

globehotelbude.com; 2D/2Tr) is a bit run down, but has room-only rates from just £30pp (sgl/sgl occ £50); breakfast costs an extra £7.50pp.

Nearby is a *Premier Inn* (☎ 0333-2346549, 🖥 premierinn.com) where, incredibly, you can get a standard double room for as little as £16.50pp (sgl occ £33) in low season, although expect to pay more than £50pp (sgl occ more than £100) in peak holiday season. Breakfast costs an extra £8.99pp. There's a café-bar area, too, which also does evening meals.

Where to eat and drink
Cafés & Bakeries There are numerous options for a coffee and a snack in Bude. Inside the castle is *Limelight Café* (daily 10am-4pm), which does sandwiches, cream teas and coffee. *The Coffee Shop* (☎ 01288-355973; **fb**; Mar-Nov daily 10am-5pm, Dec-Feb 10.30am-4pm), on Lansdown Rd, sells freshly baked goods from *Lansdowne Bakery* (**fb**; daily 9am-5pm), a long-standing, good-value bakery that does various pastries, freshly-made sandwiches (£2.95), pasties (£4.25) and bacon and sausage baps (£2.50). Nearby *Pengenna Pasties* (daily 9am-5pm) offers excellent pasties, scones and other baked goods.

On the outskirts of town, *The Coffee Pot* (☎ 01288-356142; **fb**; daily June-Sep 8am-6pm, winter 8.30am-3pm; 🐾) is a down-to-earth, friendly café with cream teas, full English breakfasts, and some roadside patio seating. On Belle Vue, *Costa Coffee* (Mon-Sat 7am-6.30pm, Sun 9am-5pm) is the first café to open in the middle of town.

Down on the canal, *The Barge* (☎ 01288-356786, 🖥 thebargebude.co.uk; **fb**; Mon-Sat 10am-5pm, Sun 10am-4pm) is a café on a boat offering salads (£9-10), sandwiches (£6.50-8.50) and cream teas (£6), as well as fish and chips (£11) and hot ciabattas (£9-10). Nearby, beside the canal lock, is *The Lock Gates Tearoom* (**fb**; summer Tue-Sun 10am-5pm) which does breakfasts (£6.50-7.50) until noon, then lunchtime sandwiches, toasties and jacket potatoes (£6-9). Cream teas are £6. Also by the

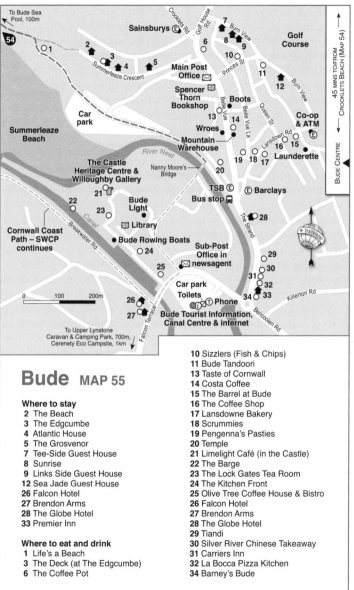

To Bude Sea
Pool, 100m

54

Sainsburys £

Crooklets Rd
Golf House Rd

7 Burn View
8
9

6

2
3 4
5
Summerleaze Crescent

Golf
Course

10
Princes St

11

12 Burn View

Main Post
Office ✉

45 MINS TO/FROM
CROOKLETS BEACH (MAP 54)

Spencer
Thorn
Bookshop

Boots

Belle Vue

13 14 Belle Vue La

Wroes

Co-op
& ATM
£

Car
park

Queen St

Summerleaze
Beach

Mountain
Warehouse

River Neet

Lansdown Rd

16 15 £

19 18 17 Launderette
20

BUDE CENTRE

The Castle
Heritage Centre &
Willoughby Gallery

Nanny Moore's
Bridge

21

22

23

Bude
Light

Library

TSB £
Bus stop 🚌

£ Barclays

The Strand

28

Cornwall Coast
Path – SWCP
continues

Canal
Breakwater Rd

● Bude Rowing Boats
24

25

Sub-Post
Office in
✉ newsagent

29

30

31
32
34 33

Killerton Rd

ROUTE GUIDE AND MAPS

0   100   200m

Car park
Toilets
26   @ ℹ Phone
27 Bude Tourist Information,
Canal Centre & internet

Falcon Terrace

Bencoolen Rd

To Upper Lynstone
Caravan & Camping Park, 700m,
Cerenety Eco Campsite, 1km

Bude MAP 55

Where to stay
2 The Beach
3 The Edgcumbe
4 Atlantic House
5 The Grosvenor
7 Tee-Side Guest House
8 Sunrise
9 Links Side Guest House
12 Sea Jade Guest House
26 Falcon Hotel
27 Brendon Arms
28 The Globe Hotel
33 Premier Inn

Where to eat and drink
1 Life's a Beach
3 The Deck (at The Edgcumbe)
6 The Coffee Pot

10 Sizzlers (Fish & Chips)
11 Bude Tandoori
13 Taste of Cornwall
14 Costa Coffee
15 The Barrel at Bude
16 The Coffee Shop
17 Lansdowne Bakery
18 Scrummies
19 Pengenna's Pasties
20 Temple
21 Limelight Café (in the Castle)
22 The Barge
23 The Lock Gates Tea Room
24 The Kitchen Front
25 Olive Tree Coffee House & Bistro
26 Falcon Hotel
27 Brendon Arms
28 The Globe Hotel
29 Tiandi
30 Silver River Chinese Takeaway
31 Carriers Inn
32 La Bocca Pizza Kitchen
34 Barney's Bude

canal, though set back slightly from the water, is *The Kitchen Front* (☎ 01288-350107, 🖳 thekitchenfront.co.uk; **fb**; Mon-Thur 10am-5pm, Fri & Sat to 3.30pm, closed Sun, winter hours variable) a quirky wartime-themed tearoom and craft workshop where you can enjoy a 1940s-style afternoon tea with vintage china and cakes made from wartime recipes.

Overlooking the river, *Temple* (☎ 01288-354739, 🖳 templecornwall.com; **fb**; lunch Wed-Sun 11.30am-2.30pm, evening daily 5.30-8.30pm, booking essential) is the hipsters choice of café, with old-school classroom table and chairs, a health-conscious menu (lunchtime small plates £4-9) and good tunes. There's a £28 set menu come evening.

If you just fancy an ice cream, it's hard to resist *Taste of Cornwall* (daily 10am-6pm) with at least 24 different flavours on offer.

Restaurants & Takeaways

Café by day, bistro by night, *Olive Tree Coffee House and Bistro* (☎ 01288-359577, 🖳 olivetreebude.co.uk; **fb**; daily 10am-4pm, summer Mon-Sat 10am-8pm) serves a good variety of gluten-free and vegetarian dishes. It's a lovely spot beside the canal, but prices aren't cheap.

More affordable, *Scrummies* (summer Mon-Sat 8am-9pm, Sun 9am-9pm, winter days/hours variable) is owned by local fisherman Cliff Bowden who catches, prepares and cooks 60-70% of the fish himself and offers a gigantic cod 'n' chips.

Just before The Strand arrives at the road bridge, American restaurant *Barney's Bude* (☎ 01288-350850, **fb**; daily noon-9pm; 🐾) offers a variety of burgers from £7.95 plus hot dogs, shakes and gelato ice cream to eat in or takeaway.

Nearby, *La Bocca Pizza Kitchen* (☎ 01288-255855, 🖳 laboccabude.co.uk; **fb**; Mon-Wed 4-9pm, Thur-Sun noon-9pm, takeaway deliveries 5-9pm) is a small pizza and pasta restaurant that also does takeaway too. The pizza here is excellent.

Also on this stretch are the two Chinese restaurants, *Tiandi* (☎ 01288-359686; **fb**; daily 5-10pm), which also does Thai cuisine, and *Silver River Chinese*

Takeaway (☎ 01288-352028; **fb**; Tue-Sun 5-10pm, closed mid Jan to mid Feb).

The best Indian restaurant in town is *Bude Tandoori* (☎ 01288-359994, 🖳 bude tandoori.co.uk; daily 5-11.30pm), which, unusually, has some outdoor seating too.

For classic British seaside fish 'n' chips look no further than *Sizzlers* (☎ 01288-356331; **fb**; daily noon-9pm), an eat-in or takeaway chippy.

In terms of location, *Life's a Beach* (☎ 01288-355222, 🖳 lifesabeach.info; **fb**; summer Sun-Tue 10am-4pm, Wed-Sat 10am-8pm, winter hours variable) is the pick of the bunch, with fabulous beach views from its terrace. The lunchtime menu includes burgers (£8-9) and baguettes (£5.50-8.50). Evening is for fine dining, including good seafood (mains £16.50-22.50, 2/3 courses £25.50/29.50), and is indoors only.

Pubs

Next to the canal, the ever-popular *Brendon Arms* (see Where to stay; food daily noon-2pm & 6-9pm, school summer hols noon-9pm) is a 150-year-old pub with plenty of garden seating out front. Next door, *Falcon Hotel* (see Where to stay) has a bar (food daily 10am-9pm; 🐾) and a restaurant (daily 6.30-9pm, Sun noon-2.30pm; booking preferred) but the menu (most mains £12.50-15) is fairly standard pub grub. The recently opened bar-restaurant *The Deck* (☎ 01288-353846, 🖳 thedeckbude.co.uk; **fb**; Tue-Sat 4-8.30pm, daily in summer), at The Edgcumbe (see Where to stay), can also be recommended.

At the bottom of The Strand, *Carriers Inn* (☎ 01288-352459; **fb** ; food Mon-Sat noon-3pm & 6-9pm, Sun noon-5.30pm; 🐾 on a lead in the bar) is even older than the Brendon Arms, although less cheery. Just along the road *The Globe Hotel* (see Where to Stay; food noon-2.30pm & 6-9pm) has a no frills pub-like bar area with cheap pub food, real ales and friendly staff.

If you just fancy a drink, it's well worth hunting down *The Barrel at Bude* (☎ 01288-356113, 🖳 thebarrelatbude.com; **fb**; Thur-Sat 4-9pm), a pint-sized smugglers bar serving Cornish craft ales, ciders and gin.

APPENDIX A: GPS WAYPOINTS

MAP	REF	GPS WAYPOINTS	DESCRIPTION [see p17]
Map 1	01	N51 12.636 W3 28.345	Hands Sculpture – start of SWCP
Map 2	02	N51 13.113 W3 30.671	Start of rugged alternative route
Map 3	03	N51 13.059 W3 31.125	Gate into and out of Holnicote Estate
Map 4	04	N51 13.383 W3 32.352	Cross metalled road
Map 5	05	N51 13.578 W3 34.057	Reunion of two trails
Map 5	06	N51 13.263 W3 34.928	Turn-off left outside Bossington
Map 6	07	N51 12.967 W3 36.986	Rejoin beach
Map 7	08	N51 13.249 W3 38.086	Arch over path and gate
Map 7	09	N51 13.263 W3 39.490	Culbone Church
Map 8	10	N51 13.325 W3 42.176	Paths to Burford and County Gate
Map 9	11	N51 13.749 W3 42.610	Reunion of two paths
Map 9	12	N51 13.806 W3 43.679	Wild Boar gateposts
Map 10	13	N51 14.096 W3 45.677	Gate into/out of Pudleep Gurt
Map 10	14	N51 14.354 W3 46.949	Turn off road
Map 11	15	N51 14.304 W3 47.445	Reunion with path from lighthouse
Map 11	16	N51 13.837 W3 49.303	Drop off road and zig-zag down to beach
Map 12	17	N51 13.755 W3 51.558	Cattle grid and gate
Map 13	18	N51 13.474 W3 52.942	Sign quoting Psalm 100:4
Map 13	19	N51 13.398 W3 53.844	Signpost to Heddon's Mouth
Map 14	20	N51 13.324 W3 55.618	Heddon's Mouth
Map 14	21	N51 13.138 W3 56.751	Gate with 'ENP' on
Map 15	22	N51 12.857 W3 58.228	Turn right onto good, wide path
Map 15	23	N51 12.538 W3 59.238	Great Hangman National Trust sign
Map 16	24	N51 12.855 W4 00.209	Top of Great Hangman, large cairn
Map 17	25	N51 12.375 W4 02.185	Combe Martin Beach
Map 17	26	N51 12.723 W4 03.838	Watermouth Valley Camping Park
Map 18	27	N51 12.966 W4 05.208	First view of Ilfracombe and Lundy
Map 19	28	N51 12.548 W4 06.853	Ilfracombe Harbour
Map 20	29	N51 11.829 W4 10.539	Lee Bridge
Map 21	30	N51 11.899 W4 11.993	Bull Point
Map 21	31	N51 11.241 W4 13.738	Morte Point
Map 22	32	N51 10.351 W4 12.448	Tourist Information Centre, Woolacombe
Map 23	33	N51 08.543 W4 13.148	Entrance to Putsborough Sands car park
Map 24	34	N51 08.529 W4 15.510	Baggy Point
Map 24	35	N51 07.985 W4 14.163	Croyde Beach
Map 25	36	N51 07.336 W4 14.376	Turn onto road, officially left but is a shortcut
Map 26	37	N51 07.082 W4 13.086	Join road
Map 26	38	N51 07.013 W4 12.229	Leave road at gate
Map 27	39	N51 05.622 W4 11.719	Turn right and enter Braunton Burrows
Map 27	40	N51 04.309 W4 11.496	Turn left onto sand footpath
Map 28	41	N51 06.019 W4 09.788	Velator Bridge
Map 29	42	N51 05.624 W4 07.393	Heanton Court pub
Map 30	43	N51 05.650 W4 06.663	Path goes under bridge
Map 31	44	N51 04.660 W4 03.499	Turn left up steps to access bridge
Map 32	45	N51 04.744 W4 07.168	Fremington Quay Café
Map 33	46	N51 04.237 W4 09.603	Main trail leaves disused railway here
Map 34	47	N51 04.318 W4 10.113	Start of jetty
Map 34	48	N51 03.384 W4 10.726	Join road after gap in wall
Map 34	49	N51 02.987 W4 10.680	Turn off road at gate (Instow)
Map 35	50	N51 02.515 W4 11.041	Pass jetty
Map 36	51	N51 00.935 W4 12.002	Bideford Long Bridge
Map 37	52	N51 02.550 W4 11.540	Wooden footbridge
Map 37	53	N51 03.125 W4 11.371	The Quay, Appledore

Map 37	54	N51 03.203 W4 12.201	Signpost high/low tide route
Map 38	55	N51 03.338 W4 13.543	Public toilets
Map 39	56	N51 02.451 W4 14.208	Westward Ho! (Leave Golf Links Rd)
Map 40	57	N51 01.139 W4 16.446	Green Cliff National Trust sign
Map 41	58	N50 59.605 W4 18.327	Gate at Peppercombe
Map 42	59	N50 59.266 W4 20.635	Buck's Mills
Map 42	60	N50 59.288 W4 21.426	Mary's Rest (huge beech tree)
Map 43	61	N50 59.171 W4 22.286	Join The Hobby Drive
Map 43	62	N50 59.895 W4 23.980	Gate into Clovelly
Map 44	63	N51 00.213 W4 24.235	Wilderness Summerhouse Cabin
Map 44	64	N51 00.621 W4 25.261	Mouthmill
Map 45	65	N51 00.759 W4 26.710	Memorial to Wellington Bomber
Map 45	66	N51 01.153 W4 28.168	Trig Point
Map 46	67	N51 01.235 W4 30.745	Radar station
Map 47	68	N51 00.154 W4 31.648	Blackpool Mill
Map 48	69	N50 59.631 W4 31.968	Hartland Quay
Map 49	70	N50 58.069 W4 31.795	Turn-off to Elmscott
Map 50	71	N50 55.988 W4 32.624	Welcombe Mouth
Map 51	72	N50 54.389 W4 33.720	Hawker's Hut
Map 52	73	N50 53.129 W4 33.531	Right turn by radio station
Map 53	74	N50 51.659 W4 33.224	Wooden footbridge at Sandy Mouth
Map 54	75	N50 50.121 W4 33.129	Lifeguard lookout

MAP KEY

🖼 Library/bookstore		● Other			
♠ Where to stay	@ Internet	CP Car park
○ Where to eat and drink	🛎 Museum/gallery	🚌 Bus station/stop
Λ Campsite	✚ Church/cathedral	━☐━ Rail line & station
⊠ Post Office	☎ Telephone	▭ Park
ⓔ Bank/ATM	☑ Public toilet	082 GPS waypoint
ⓘ Tourist Information	☐ Building	

South West Coast Path — Sand dunes — Trees/woodland
Other path — Cliffs — Bog or marsh
4 x 4 track — Cornish hedge — Sand
Tarmac road — Bridge — Stones
Steps — Fence — Lighthouse
Slope — Wall — Lifeguard cover
Steep slope — Hedge — Rescue equipment
Stile — Water — Golf course
Gate — Stream/river — Map continuation

APPENDIX B: TAKING A DOG

The South West Coast Path is a dog-friendly path and many are the rewards that await those prepared to make the extra effort required to bring their best friend along with them. However, don't underestimate the amount of work involved. Indeed, just about every decision you make will be influenced by the fact that you've got a dog: how you plan to travel to the start of the trail, where you're going to stay, how far you're going to walk each day, where you're going to rest and where you're going to eat in the evening etc.

If you're sure your dog can cope with (and, just as importantly, *enjoy*) walking 10 miles or more a day for several days in a row, you need to start preparing accordingly. Extra thought needs to go into your itinerary. Study the town & village facilities table on pp32-3 (and the advice below), and plan where to stop and where to buy food.

Looking after your dog

To begin with, you need to make sure that your own dog is fully **inoculated** against the usual doggy illnesses, and also up to date with regard to **worm pills** (eg Drontal) and **flea preventatives** such as Frontline – they are, after all, following in the pawprints of many a dog before them, some of whom may well have left fleas or other parasites on the trail that now lie in wait for their next meal to arrive. **Pet insurance** is also a very good idea for a trip such as this; if you've already got insurance, do check that it will cover the kind of walk you are planning. Perhaps the most important implement you can take with you is the **plastic tick remover**, available from vets for a couple of quid. Ticks are a real problem on the SWCP. These removers, while fiddly, help you to get rid of the tick safely (ie without leaving its head behind buried under the dog's skin).

Being in unfamiliar territory also makes it more likely that you and your dog could become separated. All dogs in the UK must, by law, be **microchipped**, but it is also a good idea to make sure your dog has a **tag with your contact details on it** (a mobile phone number would be best if you are carrying one with you).

Dogs on beaches There is no general rule regarding whether dogs are allowed on beaches or not. Some of the beaches on the SWCP are open to dogs all year; some allow them on the beach only outside the summer season (1 May to 30 Sep); while a few beaches don't allow dogs at all. (Guide dogs, by the way, are usually excluded from any bans.) If in doubt, look for the noticeboards that will tell you the exact rules. On the beaches, the rules vary: at Woolacombe (see box p130), they have an area where dogs are forbidden, another where they need to be on a lead, and a third area where they can run free. At Croyde you will have to walk across a part where dogs are banned – keep the dog on a tight lead here.

For more information about which beaches allow dogs and when, go to 🖳 visitdevon .co.uk/explore/dog-friendly and 🖳 n-somerset.gov.uk (search 'animals on the beach').

Where dogs are banned from a beach there will usually be an alternative path that you can take that avoids the sands. If there isn't, and you have no choice but to cross the beach even though dogs are officially banned, you are permitted to do so as long as you cross as speedily as possible, follow the line of the path (which is usually well above the high-water mark) and keep your dog tightly under control.

Whatever the rules of access are for the beach, remember that your dog shouldn't disturb other beach-users – and you must always **clean up after your dog**. Don't forget to bring drinking water with you as dogs can over-heat with the lack of shade.

When to keep your dog on a lead

● **On cliff tops** It's a sad fact that, every year, a few dogs lose their lives falling over the edge of the cliffs. It usually occurs when they are chasing rabbits (which know where the cliff-edge is and are able, unlike your poor pooch, to stop in time).
● **When crossing farmland**, particularly in the lambing season (around May) when your dog can scare the sheep, causing them to lose their young. Farmers are allowed by law to

shoot at and kill any dogs that they consider are worrying their sheep. During lambing, most farmers would prefer it if you didn't bring your dog at all. The exception is if your dog is being attacked by cows. Some years ago there were three deaths in the UK caused by walkers being trampled as they tried to rescue their dogs from the attentions of cattle. The advice in this instance is to **let go of the lead**, head speedily to a position of safety (usually the other side of the field gate or stile) and call your dog to you.

● **On National Trust land**, where it is **compulsory** to keep your dog on a lead.

● **Around ground-nesting birds** It's important to keep your dog under control when crossing an area where certain species of birds nest on the ground. Most dogs love foraging around in the woods but make sure it's allowed; some woods are used as 'nurseries' for game birds and dogs are only allowed through them on a lead.

What to pack

● **Food/water bowl** Foldable cloth bowls are popular with walkers, being light and compact in your rucksack. You can get also get a water-bottle-and-bowl combination, where the bottle folds into a 'trough' from which the dog can drink. Bring treats as well as regular food to keep up the mutt's morale. That said, if your dog is anything like mine the chances are they'll spend most of the walk dining on rabbit droppings and sheep poo anyway.

● **Lead and collar** An extendable one is probably preferable for this sort of trip. Make sure both lead and collar are in good condition – you don't want either to snap on the trail, or you may end up carrying your dog through sheep fields until a replacement can be found. It is worth taking a spare.

● **Medication** You'll know if you need to bring any lotions or potions.

● **Bedding** A simple blanket may suffice, or you can opt for something more elaborate if you aren't carrying your own luggage.

● **Tick remover** See p209.   ● **Poo bags** Essential (see below).

● **Hygiene wipes** For cleaning your dog after it's rolled in stuff.

● **A favourite toy** Helps prevent your dog from pining for the entire walk.

● **Corkscrew stake** Available from camping or pet shops, this will help you to keep your dog secure in one place while you set up camp/doze.

● **Raingear** It can rain a lot!   ● **Old towels** For drying your dog after the deluge.

When it comes to packing, I always leave an exterior pocket of my rucksack empty so I can put used poo bags in there (for deposit at the first bin we come to). I keep all the dog's kit together and separate from the other luggage (usually inside a plastic bag inside my rucksack). I have also seen several dogs sporting their own 'doggy rucksack', so they can carry their own food, water, poo etc – which certainly reduces the burden on their owner!

Cleaning up after your dog

It is extremely important that dog owners behave in a responsible way when walking the path. Dog excrement should be cleaned up. In towns, villages and fields where animals graze or which will be cut for silage, hay etc, you need to pick up and bag the excrement. In other places you can possibly get away with merely flicking it with a nearby stick into the undergrowth, thus ensuring there is none left on the path to decorate the boots of others.

Staying (and eating) with your dog

In this guide we have used a symbol 🐾 to denote where a hotel, pub or B&B welcomes dogs; however, this always needs to be arranged in advance and some places may charge extra. Hostels (both YHA and independent) do not permit them unless they are an assistance (guide) dog; smaller campsites tend to accept them, but some of the larger holiday parks do not. Before you turn up always double check whether the place you would like to stay accepts dogs and whether there is space for them; many places have only one or two rooms suitable for people with dogs. When it comes to **eating**, most landlords allow dogs in at least a section of their pubs, though few restaurants do. Make sure you always ask first and ensure your dog doesn't run around the pub but is secured to your table or to a radiator.

INDEX

Page references in red type refer to maps

TRAILBLAZER'S BRITISH WALKING GUIDES

We've applied to destinations which are closer to home Trailblazer's proven formula for publishing definitive practical route guides for adventurous travellers. Britain's network of long-distance trails enables the walker to explore some of the finest landscapes in the country's best walking areas. These are guides that are user-friendly, practical, informative and environmentally sensitive.

● **Unique mapping features** In many walking guidebooks the reader has to read a route description then try to relate it to the map. Our guides are much easier to use because walking directions, tricky junctions, places to stay and eat, points of interest and walking times are all written onto the maps themselves in the places to which they apply. With their uncluttered clarity, these are not general-purpose maps but fully edited maps drawn by walkers for walkers.

'The same attention to detail that distinguishes its other guides has been brought to bear here'.
THE SUNDAY TIMES

● **Largest-scale walking maps** At a scale of just under 1:20,000 (8cm or 3¹/₈ inches to one mile) the maps in these guides are bigger than even the most detailed British walking maps currently available in the shops.

● **Not just a trail guide – includes where to stay, where to eat and public transport** Our guidebooks cover the complete walking experience, not just the route. Accommodation options for all budgets are provided (pubs, hotels, B&Bs, campsites, bunkhouses, hostels) as well as places to eat. Detailed public transport information for all access points to each trail means that there are itineraries for all walkers, for hiking the entire route as well as for day or weekend walks.

Cleveland Way *Henry Stedman*, 1st edn, ISBN 978-1-905864-91-1, 240pp, 98 maps

Coast to Coast *Henry Stedman*, 9th edn, ISBN 978-1-912716-11-1, 268pp, 109 maps

Cornwall Coast Path (SW Coast Path Pt 2) *Stedman & Newton*, 7th edn, ISBN 978-1-912716-26-5, 352pp, 142 maps

Cotswold Way *Tricia & Bob Hayne,* 4th edn, ISBN 978-1-912716-04-3, 204pp, 53 maps

Dales Way *Henry Stedman*, 1st edn, ISBN 978-1-905864-78-2, 192pp, 50 maps

Dorset & South Devon (SW Coast Path Pt 3) *Stedman & Newton*, 2nd edn, ISBN 978-1-905864-94-2, 340pp, 97 maps

Exmoor & North Devon (SW Coast Path Pt I) *Stedman & Newton*, 3rd edn, ISBN 978-1-9912716-24-1, 224pp, 68 maps

Great Glen Way *Jim Manthorpe*, 2nd edn, ISBN 978-1-912716-10-4, 184pp, 50 maps

Hadrian's Wall Path *Henry Stedman*, 6th edn, ISBN 978-1-912716-12-8, 250pp, 60 maps

London LOOP *Henry Stedman*, 1st edn, ISBN 978-1-912716-21-0, 236pp, 60 maps

Norfolk Coast Path & Peddars Way *Alexander Stewart*, 1st edn, ISBN 978-1-905864-98-0, 224pp, 75 maps

North Downs Way *Henry Stedman*, 2nd edn, ISBN 978-1-905864-90-4, 240pp, 98 maps

Offa's Dyke Path *Keith Carter*, 5th edn, ISBN 978-1-912716-03-6, 268pp, 98 maps

Pembrokeshire Coast Path *Jim Manthorpe*, 6th edn, ISBN 978-1-912716-13-5, 236pp, 96 maps

Pennine Way *Stuart Greig*, 5th edn, ISBN 978-1-912716-02-9, 272pp, 138 maps

The Ridgeway *Nick Hill*, 5th edn, ISBN 978-1-912716-20-3, 208pp, 53 maps

South Downs Way *Jim Manthorpe*, 7th edn, ISBN 978-1-912716-23-4, 204pp, 60 maps

Thames Path *Joel Newton*, 3rd edn, ISBN 978-1-912716-27-2, 256pp, 99 maps

West Highland Way *Charlie Loram*, 7th edn, ISBN 978-1-912716-01-2, 218pp, 60 maps

'The Trailblazer series stands head, shoulders, waist and ankles above the rest. They are particularly strong on mapping ...'
THE SUNDAY TIMES

Orkney

Thurso

Stornoway O

Scottish Highlands Hillwalking Guide

Skye

O Inverness

Great Glen Way

O Aberdeen

Fort William

SCOTLAND

Mull

West Highland Way

Arran

Milngavie
Glasgow

Edinburgh

Berwick upon Tweed

Kirk Yetholm

Pennine Way

Hadrian's Wall Path

Bowness-on-Solway

Wallsend
Newcastle upon Tyne

N. IRELAND

Carlisle

Coast to Coast

O **Belfast**

St Bees O

Bowness-on-Windermere O

Dales Way

Robin Hood's Bay

O Filey

Helmsley

Cleveland Way

REP. OF IRELAND

Isle of Man

Ilkley
O York

O Leeds

Hull O

Pennine Way

Liverpool O
Prestatyn

Manchester O O Edale

O Lincoln

O **Dublin**

Anglesey
Bangor

O Crewe

Norfolk Coast Path & Peddars Way

Cromer
Norwich

ENGLAND

I R I S H S E A

O Nottingham

Offa's Dyke Path

Birmingham O

Knettishall Heath O

Great Yarmouth

Cardigan

Cotswold Way

WALES

Chipping Campden

The Ridgeway

Ivinghoe Beacon

London LOOP

Amroth

Pembrokeshire Coast Path

Kemble

London

Thames Path

Chepstow

Cardiff O

Bristol O

Bath

Overton Hill

Canterbury

Exmoor & N Devon Coast Path

Minehead

Winchester
Salisbury

Farnham

Dover

Bude

Exeter O

O Poole

Portsmouth O

Eastbourne

Brighton

North Downs Way

Cornwall Coast Path

Plymouth

Isle of Wight

South Downs Way

Isles of Scilly

Dorset & S Devon Coast Path

ENGLISH CHANNEL

0   50   100km
0   25   50 miles

TRAILBLAZER

British Walking Guides

SEE OVERLEAF FOR FULL TITLE LIST

Great Glen WAY

THE Ridgeway

South Downs WAY

Cornwall COAST PATH

London LOOP LONDON OUTER ORBITAL PATH

Thames Path

★ trailblazer

TRAILBLAZER TITLE LIST

Adventure Cycle-Touring Handbook
Adventure Motorcycling Handbook
Australia by Rail
Cleveland Way (British Walking Guide)
Coast to Coast (British Walking Guide)
Cornwall Coast Path (British Walking Guide)
Cotswold Way (British Walking Guide)
The Cyclist's Anthology
Dales Way (British Walking Guide)
Dorset & Sth Devon Coast Path (British Walking Gde)
Exmoor & Nth Devon Coast Path (British Walking Gde)
Great Glen Way (British Walking Guide)
Hadrian's Wall Path (British Walking Guide)
Himalaya by Bike – a route and planning guide
Iceland Hiking – with Reykjavik City Guide
Inca Trail, Cusco & Machu Picchu
Japan by Rail
Kilimanjaro – the trekking guide (includes Mt Meru)
London Loop (British Walking Guide)
London to Walsingham Camino
Madeira Walks – 37 selected day walks
Moroccan Atlas – The Trekking Guide
Morocco Overland (4x4/motorcycle/mountainbike)
Nepal Trekking & The Great Himalaya Trail
Norfolk Coast Path & Peddars Way (British Walking Gde)
North Downs Way (British Walking Guide)
Offa's Dyke Path (British Walking Guide)
Overlanders' Handbook – worldwide driving guide
Pembrokeshire Coast Path (British Walking Guide)
Pennine Way (British Walking Guide)
Peru's Cordilleras Blanca & Huayhuash – Hiking/Biking
Pilgrim Pathways: 1-2 day walks on Britain's sacred ways
The Railway Anthology
The Ridgeway (British Walking Guide)
Scottish Highlands – Hillwalking Guide
Siberian BAM Guide – rail, rivers & road
The Silk Roads – a route and planning guide
Sinai – the trekking guide
South Downs Way (British Walking Guide)
Thames Path (British Walking Guide)
Tour du Mont Blanc
Trans-Canada Rail Guide
Trans-Siberian Handbook
Trekking in the Everest Region
The Walker's Anthology
The Walker's Anthology – further tales
West Highland Way (British Walking Guide)

For more information about Trailblazer and our
expanding range of guides, for guidebook updates or
for credit card mail order sales visit our website:

www.trailblazer-guides.com

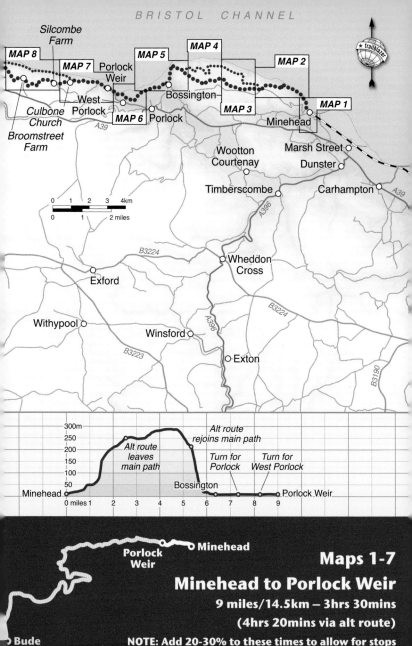

BRISTOL CHANNEL

Silcombe Farm

MAP 8

Culbone Church

Broomstreet Farm

MAP 7

Porlock Weir

West Porlock

MAP 6

Porlock

MAP 5

Bossington

MAP 4

MAP 3

MAP 2

MAP 1

Minehead

Marsh Street

Dunster

Carhampton

Wootton Courtenay

Timberscombe

Wheddon Cross

Exford

Withypool

Winsford

Exton

A39

A396

B3224

B3224

B3223

B3190

0 1 2 3 4km
0 1 2 miles

300m
250
200
150
100
50

Alt route rejoins main path

Alt route leaves main path

Turn for Porlock

Turn for West Porlock

Minehead

Bossington

Porlock Weir

0 miles 1 2 3 4 5 6 7 8 9

Minehead

Porlock Weir

Maps 1-7

Minehead to Porlock Weir

9 miles/14.5km – 3hrs 30mins

(4hrs 20mins via alt route)

NOTE: Add 20-30% to these times to allow for stops

Bude

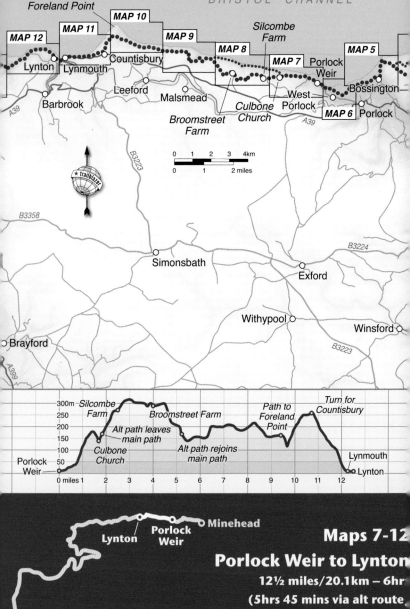

BRISTOL CHANNEL

Foreland Point

MAP 12   MAP 11   MAP 10   MAP 9

Lynton   Lynmouth   Countisbury

Barbrook

Leeford

Malsmead

Silcombe Farm

MAP 8   MAP 7

Porlock Weir

MAP 5

Bossington

West Porlock

Culbone Church

MAP 6   Porlock

Broomstreet Farm

A39

B3223

0 1 2 3 4km
0   1   2 miles

★trailblazer

B3358

Simonsbath

Exford

B3224

Withypool

Winsford

Brayford

B3223

A399

300m   Silcombe
250   Farm
200   Broomstreet Farm
150   Alt path leaves
100   main path   Path to
 50   Culbone   Alt path rejoins   Foreland   Turn for
Porlock Church   main path   Point   Countisbury
Weir   Lynmouth
                                                                  Lynton
0 miles 1   2   3   4   5   6   7   8   9   10   11   12

Minehead

Lynton   Porlock Weir

Bude

Maps 7-12

Porlock Weir to Lynton

12½ miles/20.1km – 6hr

(5hrs 45 mins via alt route)

NOTE: Add 20-30% to these times to allow for stop

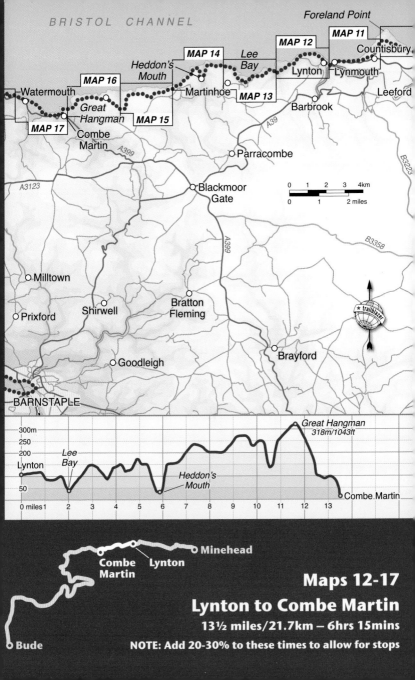

BRISTOL CHANNEL

Foreland Point

MAP 11

Countisbury

MAP 12

MAP 14 Lee Bay

Heddon's Mouth

Lynton

Lynmouth

MAP 16

Martinhoe

MAP 13

Leeford

Watermouth

Great Hangman

MAP 15

Barbrook

A39

MAP 17

Combe Martin

A399

Parracombe

A3123

Blackmoor Gate

A399

B3358

Milltown

Prixford

Shirwell

Bratton Fleming

Brayford

Goodleigh

BARNSTAPLE

★ trailblazer

300m
250
200
150
100
50

Lynton

Lee Bay

Great Hangman
318m/1043ft

Heddon's Mouth

Combe Martin

0 miles 1   2   3   4   5   6   7   8   9   10   11   12   13

0   1   2   3   4km
0   1   2 miles

Minehead

Combe Martin   Lynton

Bude

Maps 12-17

Lynton to Combe Martin

13½ miles/21.7km – 6hrs 15mins

NOTE: Add 20-30% to these times to allow for stops

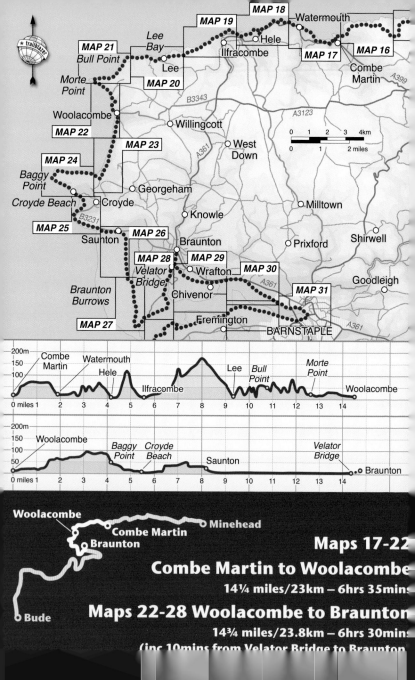

MAP 18
Watermouth

MAP 19
Lee
Bay
MAP 21
Bull Point
Morte
Point

Hele

Ilfracombe

MAP 17
MAP 16
Combe
Martin

A399

Woolacombe
MAP 22

Lee

MAP 20

B3343

A3123

Willingcott

West
Down

A361

0   1   2   3   4km
0   1   2 miles

MAP 23

MAP 24
Baggy
Point
Croyde Beach

Georgeham

Croyde

Knowle

Milltown

MAP 25
B3231

MAP 26

Saunton

Braunton

Prixford

Shirwell

MAP 28
Velator
Bridge

MAP 29
Wrafton

Goodleigh

MAP 30

MAP 31

Braunton
Burrows

Chivenor

MAP 27

Fremington

BARNSTAPLE

A361

A361

200m
150
100

Combe
Martin

Watermouth

Hele

Ilfracombe

Lee

Bull
Point

Morte
Point

Woolacombe

0 miles 1   2   3   4   5   6   7   8   9   10   11   12   13   14

200m
150
100
50

Woolacombe

Baggy
Point

Croyde
Beach

Saunton

Velator
Bridge

Braunton

0 miles 1   2   3   4   5   6   7   8   9   10   11   12   13   14

Woolacombe

Combe Martin

Minehead

Braunton

Bude

Maps 17-22

Combe Martin to Woolacombe

14¼ miles/23km – 6hrs 35mins

Maps 22-28 Woolacombe to Braunton

14¾ miles/23.8km – 6hrs 30mins
(inc 10mins from Velator Bridge to Braunton

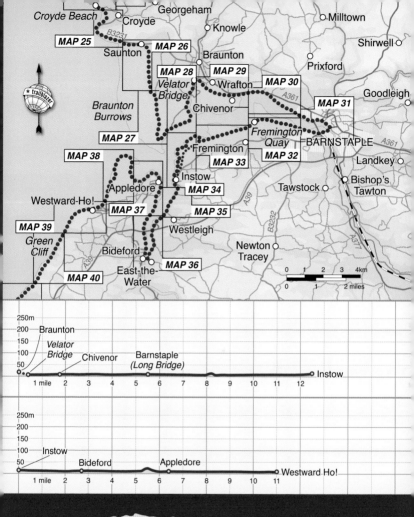

MAP 25

MAP 26

MAP 28

MAP 29

MAP 30

MAP 31

MAP 27

MAP 38

MAP 32

MAP 33

MAP 34

MAP 37

MAP 35

MAP 39

MAP 40

MAP 36

Croyde Beach

Georgeham

Croyde

Knowle

Milltown

Shirwell

B3231

Saunton

Braunton

Prixford

Velator Bridge

Wrafton

Goodleigh

Chivenor

Braunton Burrows

Fremington Quay

BARNSTAPLE

A361

Fremington

Landkey

Instow

Appledore

Tawstock

Bishop's Tawton

Westward-Ho!

Westleigh

Green Cliff

Bideford

Newton Tracey

East-the-Water

0   1   2   3   4km
0   1   2 miles

Elevation profiles

250m
200
150
100
50

Braunton

Velator Bridge

Chivenor

Barnstaple (Long Bridge)

Instow

1 mile 2   3   4   5   6   7   8   9   10   11   12

250m
200
150
100
50

Instow

Bideford

Appledore

Westward Ho!

1 mile 2   3   4   5   6   7   8   9   10   11

Minehead

Braunton

Westward Ho!

Instow

Bude

Maps 29-34

Braunton to Instow

12½ miles/20km – 5hrs
(inc 10mins to Velator Bridge)

Maps 34-39, Instow to Westward Ho!

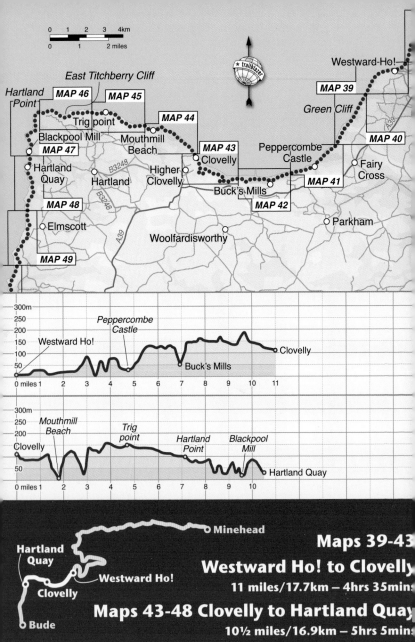